PROJECT VITRA.
Sites, Products, Authors, Museum, Collections, Signs; Chronology, Glossary.
Edited by Cornel Windlin and Rolf Fehlbaum, Basel 2008.

Birkhäuser

PROJECT VITRA.
Sites—p. 9, Products—p. 63, Authors—p. 137, Museum—p. 239, Collections—p. 269, Signs—p. 311; Chronology, Glossary—p. 365

THE LASTING DREAM

Project Vitra commenced in Basel and Weil am Rhein in the year 1957, when the company's founders, Willi and Erika Fehlbaum, began to produce furniture by Charles & Ray Eames and George Nelson. Today we continue to manufacture these furniture classics, and we are still at home in the metropolitan region of Basel. Yet over the years the Vitra project has come to embrace many more things.

The reason we call it a project is because everyone involved regards it as much more than just a matter of business. Obviously economic success was, and will remain, the foundation of the Vitra company. However, the direction of our work is guided by the project. It is based on the conviction that everyday life holds great potential for inspiration and aesthetic enjoyment, and that design can discover and develop this potential. The Vitra project serves this purpose. It manifests itself on different levels: in the company's products and interior concepts, in its architecture, collections, museum, methods of communication and, finally, in its approach to both designers and users. These tangible manifestations are the subject of this book.

Charles Eames had the most enduring influence on the Vitra project. He viewed the primary condition of design as the 'recognition of need' and warned against stylistic excesses: the designer should practice self-restraint and devote himself completely to the task of problem

Rolf Fehlbaum

solving. Yet design is ultimately a matter of individual authorship – of creative people developing unmistakably distinctive solutions based on their analysis of a problem's criteria and parameters. The designer couple Charles and Ray Eames serves as an ideal example.

For this reason, Vitra always works with designers who possess the capability of authorship – that is to say, who not only have creative skills, but who invest their work with a personal world view. Their designs bear a message that goes far beyond the impulse of merely trying to please.

The diversity of the Vitra project can seem almost confusing at times. That has never bothered us. The architectural park on the Vitra Campus in Weil am Rhein defines us as readily as the chairs and office furniture that we produce; the Vitra Design Museum with its collections, archives and miniatures belongs as much to the project as the twentieth-century classics and collages for interior living that we have developed during the past years. We are convinced that the design and arrangement, development and modification of the spaces in which we live and work is best achieved with as few boundaries as possible.

Consequently, we do not regard homes, offices and public venues as strictly separate spaces, but as related environments. Depending on the need, we create products that are as inexpensive as our plastic chairs, or as luxurious as the Eames Lounge Chair. We also move backwards and forwards, simultaneously, on the continuum of time. While we are committed to the heritage of classics in the form of re-editions, exhibitions and publications, we promote contemporary

Rolf Fehlbaum

design with equal passion. And Vitra is no less interested in ergonomics, ecology, logistics and quality assurance than in the anthropology of dwelling.

In order to deepen my understanding of interiors and interior design products, I began collecting modern furniture in the early 1980s. The progressive growth of this collection led to the idea of building a museum. A vital museum, however, calls for exhibitions. To finance their production and presentation, the exhibitions would have to be so attractive that other institutions would want to show them as well. This realization eventually led to the publication of catalogues, the organization of workshops, the acquisition of archives and the creation of unique museum products. Exhibitions organized by the Vitra Design Museum now tour around the globe.

In 1981, the opportunity suddenly presented itself to incorporate architecture into the Vitra project. A major fire had destroyed half of the factory site in Weil, making it necessary to rebuild our production facilities. Nicholas Grimshaw, architect of the first new building, also designed a master plan for the unified development of the entire premises. A short time later, however, this homogenous concept was replaced by the idea of a collage, due to an encounter with Frank Gehry. We were guided by the ideal of the Campus as a vital assemblage of public and private, industrial and cultural elements.

A present assessment of the Vitra project can only be tentative. It is a work in progress – and will continue to be so for a long time to come. As a family-owned enterprise, there is a good chance that Vitra's

Rolf Fehlbaum

unique character can be sustained into the future. In addition to the current building projects, we are pursuing other activities: the expansion into new markets in Asia, new models for communication and training, as well as Vitra Edition, which gives us the chance to experiment with exciting ideas.

The Vitra project sometimes seems like a dream to me. Why is this? It offers the opportunity to produce the things that one loves. We are able to work with some of the most creative architects, designers and graphic artists of our time. Our personal interests are compatible with the aims of the project. Every day provides a reason to look forward to the next step. And finally, all of those aspects are not only satisfying, but also tend to fulfil business expectations.

This dream has been a reality for me, and us, over the past fifty years. We owe this to the creative individuals who have collaborated with Vitra during this time. When I made my first trip to the United States in 1960, I visited Charles and Ray Eames, George Nelson and Alexander Girard. This experience established my trust in creative minds as the key to a new business model.

Yet such trust alone is not enough; additional factors play an important role. Raymond Fehlbaum, who has always maintained a low public profile, gave the Vitra project its solid foundation and structure. Others have contributed to it in a variety of different functions and furthered its advancement in what has often been an unspectacular, step-by-step process. They are natives of the metropolitan region of Greater Basel, or have found a new home here. Or they work for us

Rolf Fehlbaum

somewhere else in the world, in one of our subsidiaries. They have been involved in the project for years, sometimes even decades. In this book, which is dedicated to "creatives", they receive only marginal attention, but their contributions remain essential.

We are now looking in the direction of the next fifty years, in which we hope to further the balancing act between play and work, dream and reality. Everyday life will continue to be at the focus of our efforts in the future, and our ability to redeem the promise of our heritage will be reflected in the degree to which convincing and useful products arise from the Vitra project.

Rolf Fehlbaum is Vitra's chairman. After completing studies in social sciences, he worked as a film producer and a training consultant in the architectural field. Since taking over the leadership at Vitra in 1977, he has internationalized the company's operations, established links with leading designers, commissioned works by some of the world's pre-eminent architects and founded the Vitra Design Museum.

SITES.
Vitra Center and Vitra Campus, photographed by Paola de Pietri, Olivo Barbieri, Giovanni Chiaramonte, Gabriele Basilico — p. 12

Playing seriously by Luis Fernández-Galiano — p. 55

PROJECT VITRA

SITES.

SITES

Vitra's core operations are located in the metropolitan area of Basel, with the Vitra Center (headquarters and product development) in Birsfelden, Switzerland, and the Vitra Campus (factory buildings, logistics, the Design Museum and various cultural facilities) in Weil am Rhein, Germany. Both the Vitra Center and the Vitra Campus are known for their contemporary architecture. These buildings have symbolized the company's rigorous standards and distinctive identity for a quarter of a century.

SITES   Vitra Center, Birsfelden   12

Paola de Pietri

Vitra's first production unit was built in Birsfelden, near Basel, in 1957. The Vitra Center, designed by Frank Gehry to house the company's administrative headquarters, was built beside the production block in 1994. On the edge of a residential and industrial zone, the complex is separated from the Hardwald forest recreational area by a motorway slip road and the railway.

SITES　　　　　　　　Vitra Center, Birsfelden　　　　　　　　　　　　　　　　13

SITES Vitra Center, Birsfelden 14

Olivo Barbieri

The Vitra Center in Birsfelden consists of an office tract and in front of this the 'villa', which houses the reception area, cafeteria, staff restaurant and conference rooms. Within the Vitra complex, the 'villa' is the hub of social interaction and communication.

SITES — Vitra Center, Birsfelden

SITES   Vitra Center, Birsfelden   16

Olivo Barbieri   The offices and 'villa' are joined together by a generously proportioned lobby zone, the two outer walls of which consist entirely of glass, and which is traversed inside by bridge-like walkways. On the forecourt pavement a yellow arrow points visitors to the main entrance.

SITES

Vitra Center, Birsfelden

SITES Vitra Center, Birsfelden 18

Giovanni Chiaramonte   View from the Hardwald woods across the motorway slip road (not visible from this point) to the Vitra grounds in Birsfelden. On the left can be seen the curving roof segments of the 1950s factory building, which now houses the company's development unit.

SITES Vitra Center, Birsfelden 19

SITES | Vitra Center, Birsfelden | 20

Paola de Pietri — Aerial photograph of the Vitra Center clearly showing the expansive, asymmetrical roof covering the lobby zone between the 'villa' and the office tract.

SITES

From Birsfelden to Weil am Rhein

21

Paola de Pietri

Vitra's two sites in Birsfelden and Weil am Rhein are seven kilometres from one another. On the motorway the journey across the Swiss/German border takes around 15 minutes.

SITES From Birsfelden to Weil am Rhein 22

Paola de Pietri Weil am Rhein lies at the foot of the Tüllinger, a long sweeping hill with orchards and vineyards on its western slopes.

| SITES | Vitra Campus, Weil am Rhein | 23 |

Paola de Pietri

Aerial view of the north-eastern edge of the Vitra Campus in Weil am Rhein. On the left is Tadao Ando's Conference Pavilion set in a meadow dotted with cherry trees, and behind it a production building designed by Nicholas Grimshaw. On the upper right are the Vitra Design Museum and another factory building, both designed by Frank Gehry.

SITES — Vitra Campus, Weil am Rhein

Nicholas Grimshaw, Claes Oldenburg & Coosje van Bruggen, Frank Gehry, Tadao Ando, Zaha Hadid, Álvaro Siza, Jean Prouvé, Richard Buckminster Fuller, Jasper Morrison, Herzog & de Meuron, SANAA

Architects and designers of the buildings and installations on the Vitra Campus, Weil am Rhein, 1981–2009

SITES   Vitra Campus, Weil am Rhein   25

Paola de Pietri   Aerial view of the Vitra Campus in Weil am Rhein from the south-west. The old factory building in the lower right corner of the grounds will be replaced with a new building by SANAA in 2009.

SITES   Vitra Campus, Weil am Rhein   26

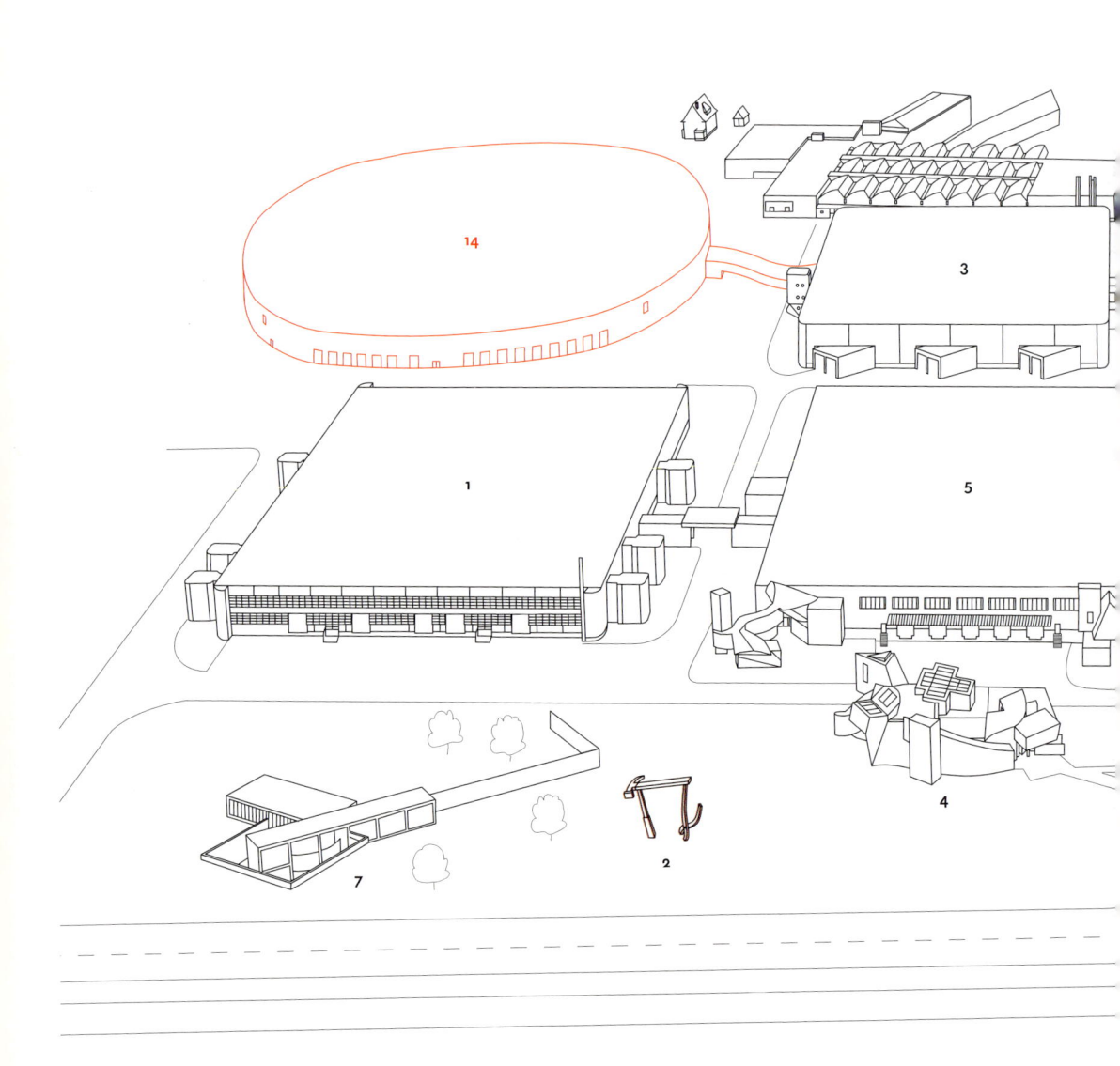

1 Factory hall, Nicholas Grimshaw, 1981
2 "Balancing Tools", Claes Oldenburg and
   Coosje van Bruggen, 1984
3 Factory hall, Nicholas Grimshaw, 1987
4 Vitra Design Museum, Frank Gehry, 1989
5 Factory hall, Frank Gehry, 1989
6 Gate, Frank Gehry, 1989
7 Conference Pavilion, Tadao Ando, 1993

| SITES | Vitra Campus, Weil am Rhein | 27 |

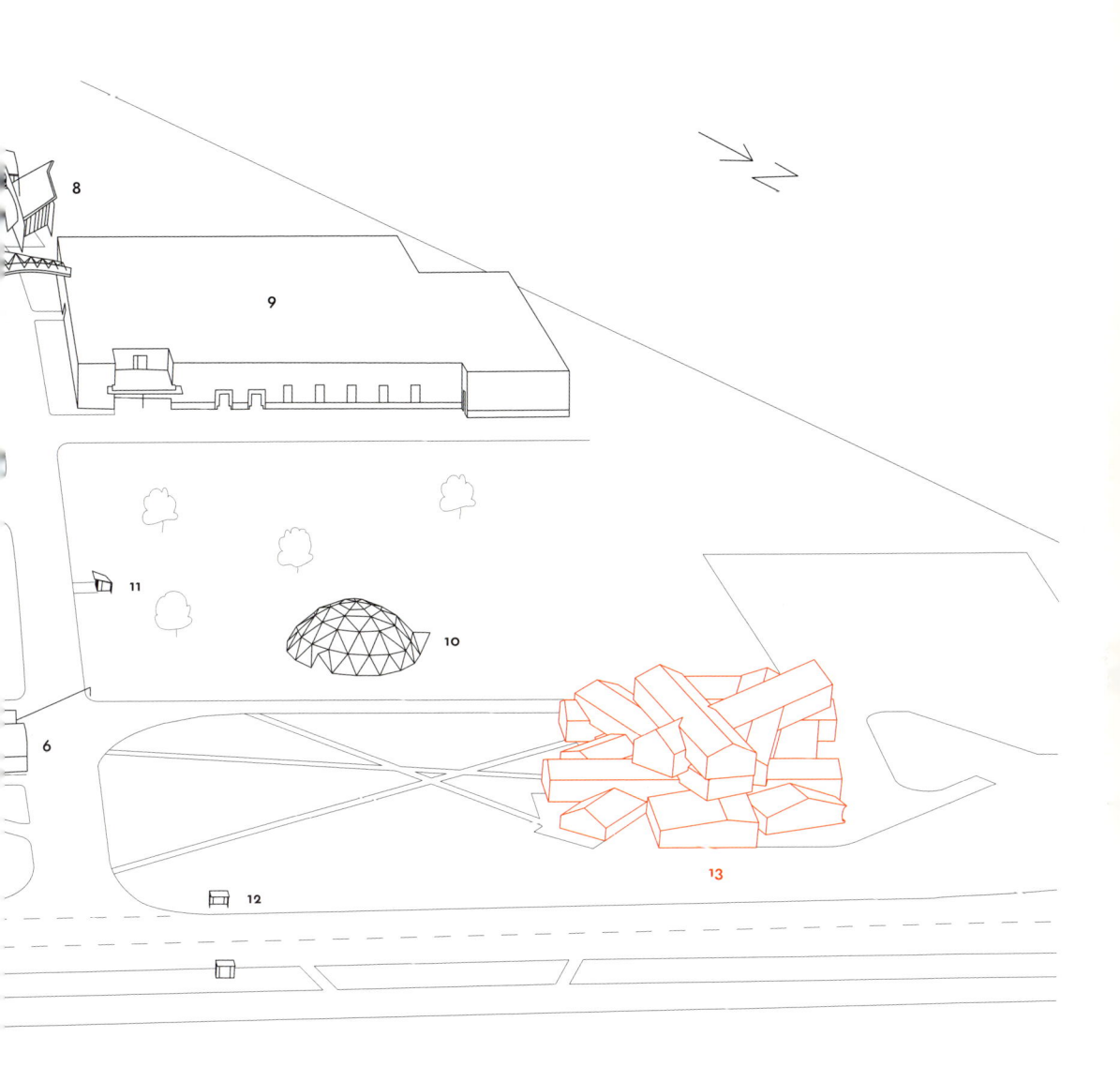

8 Fire Station, Zaha Hadid, 1993
9 Factory hall, Álvaro Siza, 1994
10 Dome, Richard Buckminster Fuller (c.1950), installed 2000
11 Petrol station, Jean Prouvé (1953), installed 2003
12 Bus stop, Jasper Morrison, 2006
13 VitraHaus, Herzog & de Meuron (under construction), 2009
14 Factory hall for Vitrashop, SANAA (under construction), 2009

SITES Vitra Campus, Weil am Rhein 28

Giovanni Chiaramonte   "Balancing Tools", a sculpture by Claes Oldenburg and Coosje van Bruggen, was set up in the Vitra grounds in 1984 as a 70th birthday present to company-founder Willi Fehlbaum from his sons. Ando's Conference Pavilion and Gehry's Vitra Design Museum both followed some time after and now form a superb backdrop.

SITES — Vitra Campus, Weil am Rhein — 29

SITES Vitra Campus, Weil am Rhein 30

Olivo Barbieri

The asphalt footpath between the Vitra Design Museum and Tadao Ando's Conference Pavilion was carefully laid out to enhance visitors' awareness of the architectural and functional differences between the two buildings.

SITES

Vitra Campus, Weil am Rhein

SITES | Vitra Campus, Weil am Rhein | 32

Olivo Barbieri | An L-shaped concrete wall leads visitors to the Conference Pavilion entrance and conceals the rest of the Vitra Campus.

SITES — Vitra Campus, Weil am Rhein — 33

SITES   Vitra Campus, Weil am Rhein   34

Paola de Pietri   Because cherry trees are the object of deep veneration in Japanese culture, Tadao Ando took great care to protect them when planning his Conference Pavilion, and only three of the trees had to be felled.

SITES   Vitra Campus, Weil am Rhein   35

SITES — Vitra Campus, Weil am Rhein — 36

Paola de Pietri — The Vitra Design Museum seen from the back against the long sweep of the Tüllinger hill.

SITES Vitra Campus, Weil am Rhein 37

SITES   Vitra Campus, Weil am Rhein

Gabriele Basilico

For his production building behind the Vitra Design Museum, Gehry adopted a plain, restrained style, venturing into more expressive sculptural forms only in the access areas on the north-eastern corners.

SITES   Vitra Campus, Weil am Rhein   39

Gabriele Basilico   A curving ramp, conveying a sense of flowing movement, leads to the upper floor of Gehry's production building.

SITES — Vitra Campus, Weil am Rhein — 40

Gabriele Basilico — The stele-like tower supports the ramp to the upper floor of the production building and forms a shaft through which light flows in.

SITES — Vitra Campus, Weil am Rhein — 41

Gabriele Basilico — The factory buildings, designed by Nicholas Grimshaw in the 1980s, with their cladding of horizontally ribbed metal panels.

SITES | Vitra Campus, Weil am Rhein | 42

Gabriele Basilico — Facade details of Grimshaw's factory buildings

| SITES | Vitra Campus, Weil am Rhein | 43 |

Gabriele Basilico

SITES — Vitra Campus, Weil am Rhein — 44

Olivo Barbieri — The second of Nicholas Grimshaw's factory buildings, which was constructed in 1987, with Álvaro Siza's 1994 building in the background.

SITES   Vitra Campus, Weil am Rhein   45

SITES — Vitra Campus, Weil am Rhein — 46

Olivo Barbieri

Siza designed this bridge-like roof to link his own and Grimshaw's factory buildings, and it was put in place in 1994. On its long arm of steel girder tracery, the roof is lowered only when it is raining and otherwise remains raised to allow an unobstructed view of Zaha Hadid's Fire Station.

Vitra Campus, Weil am Rhein

SITES — Vitra Campus, Weil am Rhein

Olivo Barbieri

The Fire Station was designed by Zaha Hadid, built in 1993, and is now used for cultural activities. The right-hand half of the building with its upward sweeping spear-shaped portico was formerly the garage for the fire engines. The left-hand side housed training rooms and other facilities for the firemen.

Vitra Campus, Weil am Rhein

SITES   Vitra Campus, Weil am Rhein   50

Olivo Barbieri   View of the Fire Station from the south showing the three interlocking wedge-like blocks that form the whole.

SITES — Vitra Campus, Weil am Rhein — 51

SITES Vitra Campus, Weil am Rhein

Giovanni Chiaramonte   A view of the Vitra Campus in Weil am Rhein from the Tüllinger hillside.

SITES Vitra Campus, Weil am Rhein

SITES   Vitra Campus, Weil am Rhein   54

Olivo Barbieri   The Vitra Campus by night with the lights of Basel in the background.

PLAYING SERIOUSLY

The Vitra Campus is a playing field – but for serious games. An industrial park in the heart of Europe does not at first sight appear to be the appropriate place for risk architecture; however, both technical innovation and artistic exploration are aspects of a desire to experiment that has resulted in an amazing collection of signature architecture in Weil am Rhein. From the dynamic forms of the Vitra Design Museum by the Californian Frank Gehry or the rushing forms of the Fire Station by the Anglo-Iraqi architect, Zaha Hadid, to the latest projects by the Japanese Kazuyo Sejima and Ryue Nishizawa, or the Swiss Jacques Herzog and Pierre de Meuron, major world architects have helped to turn the dream of the entrepreneur and collector, Rolf Fehlbaum, into reality by creating a site near Basel that is committed to experimentation and artistic excellence.

In Sydney Pollack's documentary on Frank Gehry, musician Bob Geldof, lost in thought, talks about being thunderstruck by the fleeting glimpses of the dancing forms of the Design Museum, his vision groggy with tiredness and the steamed-up glass of his tour bus, and this sensation of sudden discovery has struck visitors to the Campus ever since Gehry completed his most emblematic work in 1989. The year in which the Berlin Wall fell was also the year Vitra entered the history of architecture: this was the year in which "Arquitectura Viva" first dealt with the Campus, and the year in which I first heard admiring reports of the

Luis Fernández-Galiano

most forward-thinking pioneers who were on a pilgrimage to Weil am Rhein, while I was living in Los Angeles as a Visiting Scholar at the Getty Center.

Philip Johnson, whom I had got to know through Frank Gehry, was even then an enthusiastic follower of the Santa Monica architect, one of the seven artists included in his 'deconstructivist' exhibition at the MoMA the year before, but Johnson's trip to Basel did not come until a decade later. When at last he visited Basel and Weil in 1999, he wrote: "The Vitra collection of architecture by the great architects of the present day is unique in the world. Since the Weissenhofsiedlung in Stuttgart in 1927, there has not been a gathering in a single place of a group of buildings designed by the most distinguished architects in the Western world."

It was inevitable that the New York master was reminded of his own farm in Connecticut, where he had rounded off his career with a series of small structures in a similar way to the way in which Vitra brings together international architecture on its campus, with a mixture of personal ambition and openness to the general public – another point of contact between the two concepts at Weil and New Canaan.

In the spring of 2007, eighteen months after Johnson's death at ninety-eight in January 2006, his property at New Canaan, which he donated to the American National Trust, was opened to the public. Everyone who comes here to see the legendary Glass House which the American built in 1949 as a homage to his mentor, Mies van der Rohe, has to go through the sculpted Gatehouse built by Johnson as a homage to Gehry almost half a century later. By comparison, Vitra does not have such a long architectural history, although between the initial design in 1981 and the scheduled completion of the last commissions in 2009 there are almost three decades of architectural masterpieces. However, both the diversity of the styles and the importance of some of the works in the individual careers of their creators give Vitra a uniqueness that the critical generosity of Johnson highlighted.

After a fire in 1981, the factory area was reconstructed and, in later years, extended with the collaboration of a host of famous architects. The British architect, Nicholas Grimshaw, built the new factory halls in the years after the fire, while the Czech architect, Eva Jiricna, and the Italian, Antonio Citterio, were involved in parts of the rebuilding work. In 1989, Gehry completed the work on a factory hall and the Vitra Design Museum, which was his first work in Europe and the start of an extraordinarily influential stage in his career. Between 1993 and 1994, the Portuguese Álvaro Siza constructed another factory hall, the Japanese Tadao Ando a conference pavilion – also his first work in Europe –, and Zaha Hadid, a fire station, her very first building after coming to fame by winning first prize in the 'Peak Leisure Club' competition in 1982.

    In later years, the site was extended with the creation of a number of smaller buildings – a dome-shaped tent construction by Richard Buckminster Fuller, a petrol station by Jean Prouvé and a bus stop by Jasper Morrison. In 2006 work was begun on two further constructions – to be completed in 2009. One, an unusual round factory building with loading ramps all around it where transport vehicles can be docked, designed by the Tokyo-based studio, SANAA (Kazuyo Sejima and Ryue Nishizawa). In addition to this, Herzog & de Meuron designed

Luis Fernández-Galiano

"Balancing Tools" by Claes Oldenburg and Coosje van Bruggen, 1984

Dome by Richard Buckminster Fuller (c. 1950), installed 2000

the VitraHaus, a large showroom for products in the Vitra Home Collection, which combines typical motifs found in their latest creations, such as the classic pitched roof and a stacking of forms. Including the Swiss practice, five architectural studios that have been awarded the prestigious Pritzker prize are now represented on the Vitra Campus; the significance of this lies in the fact that in all cases, apart from the last one, the works were commissioned before the prize was awarded – a clear indication of Fehlbaum's nose for talent.

Even without taking into account Vitra's other buildings – Antonio Citterio constructed another factory building in the German town of Neuenburg and Frank Gehry designed the Vitra Center in the Swiss town of Birsfelden, near Basel –, the buildings at Weil am Rhein form such an unusual and cosmopolitan concentration of architecture in their brilliance and novelty that they were immediately included in the architectural tours of the area, already important because of its proximity to Le Corbusier's Notre-Dame-du-Haut chapel in Ronchamp and because of the Goetheanum by Rudolf Steiner in Dornach. Before taking over the family business, Rolf Fehlbaum completed a doctorate with a thesis on the utopian socialist, Saint-Simon – an aristocrat in

Petrol station by Jean Prouvé (1953), installed 2003

Bus stop by Jasper Morrison, 2006

Napoleonic times who was an advocate of the new religion of industry. With such worship of science and technology, Fehlbaum must have felt inspired.

The initial buildings constructed by Nicholas Grimshaw were in the high-tech tradition, unadorned, functional and precise elements which characterized much of British architecture. However, giving the commission for the Museum to Frank Gehry broke away from this essential line. The building constructed by the Californian – himself a chair designer – to house the company collection is characterized by its sculptural, broken forms in a shell made of white plaster and zinc plate, with an unexpected and highly complex interior full of luminous expressiveness. Opposite the gigantic polychrome tools by his friend, Claes Oldenburg – with whom he had already worked on the famous Chiat Day building in Los Angeles, whose facade incorporates the sculptor's gigantic prisms –, Gehry's small construction, designed without any help from the CATIA software which he would later find so useful, rose up like a playful formal and intellectual challenge. Echoes of the impression it made can be seen today in numerous works of architecture, including, of course, the most famous example, the Guggenheim Museum in Bilbao, also built by Gehry.

Luis Fernández-Galiano

But if the Design Museum was a stylistic shock, the buildings completed between 1993 and 1994 also had considerable repercussions. The factory hall by Álvaro Siza is a purist cube of bricks with monumental vertical cavities and a sculpted roof construction. It is totally unspectacular in comparison with the major ambitions of the overall design and, with the characteristics that appear in all his works, serves as a neutral background for the gestural work of Zaha Hadid. The Conference Pavilion by Tadao Ando has the characteristic precision of the Osaka architect. The master of concrete and light had not until then had an opportunity to build in Europe, if you exclude the now nonexistent pavilion for the Seville Expo in 1992. For Vitra, he produced a building sunk into the ground, organized around a square inner courtyard sunk into the lawn and consisting of a cylinder and two cuboids linked together elegantly and with calm clarity and beauty.

In the same stage of construction, Zaha Hadid also built her very first building – up until then, she had only designed a restaurant interior in Japan. After ten years of continuously being one of the architectural avant-garde, she was suddenly catapulted onto the cover of professional journals as a result of the Fire Station building. On a factory site, which was once destroyed by fire, a building of that kind enjoys great prestige – even though it lost its original function when the fire brigade subsequently moved to the city of Weil and it is now used for exhibitions. The dynamic, explosive construction suggests speed of response by the fire engines while at the same time touching on the incendiary with the violence of its projectile velocity.

The inclined, unstable elements of reinforced concrete aptly reflect the Anglo-Iraqi architect's interest in Russian Suprematism –

Luis Fernández-Galiano

VitraHaus by Herzog & de Meuron (rendering, due for completion in 2009)

Factory hall for Vitrashop by SANAA (rendering, due for completion in 2009)

a fondness which she learned from her professor, Rem Koolhaas, at the Architectural Association in London, where Hadid made her home. However, the anti-gravitational construction required the use of so much steel that the concrete covering essentially has no other purpose than to protect the metal against corrosion. For an architect known up to then only for her futuristic drawings of stretched, suspended, geometrical forms who stated that she was convinced that buildings could float, the materialization – contrary to all expectations – of the Vitra Fire Station was a milestone that turned the little building into a very influential work. Like Gehry, she was originally asked by Fehlbaum to design chairs and, like him, she ended up building structures of pivotal architectural influence.

These dynamic constructions, which cross cultural and stylistic frontiers, are metaphors for a world undergoing radical change. They represent, on the one hand, the hectic movement of people, towns, information and images which entwine the planet with their vertiginous flows, but they also represent the growing instability and nomadic life that characterize modern economies and society, whose imbalances further precipitate changes and fractures. Gehry's forms in motion and Hadid's accelerated architecture, as well as the expansive, light-footed dynamism of SANAA or the swaying balance in the buildings of Herzog & de Meuron, are architectural explorations of a world in motion, playful structures that can make many people smile while still being serious. Architecture is in motion but, like the world, we do not really know where it is going.

Luis Fernández-Galiano is an architect and professor at the architecture academy of the Universidad Politécnica in Madrid. He is active as a guest professor at numerous universities in Europe and the United States, as a jury member in many major competitions (for example, Venice Architecture Biennale, 2002), as a curator and author, and as the editor of the magazines "AV Monografias" and "Arquitectura Viva".

PRODUCTS.
Collections, editions, systems, photographed and staged by Maurice Scheltens and Liesbeth Abbenes — p. 66

<u>Public</u>, <u>Office</u>, <u>Home</u> by Rolf Fehlbaum — pp. 101, 114, 128

PRODUCTS.

Project Vitra dates back to 1957 when the company, based in Birsfelden near Basel, began producing designs by Charles & Ray Eames and George Nelson. Since then, Vitra has focused all of its energy on developing and manufacturing exceptional furniture that is both durable and aesthetically unique. Vitra, whose three divisions (Public, Office and Home) often overlap, is continually expanding its range of products and concepts for the workplace as well as public and private spaces.

PRODUCTS   Charles & Ray Eames Collection   66

PRODUCTS   Charles & Ray Eames Collection   67

PRODUCTS   Charles & Ray Eames Collection   68

PRODUCTS   Charles & Ray Eames Collection   69

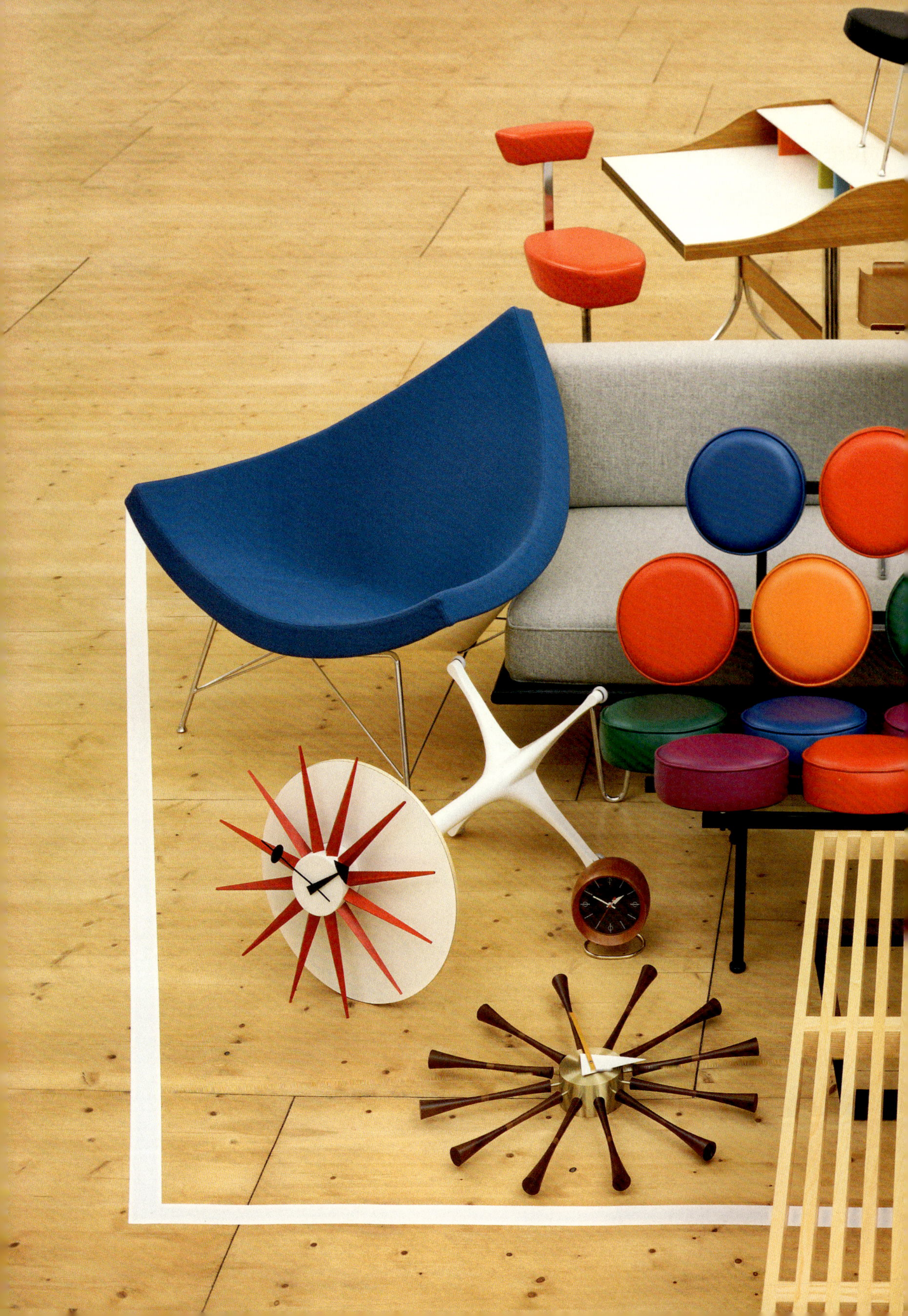

PRODUCTS   George Nelson Collection   71

PRODUCTS   Jean Prouvé Collection

PRODUCTS   Jean Prouvé Collection   73

PRODUCTS   Verner Panton Collection

PRODUCTS　　　Verner Panton Collection

PRODUCTS   Jasper Morrison Collection   76

PRODUCTS   Jasper Morrison Collection   77

PRODUCTS Maarten Van Severen Collection 78

PRODUCTS   Maarten Van Severen Collection

PRODUCTS   Ronan & Erwan Bouroullec Collection

PRODUCTS Ronan & Erwan Bouroullec Collection 81

PRODUCTS   Hella Jongerius Collection   82

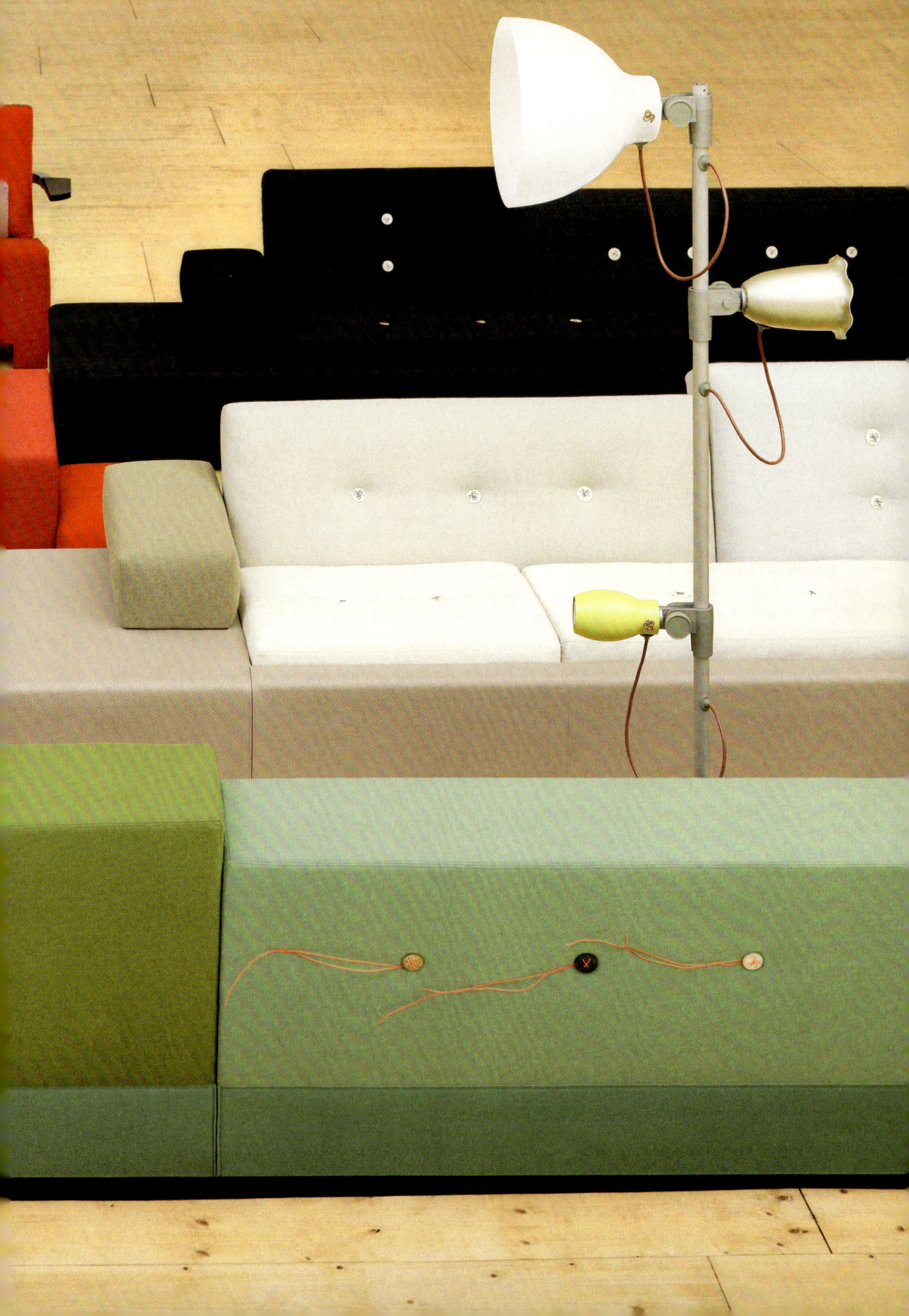

PRODUCTS Vitra Design Museum Collection

Left line, from bottom to top: Children's Chair (Eames); Elephant Stool (Yanagi) + Wooden Dolls (Girard); Prismatic Table (Noguchi) + Ball Clock (Nelson); Elephant Stool (Yanagi); Butterfly Stool (Yanagi) + Geometri Pillow (Panton); Rocking Stool (Noguchi) + Tripod Clock (Nelson).
Middle, from bottom to top: Uten.Silo (Becker); Nesting Tables (Albers) + Miniatures; Akari Light

PRODUCTS   Vitra Design Museum Collection   85

Sculptures (Noguchi); Colonial Table (Bellmann) + Sunflower Clock (Nelson); Hang it all (Eames).
Right line, from bottom to top: Children's Chair (Eames); Elephant Stool (Yanagi) + Talulah the
Toucan (Nelson); Prismatic Table (Noguchi) + Petal Clock (Nelson); Elephant Stool (Yanagi);
Butterfly Stool (Yanagi) + Checker Pillow (Girard); Rocking Stool (Noguchi) + Tripod Clock (Nelson).

PRODUCTS   Editions and sculptural objects (a selection)   86

From left to right: Coffee Table (Noguchi); Bad-Tempered Chair (Arad); Low Table Set (Gehry); How High The Moon (Kuramata); Red Beaver (Gehry); Wiggle Side Chair + Side Chair (Gehry); Freeform Sofa (Noguchi); La Chaise (Eames); BaObab (Starck); W.W. Stool (Starck); Hocker (Herzog & de Meuron); Ravioli Chair (Lynn).

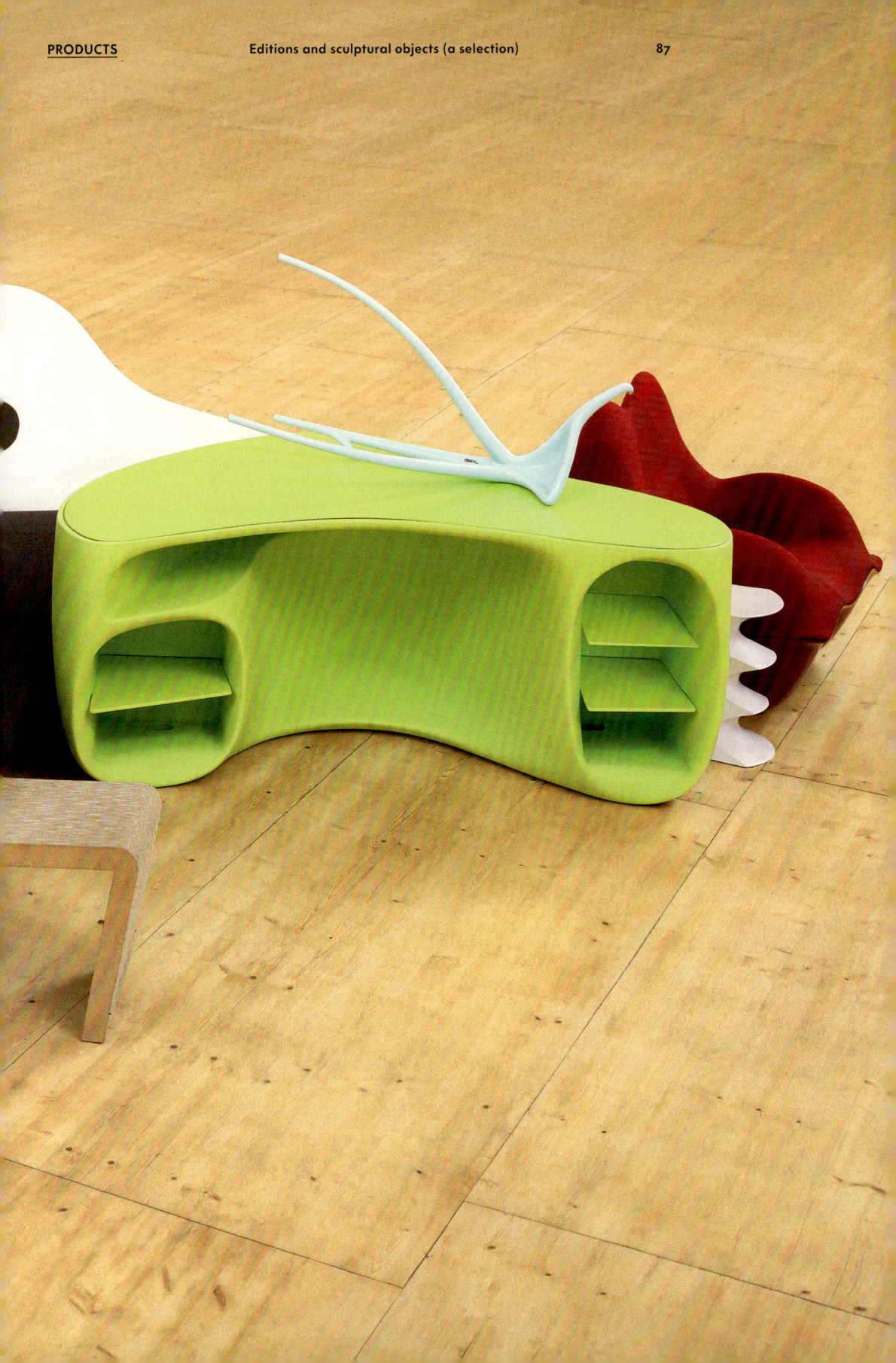

PRODUCTS · Editions and sculptural objects (a selection) · 87

PRODUCTS   Alberto Meda Collection (a selection)   88

PRODUCTS Alberto Meda Collection (a selection)

PRODUCTS Antonio Citterio Collection (a selection)

PRODUCTS Antonio Citterio Collection (a selection) 91

PRODUCTS   Ad Hoc office system by Antonio Citterio   92

PRODUCTS　　　　Ad Hoc office system by Antonio Citterio

PRODUCTS   Ad One office system by Antonio Citterio   94

PRODUCTS   Ad One office system by Antonio Citterio

PRODUCTS Joyn office system by Ronan & Erwan Bouroullec 96

PRODUCTS   Joyn office system by Ronan & Erwan Bouroullec   97

PRODUCTS   Level 34 office system by Werner Aisslinger

PRODUCTS — Level 34 office system by Werner Aisslinger

PRODUCTS

…Akari, Alcove, Algue, Amoebe, Antony, BaObab, Bar Boy, Bovist, Box, Butterfly, Cité, Coconut, Compas, Freeform, Guéridon, Heart Cone, How High The Moon, Hula Hoop, La Fonda, Loulou, Marshmallow, Polder, Potence, Ravioli, Red Beaver, Self, Standard, Trapèze, Wiggle…

A selection of product names from Vitra collections

PUBLIC, OFFICE, HOME

Whether conceived for the public sphere, the office environment or the private home, objects often appear in unanticipated ways and in unexpected places. They are like actors on a stage whose essential character remains elusive, in spite of our speculations about it. They illustrate alliances, frictions and conflicts stemming from the respective venue and its particular conventions, while demonstrating the degree to which reality can resist the ideals of design. And they fall into the hands of users with preconceived notions about what they purchased, why they bought it and what practical or symbolic gain they expect from it. This uncertainty is a necessary part of any attempt to achieve an impact with industrially manufactured products. But the physical and conceptual quality of a piece of furniture increases its chances of establishing a dignified and persuasive presence in its eventual real-world setting. Vitra bases its developmental concepts on the continual reflection of current and projected living conditions. They take into account the circumstances of everyday existence, as well as the needs and requirements that can be deduced from it. The product range of Vitra Home thus aims to facilitate an intentionally heterogeneous collage in the home defined by personal motives, while Vitra Office promotes the blending of work and life in the office, of networking and privacy. Vitra Public, in turn, pursues the goal of setting quality standards in public spaces, thereby serving as a model for others and making an enduring contribution to social well-being.

Rolf Fehlbaum

VITRA PUBLIC – THE OUTSIDE WORLD

The public sphere today encompasses far more than public space in the traditional sense of the term. It also includes areas with circumscribed public character, such as a corporate lobby, conference room facilities, the interior of a restaurant or an airport. Vitra products are also indispensable components of the staged environments transmitted all over the world by means of modern media, such as TV studios, any of countless talk-show sets or many other places where daily happenings are viewed through a camera lens.

It is in such areas of the public sphere that our products find their largest audience. Public zones are continuously perceived and experienced – though the attentiveness tends to be fleeting, that of someone ambling through and lost in thought. A well-designed public space makes it possible to experience how design and architecture can influence one's mental state and mood. Therefore the organizations that occupy and oversee public zones are obliged to act with great care and forethought. They must provide facilities that manage to accommodate the needs of a largely unknown public in places where issues of personal comfort and satisfaction usually go unaddressed.

Such a level of care requires decisive intentions and measures. The myriad sensory signals in an urban environment or in an airport, for instance, often lead to overstimulation followed by fatigue and confusion. Vitra's objective for furnishing these public spaces is,

Rolf Fehlbaum

therefore, to avoid further agitation through the use of familiar products (especially classics) or of new designs with a more reserved appearance.

In this manner, the furnishing of a lecture hall, public administration building, airport, church, café, museum, library or parliament can enhance the public perception of values like quality, authenticity and longevity. In Europe, for instance, no chair is as widespread in the conference sector as the Eames Aluminium Chair. Its design embodies clarity, directness and elegance, and we are of the opinion that these qualities have a positive influence on the content and atmosphere of an event. While difficult to prove, this can be experienced intuitively upon entering a space that is furnished with these chairs.

Another defining characteristic of the public sphere is that its facilities are subjected to frequent abuse. We know what it means for a product to be exposed to years of public use and have learned to work with these standards. At the same time, however, the durability needed to withstand such usage should not yield the slightest compromise in terms of the design ambitions and message of Vitra's products.

Finally, public facilities constitute environments in which the user is unable to exert any influence. At home, the individual decides how the space is to be furnished. And in the office, even an interior arrangement that is disliked by employees can be altered and personalized through small interventions. In the case of furnishings in the public sphere, however, visitors and users have to take things as they come.

Rolf Fehlbaum

Charles Eames articulated the engaging notion that every design task should be approached with the attitude of a good host who competently anticipates the desires of his or her guests. This 'guest-host relationship' is especially relevant with regard to the design and outfitting of public spaces.

Rolf Fehlbaum

__PRODUCTS__   Vitra Public   105

Aeroporto Francisco Sá Carneiro, Porto, 2005

Pearson International Airport, Toronto, 2005–2006

Prince George Airport Authority, 2004    Munich Airport, 2003    Dubai International Airport, 2000

Nasjonalbiblioteket, Oslo, 2005    University Library, Utrecht, 2004

PRODUCTS   Vitra Public   106

The Seattle Public Library, 2004

Allerheiligen Hofkirche, Munich, 2003

Augustinus Muziekcentrum, Antwerp, 2006

Weil am Rhein Church, 1993

St Bartholomew Church, Chodovice, Czech Republic, 2006

…Allerheiligen Hofkirche, Atomium, Centre Pompidou, Deutscher Bundestag, Kunsthaus Graz, LA Philharmonic Concert Hall, Nasjonalbiblioteket Oslo, Palais de Justice Nantes, Pinakothek der Moderne München, Seattle Public Library, Tate Modern, University Library Utrecht…

A selection of projects for public spaces

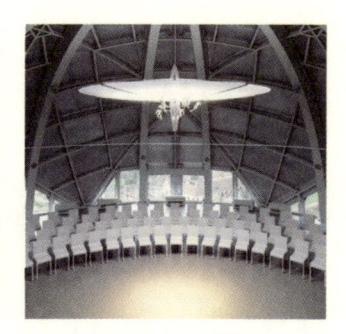

PRODUCTS   Vitra Public   108

Atomium, Brussels, 2006

EXPO 2000, Hanover, 2000

Kunsthaus, Graz, 2003

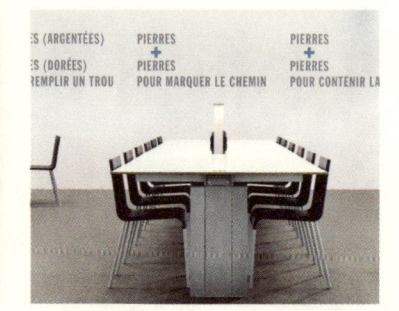

Centre Pompidou, Paris, 1997–1999   Pinakothek der Moderne, Munich, 2002

PRODUCTS　　　Vitra Public　　　109

MAK, Vienna, 2006

Wapping Project, London, 2004

Sushi West, Paris, 2004

Wox Restaurant, Abdoun, Amman, 2003

Bed Supperclub, Bangkok, 2004

Hotel Überfluss, Bremen, 2005

Hotel Julien, Antwerp, 2004

G-Star International, Amsterdam, 2004

Mexx International, Amsterdam, 2004

Philips International Headquarters, Amsterdam, 2001–2003

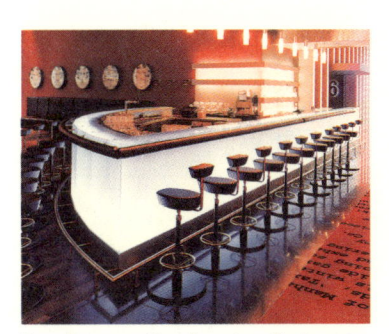

Sony European Headquarters, Berlin, 1999

The National Belgian Railway Company, Brussels, 2001

Marks & Spencer, London, 2004

PRODUCTS Vitra Public

The Reichstag, Berlin, 1999

Sachsen Parliament, Dresden, 1997

Marseille City Hall, 2006

Lower Austria Parliament, St Pölten, 1996

Basel City Hall, 2001

Gruppo IPI, La Bolla, Turin, 1994

Institut du Monde Arabe, Paris, 1990

The National Belgian Railway Company, Brussels, 2001

F. Hoffmann-La Roche Training Centre, Buonas, 2002

Novartis, Basel, 2006

…Allianz, Apple, BBC, BMW, Cartier, Coca-Cola, Commerzbank, DaimlerChrysler, Deutsche Bank, Exxon Mobil, Google, Hoffmann-La Roche, IBM, L'Oréal, Lufthansa, Microsoft, Motorola, Nestlé, Novartis, Philips, Prada, Shiseido, Sony, Swiss Re, Toyota, UBS, Vodafone, VW, Warner Bros…

A selection of projects for offices

| PRODUCTS | Vitra Office | 112 |

Reliance Infocomm Ltd., Mumbai, 2003

Commerzbank, Frankfurt, 2001

The Fashion Institute of Design & Merchandising, Los Angeles, 2004

Sony Design Center, Los Angeles, 2004

Editoriale Domus, Quattroruote, Rozzano, 2006

Reynolds Porter Chamberlain LLP, London, 2006

Marks & Spencer, London, 2004

PRODUCTS Vitra Office 113

BBC, London, 2004    BBC, Birmingham, 2004

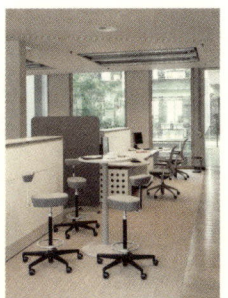

Mensura, Brussels, 2003    Deloitte, Prague, 2005

Novartis, Basel, 2005     Nestlé Nespresso, Sion, 2006–2008

Barcode-House, Munich, 2005

VITRA OFFICE – THE OFFICE WORLD

The office has a reputation for being a rather unpleasant place, characterized by discipline, uniformity and hierarchy, as well as the banishment of anything evocative of real life. Or is this interpretation merely a distorted image from the past – a reflection of the accumulated office disasters from "The Trial" by Kafka to Billy Wilder's "The Apartment" up to the open bullpens of the 1960s?

Jacques Tati, "Playtime", 1967

We know the office disaster stories. At the same time, we know they can be avoided. For thirty years, we have made the office our daily preoccupation. We work on new products, experiment with office concepts in our own facilities and read everything directly or indirectly related to the office – ergonomic aspects, technical details, cultural issues. We survey our customers, analyze our successes as well as our flops and visit all the offices we can.

The goal is easily summarized: a better office. Yet what does

Rolf Fehlbaum

'better' mean? The office should become better for the operators, that is, for companies and institutions. First and foremost this means that it should be made more productive. But the user, the office worker, should also feel comfortable and at ease. Can solutions be found to serve the interests of both parties simultaneously? And how important is the office environment compared to other factors of productivity such as organization, wages, training and quality of management? Is the furnishing of an office ultimately a matter for organizational experts, or should it concern everyone?

In finding answers to these questions, we draw on three hypotheses.

Firstly, the objects and spaces that surround us are senders of messages. They influence our feelings, our moods and – when subjected to these surroundings in the office day in, day out, over a stretch of many hours – our behaviour as well. Hence, office furnishings are more than just functional equipment or superficial decor, and our role is to understand, enhance and direct the signals they send.

Secondly, the interests of management and employees are seldom contradictory when it comes to furnishings. The way that management deals with office matters, however, tends to be authoritarian. Desires of employees that could easily be fulfilled often go unrecognized, and potential conflicts of interest are rarely the subject of open discussion. Such an approach makes it impossible to achieve simple, non-coercive solutions and forfeits the opportunity to create an office environment that motivates employees and thus helps raise productivity.

Thirdly, an office interior does not 'lie'. It unavoidably expresses the character of a company, its strengths and weaknesses, its working

Rolf Fehlbaum

Orson Welles,
"The Trial", 1962

"The Office",
BBC series, 2001

style, its ambitions. What must be realized, however, is that it does not merely reflect the company but can also exert an impact on its character. And when anchored in new ideas and principles, a new building or office interior can alter the organization of a company as well as how it is perceived.

In the best-case scenario, a well-furnished office can enhance the quality of teamwork and increase productivity. It will motivate individuals and positively influence the character of the company – its identity – thereby achieving an impact both internally and externally. Seen this way, the office becomes a central concern for every company. It has long been about more than just furniture, focusing on working

Rolf Fehlbaum

styles, business models, personnel management and recruiting too. Yet it also constitutes the greatest reserve of untapped productivity left to Western economies, now that the outsourcing of production processes has largely been exhausted.

Before coming to this understanding, however, the office underwent a long evolutionary process. Ever since there have been offices, the organizers of these spaces have been preoccupied with the design of office environments. Such efforts long focused on the Tayloristic rationalization of workflows. In the socio-political discussions of the 1970s, the influence of social democracy in Europe led to new calls for the 'humanization of work', with specific demands placed on the ergonomics and quality of workspaces. The realization of office environments upholding these principles, however, remained a topic for specialists. It was only with the now prevalent regard for the intellectual capital of a society and with the recognition of the central role played by so-called knowledge workers in advancing productivity that the office also became a matter of interest to chief executive officers.

Reception area for Interpolis insurance company, Tilburg (NL), Jurgen Bey, 2003

Rolf Fehlbaum

In the process of reconsidering previously held notions, the open-plan office is now experiencing a renaissance even in countries like Germany, where experiments with this configuration in the 1960s met with radical rejection because of their failure to accommodate the human need for privacy and protection. The open-plan schemes that companies are currently working with have been reformed and refined. The sole characteristic they share with the early office landscapes is their exploitation of the communication benefits of open spaces. Vitra has dedicated itself to the civilization of the open plan and supports modes of working that correspond to this goal.

The Vitra project began in 1957 with the licensed production of designs that Charles & Ray Eames and George Nelson had developed for the American furniture manufacturer Herman Miller. In particular, George Nelson played a pioneering role in shaping the office. The explosive power of his ideas is difficult to identify nowadays because the new typologies he created soon became widely established. A prominent example of this is the L-shaped desk. Since the nineteenth century,

L-shaped desk,
George Nelson, 1947

Rolf Fehlbaum

a desk with a working surface resting on two pedestals or cabinets had been a standard feature of every office. In 1947, George Nelson designed a desk with a single cabinet and a second element positioned at a 90° angle that provided an additional work surface for a typewriter and paperwork. With this novel configuration, he had created a new workplace type, with the 'workstation' taking the place of the desk.

George Nelson was also involved in the inaugural manifestation of another fundamentally new idea, even if only half-heartedly. The work in question is AO 1 – the attractive yet economically untenable precursor to the Action Office. Nelson acted as the designer on this project while Robert Propst served as concept developer. The unsuccessful outcome of this unequal and mismatched partnership was followed by the AO 2, with which Nelson was no longer involved. The design of the AO 2, later simply referred to as AO, was rather

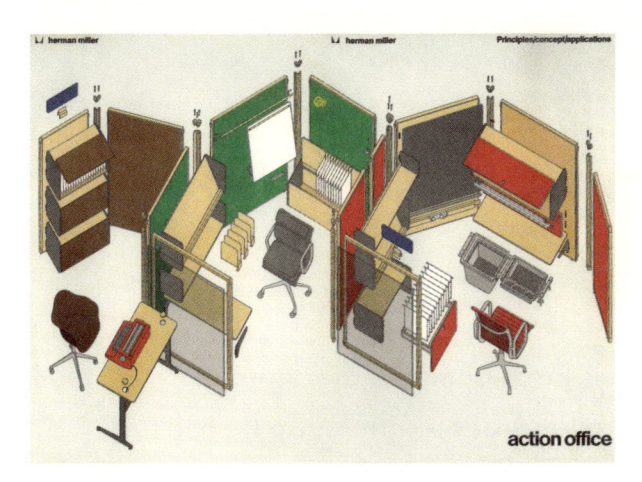

Action Office,
Herman Miller brochure, 1974

uninspired. The concept met with great success, however, going on to redefine the office environment in the United States from its inception in 1967 and restructuring the entire office furniture industry.

Rolf Fehlbaum

In all these developments, Vitra acted as the licensed producer for Europe and not as the initiator. It was not until 1968 that it launched its first independently developed product, the Panton Chair. While the Panton Chair had nothing to do with the office, it strengthened the company's self-confidence in pursuing its own projects. In 1976, Vitramat followed as the first office chair developed directly by Vitra – with the aim of imbuing the office chair 'machine', previously dominated by ergonomic aspects, with an aesthetically compelling form. The designer was Wolfgang Müller-Deisig, an unknown at the time. The chair's innovative synchronized mechanism was engineered by Egon Bräuning, who later headed product development at Vitra.

"Vitramat",
product brochure, 1976

In the years since, office chairs have been a major area of activity for Vitra. In the 1980s, the collaboration with Mario Bellini led to products that were the first to bring qualities of domestic interiors into the office. Later developments included projects with Antonio Citterio, Alberto Meda and most recently with Ronan & Erwan Bouroullec. The Worknest chair by the Bouroullec brothers

(2006) decidedly counters the recent ideal of the office chair as a conspicuously functional machine by interpreting functionality as an integrated feature.

For the long term, however, Vitra was not content in the limited role of chair manufacturer – it also wanted to have a voice in the overall design of office interiors. Unlike the chair, a self-contained and universally employable object, office furniture express ideas about interior space and embody values and convictions. Office spaces can intimidate through their monumentality; they can express hierarchical or egalitarian structures; they can embolden or stifle individual initiative. This ideological content often remains hidden, however, due to the fact that the office furniture industry by and large merely serves up the conventions of the prevailing organizational models without criticism or reflection. Vitra, by contrast, has always been interested in revitalizing and redefining the modes of working and the organizational forms of companies.

    The first approach taken was Metropol, a system that Vitra created in collaboration with Mario Bellini. As a designer for Olivetti, Bellini was familiar with the progress of information technology and anticipated that it would become an integral part of our lives. He therefore rejected the idea of developing technologically motivated 'computer furniture' for a specific generation of office machines, instead seeking to create an intelligent desk capable of easily assimilating the inevitable technological advances of the future.

    This was followed by the Ad Hoc programme created by Antonio Citterio: an office with a fresh spirit and technical straightforwardness,

"Metropol",
product brochure, 1988

a flexible module system that can accommodate all areas of the office and be broken down into reconfigurable elements. Colour found its way into the office, and over the years a comprehensive programme took shape covering all office types from individual workstations to constellations with several people up to bench systems.

Another important step towards a new work environment was Joyn by the Bouroullec brothers – a furniture system that explicitly set out to promote communication in the workplace. In responding to the complexity of the environment and the uncertainties that nearly every company has to grapple with, personal responsibility and networking present themselves as a key strategy. Each employee has to define his or her own job within the scope of a broadly cast assignment and must feel responsible for a range of tasks that might in some cases extend beyond the stated parameters.

As a result, organizations are dependent on communication as never before. Going into the office – as opposed to working undisturbed from home – represents the pivotal basis for this exchange.

Rolf Fehlbaum

Through this interaction, the group develops its own intelligence. The old office founded on the division of labour and the hierarchical accretion of individual results is being supplanted by a marketplace of knowledge. An essential insight is that the organization as a whole knows more than the management. This is one of the reasons why the oft-predicted disappearance of the conventional office and its transfer to the home workplace has failed to occur.

For this new practice to become established, the office has to change. The example of urban development provides a useful model. Interaction and communication do not simply happen on their own. A vital urban neighbourhood is a place where people who are essentially strangers can strike up useful relationships. Yet this only occurs if they do not remain entrenched in their homes, but instead circulate in the outside world – in parks, cafés, bookshops or open-air markets – where they are able to engage in and benefit from random encounters. Precisely the same thing has to happen in the office.

Equally important as the hardware is the planning of offices. We use our own offices as a laboratory for experimentation. In so doing, we have learned that a good office planner has to be an organizer as well as a psychologist and interior designer. Moreover, companies need to be prepared to invest time in workshops. This commitment is the only way to avoid the mistakes of authoritarian planning, prepare employees for the new environment and ensure the acceptance of new facilities.

These facilities are spatially divided into zones for concentrated group work, zones for retreat to accommodate solitary work, zones with elements from domestic interiors for informal meetings, a library, a café and conference zones that can be partitioned off. Such a loosening of structures and diversity of furnishings is made possible through the deliberate incorporation of home furniture and accessories from Vitra. In adopting this approach, the office recognizes and embraces the fact that we not only work here but live here as well.

Not long ago, we came up with a fitting name for this conception of the office: Net 'n' Nest. The essential importance of networking is no longer questioned. The need for nesting, for retreat, demarcation and shelter, on the other hand, is generally not discussed because it seems backwards or even autistic. Yet, in fact, nesting is the natural counterpart to networking.

The Net 'n' Nest approach addresses both of these poles, which are present in every good office. Moreover, such exemplary offices present a unique collage corresponding to the specific characteristics of the respective company. Together with their clients, the architect or planner is the creator of this collage. To foster and facilitate this creative process, Vitra provides an extensive catalogue of potential solutions, with numerous chairs and systems, the entire Home Collection and our line of classics. This fount of possibilities offers an endless variety of individual solutions.

The long path from Vitramat to Net 'n' Nest was covered in many small steps. There were a number of important stimuli along the way, however, that promoted this development and firmly propelled it forwards.

The most important inspiration came from the exhibition "Citizen Office", which the Vitra Design Museum organized in 1993 in coop-

Rolf Fehlbaum

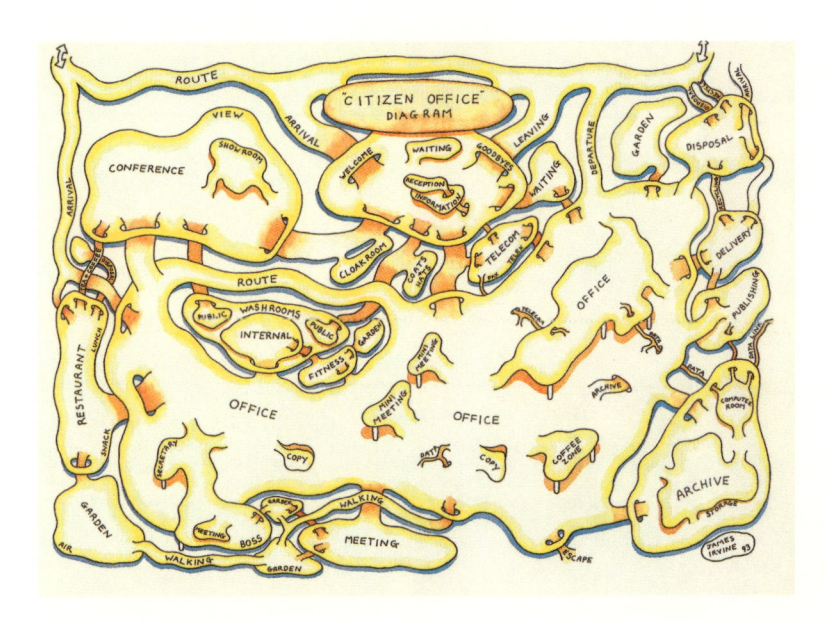

James Irvine, 1993 diagram of office configurations for the Vitra Design Museum's "Citizen Office" exhibition

eration with Ettore Sottsass, Andrea Branzi and Michele De Lucchi. It provided a new vision of the office.

The most important encounter was with George Nelson, who personified the unity of conceptual thinking, social analysis and design competence like no one else – particularly with regard to the office.

George Nelson and Rolf Fehlbaum, c. 1965

Rolf Fehlbaum

Administration building of
insurer Centraal Beheer,
Apeldoorn, 1970–1972.
Architect: Herman Hertzberger

The most important office interior was Centraal Beheer by Herman Hertzberger, the concrete embodiment of an office utopia in the late 1960s and early 1970s.

The most important experiments with our own environment were realized since 1997 with London-based designer Sevil Peach.

The most important social insight culled from these and other experiences was that many people lack opportunities for social contact, making the workplace the most significant site of interpersonal exchange. The office is the arena where a vital part of life unfolds,

Rolf Fehlbaum

not merely an auxiliary offshoot. As a space, it should be far more than just a set of office chambers.

The most important book was "The Office: A Facility Based on Change" by Robert Propst, the father of the Action Office. As a counterpoint to this way of thinking, however, it is advisable to read "A Pattern Language" by Christopher Alexander (with whom we attempted to realize an office furnishing system 'with soul').

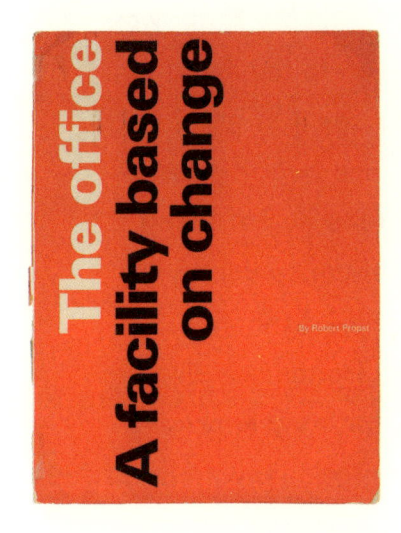

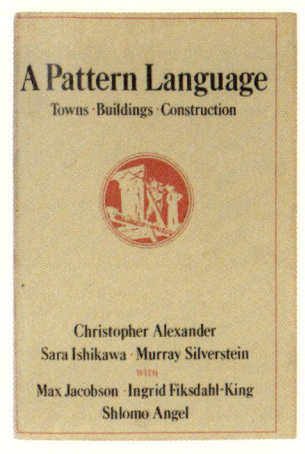

Books by Robert Propst (left) and Christopher Alexander (right)

The most important economic challenge facing the countries of Europe and the United States is to secure their own survival through creativity. Yet creativity can only flourish in a hybrid landscape of interaction and retreat, of multiple work options, moods and stimulations. This also defines the task facing Vitra: the development of an office environment in which creative work can flourish.

Rolf Fehlbaum

VITRA HOME – PRIVATE COLLAGES

Going back to its earliest days as a company, Vitra has always been concerned with domestic living and the home environment. All the same, a dedicated line of products for this sector has only been available in the last few years. This chronological discrepancy can be explained by looking at the orientation of the company. It reflects a history that owes less to the furniture and the designers themselves than to the living conditions of our society and its driving economic forces.

The Eames and Nelson furniture, with which Vitra began production in the late 1950s, was first primarily employed in the home. At the same time, these designers, bearing a tremendous influence during the formative years of the company, made no fundamental distinction between the outfitting of working and living spaces. Hence, we always felt connected to the home environment even after the truly engaging themes for Vitra were found in the office world. Technical innovations, new types of organizational concepts and deeper insights into identity formation and worker motivation led to radical changes, while the domestic sphere increasingly became a place of retreat, a private space, not an economically productive one. Originally triggered by the transition from an agrarian society into an industrial society and its form of production based on the division of labour, this process was additionally reinforced by the continually growing significance of services and their characteristic organizational forms.

This tendency did not change direction until modern information technology ushered in a paradigm shift, which was accompanied by

Rolf Fehlbaum

From: "Select, arrange", Vitra Home catalogues, 2005–2007

new freedoms. Today we can work almost anywhere. Some forecasts even heralded the private home as the most important future workplace and envisaged something akin to a revolution in the conditions of employment. While social developments have evolved in this direction, they have proven to be more moderate and multifaceted than those earlier predictions. However, in addition to our household chores, many of us now also perform at least some professional work activities from our home computer connection. Moreover, we all make continuous use of electronic media to listen to music and watch television, for education, recreation and creative purposes.

With the definitive transition to a post-industrial society, private and public aspects thus intermingle in a new way, which also impacts on the way we live. The intertwining of work and domestic living, the expansion of leisure activities as well as the far-reaching penetration of the media and the networking of everyday life demand new functions and forms of expression in many areas, in particular in the home environment.

Another important factor is that the static biography of the traditional nuclear family no longer provides meaningful orientation and standards for design. Nowadays more and more people in Western societies live alone. Relationships and living arrangements are subject to frequent change. The patchwork of lifestyles engenders a tangle of often controversial expectations regarding the value and flexibility of the home.

Hence, the new home environment needs to represent much more than a snug cocoon that encases its occupants. It should be a productive space in which inhabitants can play, learn, cook, eat, relax,

Rolf Fehlbaum

PRODUCTS   Vitra Home   131

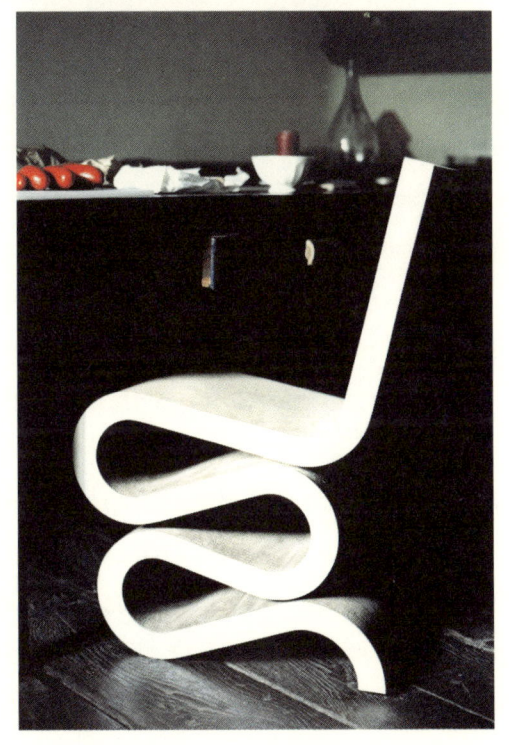

From: "Select, arrange", Vitra Home catalogues, 2005–2007

converse and occasionally even work. The outfitting of the home must accommodate this diversity with practical yet inspiring arrangements of furniture, objects, carpeting, lighting, textiles and technical devices for work and recreation. And the actively engaged individuals who live in these spaces are only conditionally interested in the changing fashions of design. They reject anything pretentious, instead opting for 'good goods' – enduring pieces with character. After all, they do not plan on redecorating year after year but are seeking a sensible balance between aesthetic risk and reliable use and function.

Several years back, these thoughts informed our considerations for a new model of domestic living. To reflect our accumulated knowledge in the areas of social behaviour and design, we chose the concept of a collage. This concept proceeds from the idea that responsibility for the master plan of an individualized home environment never resides with the manufacturer but with the user. Accordingly, there will never be a typical Vitra home. Individuals put together their own personal universe as a composite of heterogeneous elements. And for this process, they require neither aesthetic systems in the sense of standard furnishing schemes nor superimposed ideologies, but strong and autonomous products that can still be compatibly combined.

My first experience with the collage concept came when I was nineteen years old. On a visit to Charles and Ray Eames at their home in Pacific Palisades, I stood surrounded by a fascinating collage of furniture, objects, textiles, folk art, pictures and plants that took me on a journey through various ages and cultures. It had an improvised feeling about it and yet one could palpably sense the guiding hand that had carefully selected and ordered the elements. Individual items took

PRODUCTS   Vitra Home   133

From: "Select, arrange", Vitra Home catalogues, 2005–2007

on an increased familiarity and buoyancy through the way they were inserted into the whole. This space was unmistakably the centre of Charles and Ray's private existence, yet it also managed to effortlessly convey its unique enchantment to larger audiences – as I had the opportunity to experience a few years later at a picnic with seventy-five guests from all over the world.

A collage is anything but a cobbled-together patchwork. It is also far more than a mere aggregate of furniture and accessories in varying styles, languages and impressions. Our understanding of a collage is an arrangement founded on an individual coordinate system. A collage creates synergies between the objects chosen to furnish a particular space. The Vitra Home Collection brings together well-established icons and reissued works from major twentieth-century designers, as well as designs from the vibrant generation of contemporary authors. It includes furniture for all budgets, from inexpensive articles to luxury objects, in a variety of manufacturing techniques ranging from traditional handicrafts to highly innovative technologies and materials.

This breadth is the focus of our efforts. For a collage cannot come pre-packaged or prescribed. It only achieves coherence and harmony as a personal creation. It is therefore essential that people are given opportunities to make qualified selections that trace and reflect notions of their own identity. A home that evolves from such opportunities is the only place where we can truly be ourselves.

Rolf Fehlbaum

| PRODUCTS | Vitra Home | 135 |

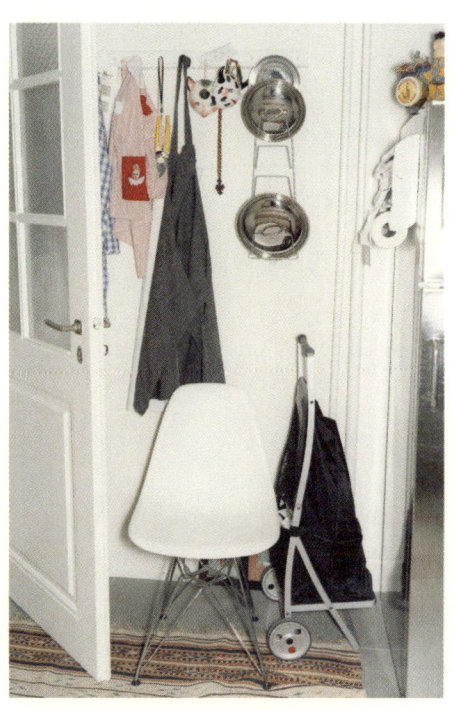

From: "Select, arrange", Vitra Home catalogues, 2005–2007

| PRODUCTS | Vitra Home | 136 |

From: "Select, arrange", Vitra Home catalogues, 2005–2007

AUTHORS.
Designers and architects: 20 portraits — p.140

<u>Design processes. Individual authorship at Vitra</u> by Rolf Fehlbaum — p. 223

AUTHORS.

AUTHORS

Vitra sees designers not simply as contractors but as authors. The relationship of trust between these authors from all corners of the world and Vitra, who shares their ambitions, is at the very heart of the company's product development process. Collaborations are always a subtle synthesis of artistic freedom, production know-how and industry knowledge. This philosophy has shaped the company's culture since its early partnerships with seminal designers like Charles & Ray Eames and George Nelson.

AUTHORS

…Charles & Ray Eames, George Nelson, Alexander Girard, Tibor Kalman, Frank Gehry, Tadao Ando, SANAA, Jasper Morrison, Zaha Hadid, Hella Jongerius, Maarten Van Severen, Ronan & Erwan Bouroullec, Jean Prouvé, Mario Bellini, Antonio Citterio, Alberto Meda, Verner Panton, Herzog & de Meuron…

A selection of designers and architects working with Vitra since the 1950s

Charles & Ray Eames

Charles and Ray Eames in 1959 on their way to Moscow for the "American National Exhibition". Charles is holding the film reels for "Glimpses of the USA" – a multiscreen presentation developed by the Eames Office that drew huge crowds at the exhibition.

Charles & Ray Eames

Charles & Ray Eames worked successively with three-dimensional moulded plywood, fibreglass-reinforced plastic and wire in their early, pioneering series. It was with the production of these pieces in Europe that Vitra's story as a furniture manufacturer began.

Charles & Ray Eames

Charles & Ray Eames not only designed their furniture but set up and took the photographs that were then used to advertise them. These shots from the 1940s and 1950s appeared in advertisements and exhibitions for Herman Miller.

Charles & Ray Eames — Preparations for a photo shoot of the Aluminium Group in a car park next to the Eames Office, in Venice, Los Angeles, c. 1959.

Designers and architects

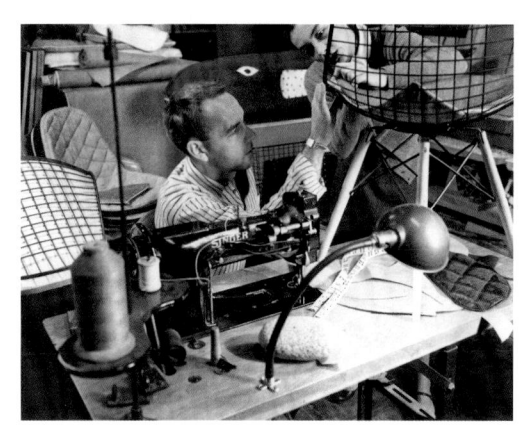

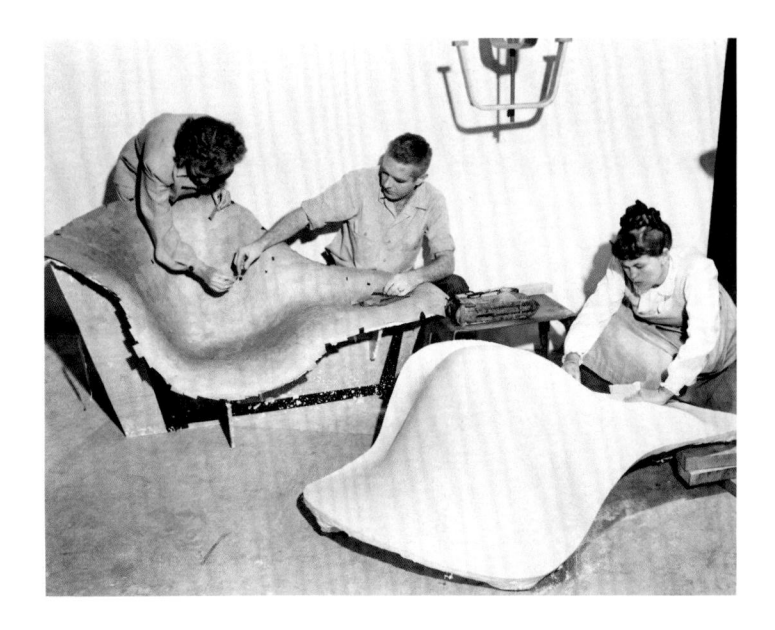

Charles & Ray Eames

The Eameses attached great importance to having their own workshop. It was here that they shaped and researched materials in an often protracted trial-and-error process until they were ready for mass production.

Charles & Ray Eames

The Eames House, built in 1949, is regarded as a key work of twentieth-century architecture. It consists entirely of prefabricated, mass-produced building elements which were selected and assembled by the couple according to a specific plan.

Charles & Ray Eames

The Eames Office, 901 Washington Boulevard in Venice, Los Angeles, was an office, atelier, model workshop, production facility, photo and film studio, darkroom, archives and storehouse all rolled into one. These pictures were taken in 1959 for a feature on the Eames Office in "Vogue" magazine.

Charles & Ray Eames

From the end of the 1950s, the Eames Office began spending more and more time on exhibition designs and slideshow productions. This picture shows the Eameses shooting "Powers of Ten" – a breathtaking pictorial journey into the relative size of things, from the microscopic to the cosmic, developed in 1968.

Charles & Ray Eames — The slogan "Take your pleasure seriously" sums up the Eameses' love of games and the importance of play in the learning process. They designed several toys, including The Toy (top and bottom left) and House of Cards (bottom).

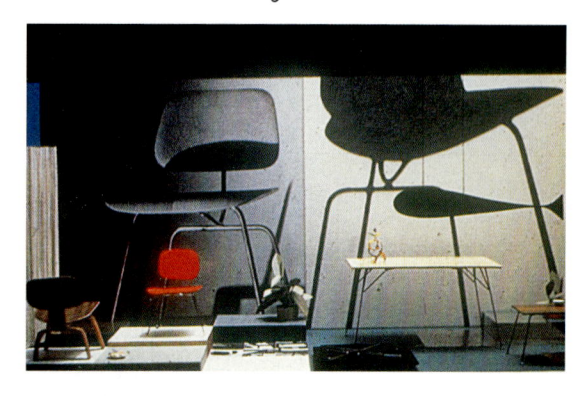

Charles & Ray Eames

For many years the Eameses were also regularly involved in designing showrooms for Herman Miller. The atmospheric vibrancy of their installations featuring furniture, objects, plants and pictures continues to inspire Vitra to this day. Window display from 1950 (top), Herman Miller Showroom in 1961 (middle) and 1963 (bottom).

Charles & Ray Eames

Erika and Willi Fehlbaum visiting the Eames Office. In the background we see the "History Wall" from the "Mathematica" exhibition produced in 1961. Such visits gave the Fehlbaums a deep understanding of the design process and formed the bedrock of the exceptionally close, decades-long collaboration between Vitra and Charles & Ray Eames.

Willi Fehlbaum im Jahre 1957: Unterzeichnung des Lizenzvertrages mit Hermann Miller in ~~New York.~~ den USA.

Herman Miller

Herman Miller, founded in Zeeland, Michigan, by D. J. DePree in 1923, has been famous for its collaborations with leading designers since the mid 1940s. The signing of a license agreement to produce the Herman Miller Collection in 1957 signalled the launch of Vitra as a furniture manufacturer.

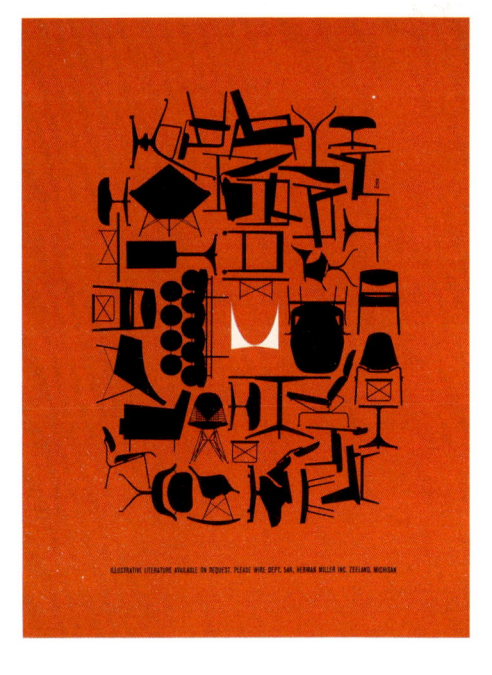

Designers and architects

153

Herman Miller

Entrepreneur D. J. DePree (seated, left) in 1975 with the Herman Miller design team (from left to right): Robert Propst, George Nelson, Alexander Girard, Ray Eames and Charles Eames. Herman Miller advertisement (bottom right) in 1962. From the same year, an advertisement by Armin Hofmann for the Herman Miller Collection produced by Vitra in Switzerland (top).

AUTHORS | Designers and architects | 154

George Nelson — Arrangement of Eames chairs by George Nelson for the 1964 Herman Miller catalogue.

AUTHORS   Designers and architects   155

George Nelson

George Nelson and the Eameses worked on many other projects in addition to their cooperation with Herman Miller. Here we see them preparing the "American National Exhibition", which took place in Moscow in 1959. Nelson was a member of the organizing committee. The Eameses showed their multi-screen presentation "Glimpses of the USA" at this event.

George Nelson

George Nelson – surrounded by pieces from the Action Office 1 series launched in 1964 – was a key figure in the American mid-century design movement both as a designer, publicist and theorist, and as design director at Herman Miller, where he worked with Charles and Ray Eames, Alexander Girard, and Isamu Noguchi.

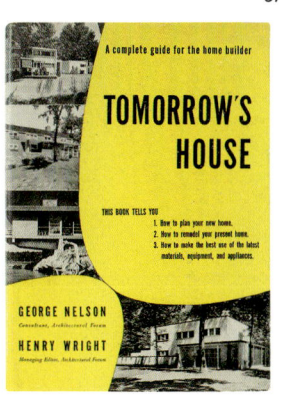

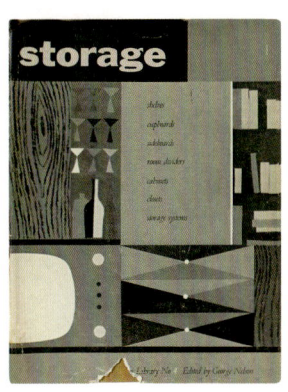

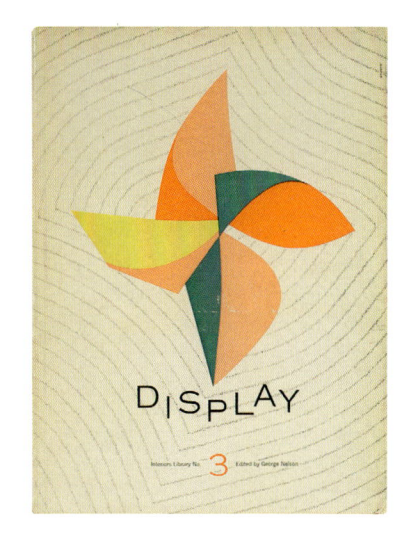

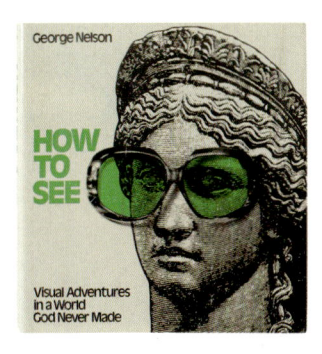

George Nelson

Some examples of George Nelson's extensive and wide-ranging writing. His essays and books not only helped shape the debate among specialists but also raised the general public's awareness of contemporary design issues and problems.

George Nelson

Nelson's main strength was concept-building. At the root of much of his work was his analysis of social needs. As early as 1945 he published an illustrated article in "Life" magazine about the storage problems associated with the ever-expanding household paraphernalia of America's middle classes.

Comprehensive storage system, rear hanging

George Nelson — Thereafter Nelson invested a great deal of energy into researching and designing storage furniture. One of the results of this work, his Comprehensive Storage System launched by Herman Miller in 1959, is pictured here.

George Nelson — Office furniture engrossed Nelson throughout his career. The individual elements of the Action Office (1964) – shown here in an advertisement produced by Nelson's office for Herman Miller – were conceived as modules for an office furniture system defined by its flexibility and expandability.

George Nelson

Especially in the late 1940s and 1950s, George Nelson presented a series of iconic furniture designs, including the Wall Clocks (top left), the Swag-Leg Chair in 1954 (bottom), and the Coconut Chair and Ottoman in 1955 (top right).

AUTHORS   Designers and architects   162

Alexander Girard

Alexander Girard – shown here in his studio in 1972 – was responsible for colours, textiles, patterns and decor at Herman Miller. His adopted home of Santa Fe, New Mexico, was close to many South American countries whose indigenous cultures were the main source of inspiration for his work.

Alexander Girard — Advertisement for Girard's 1960 textile collection for Herman Miller (above left). Pieces from the Textiles and Objects Shop designed by Girard (top right). Girard's home (below) housed a huge collection of folk art from all over the world which is today displayed in the Museum of International Folk Art in Santa Fe.

Alexander Girard

In the mid 1960s, Girard worked closely with the legendary American airline Braniff Airlines. He created a collection of tables and chairs for the company's airport lounges, which he also designed and decorated. Later, Herman Miller produced these models for the wider market.

Alexander Girard

Charles & Ray Eames designed the La Fonda Chairs for the La Fonda del Sol restaurant in New York, which Alexander Girard had decorated, with upholstery also by Girard (top). A Braniff Airlines lounge designed by Girard (middle) and Girard's colour scheme for Braniff's aeroplanes (bottom). The uniforms were designed by Emilio Pucci.

Tibor Kalman

Graphic designer Tibor Kalman (seated on the sofa), with whom Vitra worked very closely during the 1990s, visiting Rolf Fehlbaum and Federica Zanco in Basel. The drawing is by Kalman's wife, Maira.

AUTHORS   Designers and architects   167

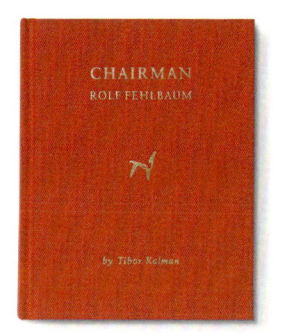

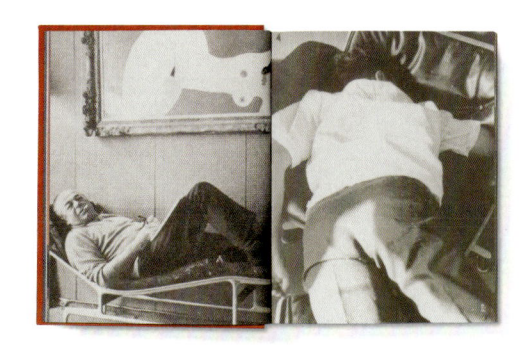

Tibor Kalman

Among the many publications Kalman designed for Vitra is "Chairman Rolf Fehlbaum", a picture portrait of the company and Rolf Fehlbaum. A few spreads from the 592-page volume are reproduced here. This work illustrates just how personal and close Kalman's relationship with Fehlbaum was.

Frank Gehry — Dynamism, expressivity, vitality and wit are the hallmarks of Los Angeles-based architect Frank Gehry's work – and of Gehry himself. Here we see him doing a stability check on his corrugated cardboard furniture in the 1970s.

AUTHORS   Designers and architects   169

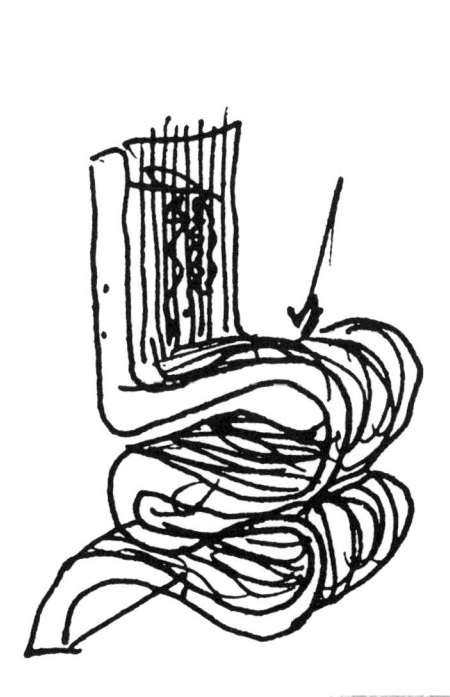

Frank Gehry

Gehry was well known for his cardboard furniture designs long before his distinctive, warped architecture-sculptures grabbed international headlines. His Easy Edge line, produced between 1969 and 1973, was marketed via American department stores at the time. Today, they are much sought-after collector's items.

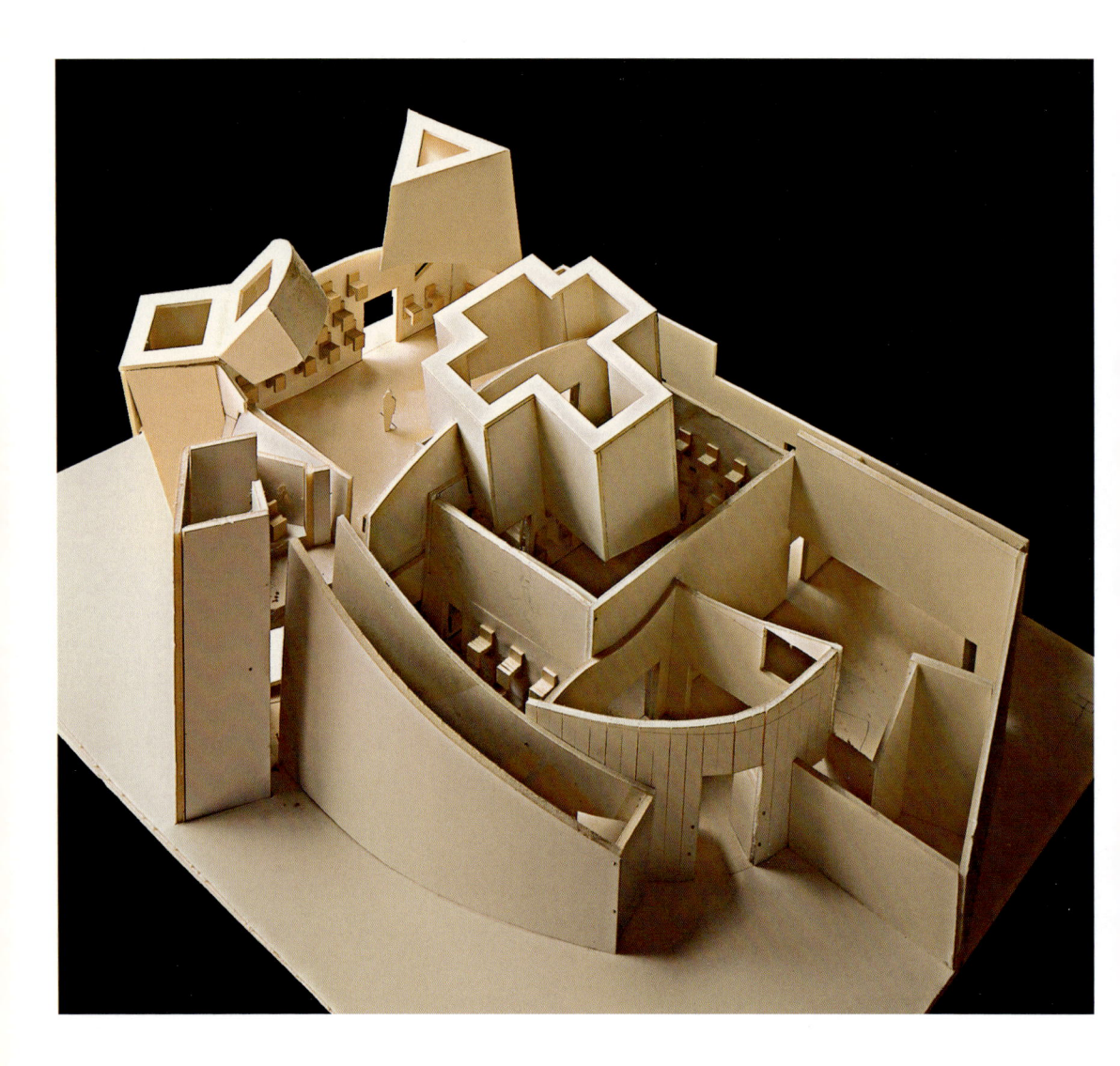

Frank Gehry

The Vitra Design Museum, completed in 1989, was the first building the architect built in Europe. The working model shows the complexity of this structure. The unusual cross-shaped roof light above the central gallery rooms is clearly discernible.

| AUTHORS | Designers and architects | 171 |

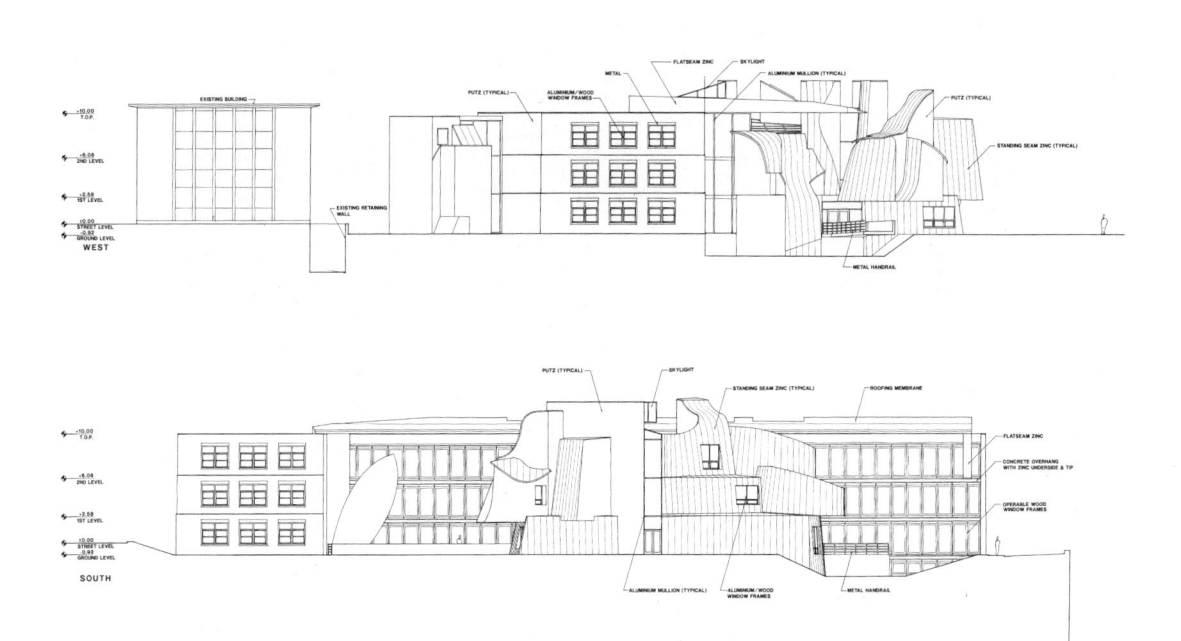

Frank Gehry

Five years after finishing the Museum, Frank Gehry embarked on another building for the company: the Vitra Center in Birsfelden. The craggy structure of the 'villa', located in front of the administration building, houses a reception area, canteen and meeting rooms.

Tadao Ando

Stylistically, the work of Japanese architect Tadao Ando is diametrically opposed to Gehry's dynamic, expressive creations. His minimalist structures, which emanate a sense of elegant, almost meditative simplicity, may now be seen in many locations around the globe.

AUTHORS Designers and architects 173

Tadao Ando

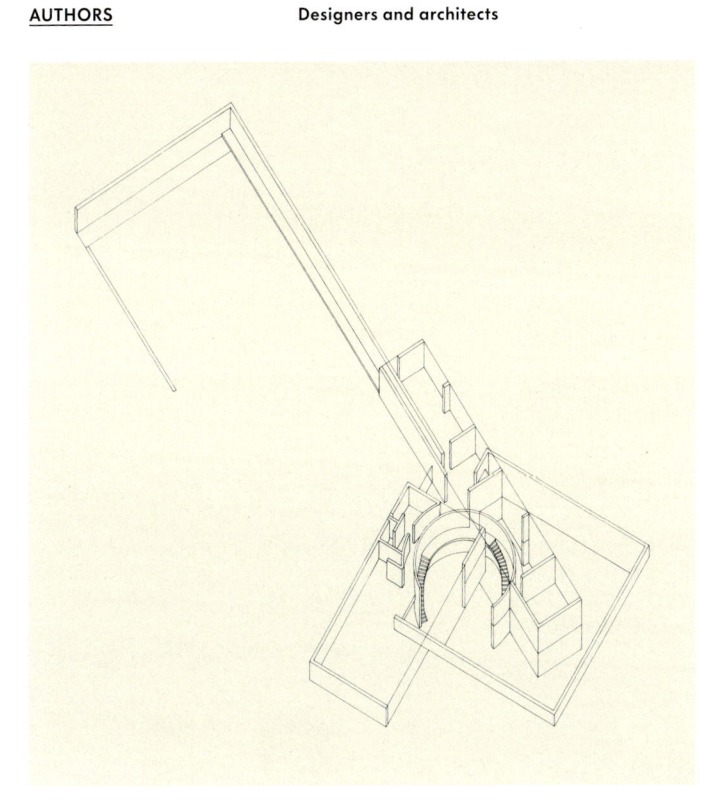

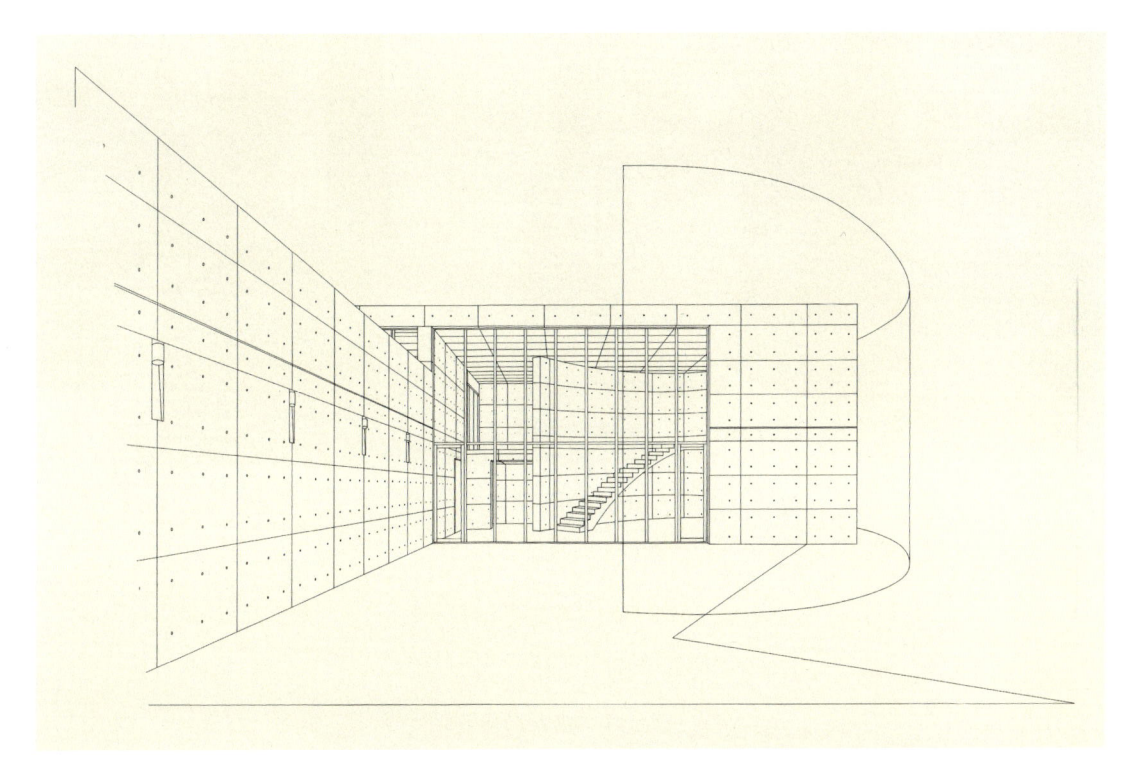

The first structure Tadao Ando built outside Japan was for Vitra. The plans for his Conference Pavilion, completed in 1993 and located very close to Gehry's Museum on the Vitra Campus in Weil, highlight the clean, geometric lines of this design.

AUTHORS Designers and architects 174

SANAA Kazuyo Sejima and Ryue Nishizawa founded their architectural practice, SANAA, in Tokyo in 1995. Their projects, which are generally both minimalist and poetic in style, are often startling departures from established building typologies.

| AUTHORS | Designers and architects | 175 |

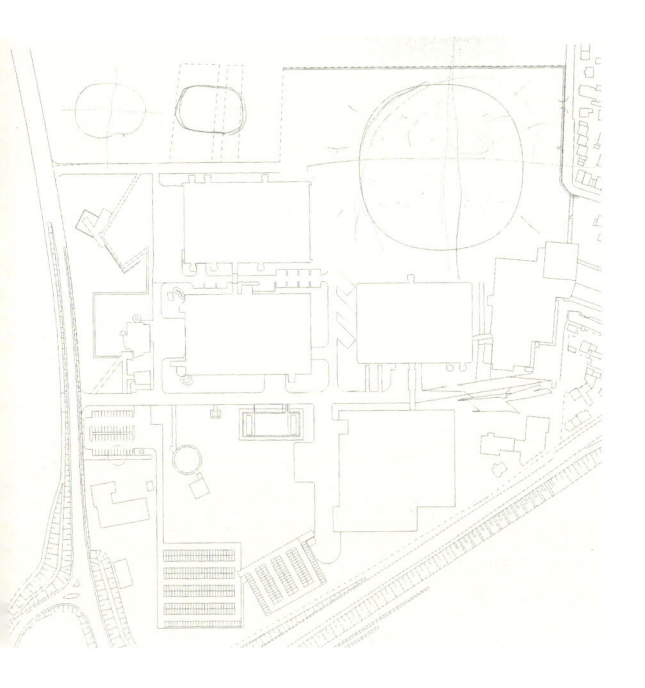

SANAA

SANAA has designed an almost entirely circular factory building for Vitrashop on the Vitra Campus in Weil am Rhein, due for completion in 2009. Sketches, a photo montage and a model photo illustrate the current project status.

Jasper Morrison

Jasper Morrison has been running his own design studios in London (since 1986) and Paris (since 2002). His work is defined by a search for simplicity and a preference for clear, pure forms. He began collaborating with Vitra in 1988 and the first joint product was the Ply-Chair.

AUTHORS   Designers and architects   177

Jasper Morrison

Morrison avoids public appearances. In 1988 he gave a 'lecture' in Milan during which he did not utter a single word but simply showed 160 images of things that had influenced or inspired his work. This presentation, a few excerpts of which are reproduced here, was later published as a picture book ("A World Without Words").

Jasper Morrison

The installation "Some New Items for the Home", staged in Berlin in 1988 and for which Morrison designed the Ply-Chair Vitra would later manufacture, was seen by many as a statement against postmodernism. It represented a radical break with the past and signalled the beginning of the New Simplicity movement.

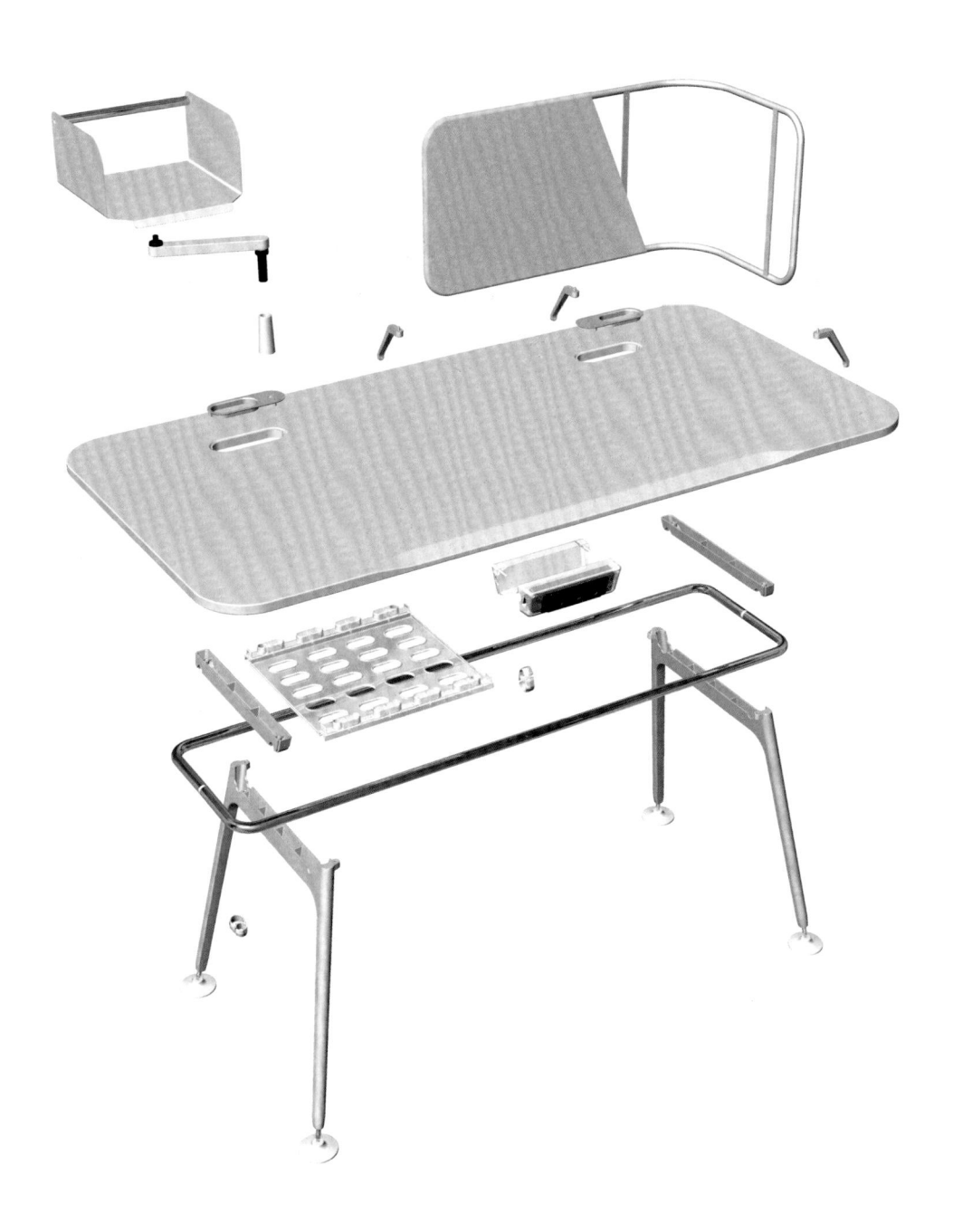

Jasper Morrison

ATM (Advanced Table Module), which Morrison designed jointly with Vitra and which has been on the market since 2003, was his answer to the question: "What do we need for a table to be functional and what can we realistically leave out?" The result is a practical, formally restrained, no-nonsense work table.

AUTHORS Designers and architects 180

Zaha Hadid

Zaha Hadid at a Vitra workshop in Weil am Rhein in 1991 with (from left to right) Werner Blaser, Nicholas Grimshaw, Frank Gehry and Peter Degen. Today Hadid receives commissions from all over the world. For many years, her architectural visions were considered too elaborate to be implemented.

Zaha Hadid

Zaha Hadid's Fire Station at the Vitra Campus in Weil, two design drawings and a model of which are reproduced here, was completed in 1993 and proved once and for all that Hadid's buildings could be translated into bricks and mortar.

Hella Jongerius

Hella Jongerius founded her studio JongeriusLab in 2000 in Rotterdam. The designer – seen here working on a leather version of the Polder Sofa she designed in 2007 – has become a linchpin of Vitra's Home Collection in a very short time thanks to her unique creations.

AUTHORS	Designers and architects	183

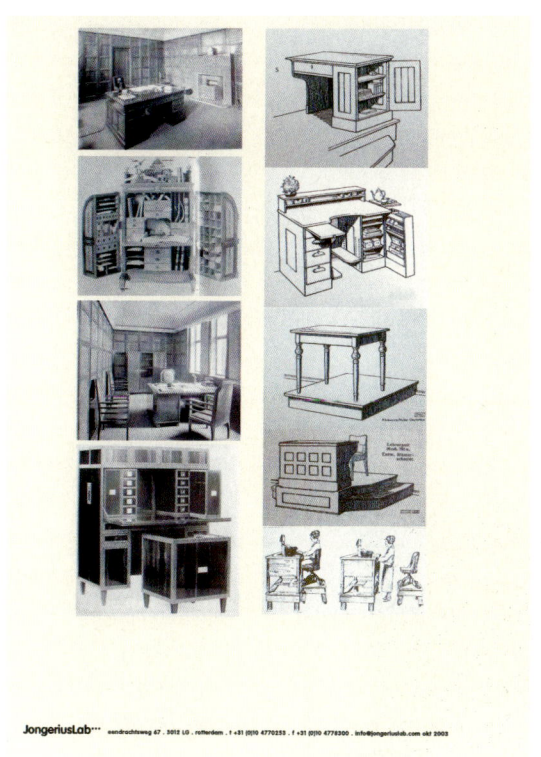

Hella Jongerius	Conducting extensive research into furniture typologies and capturing these on paper is a key part of Hella Jongerius' design method.

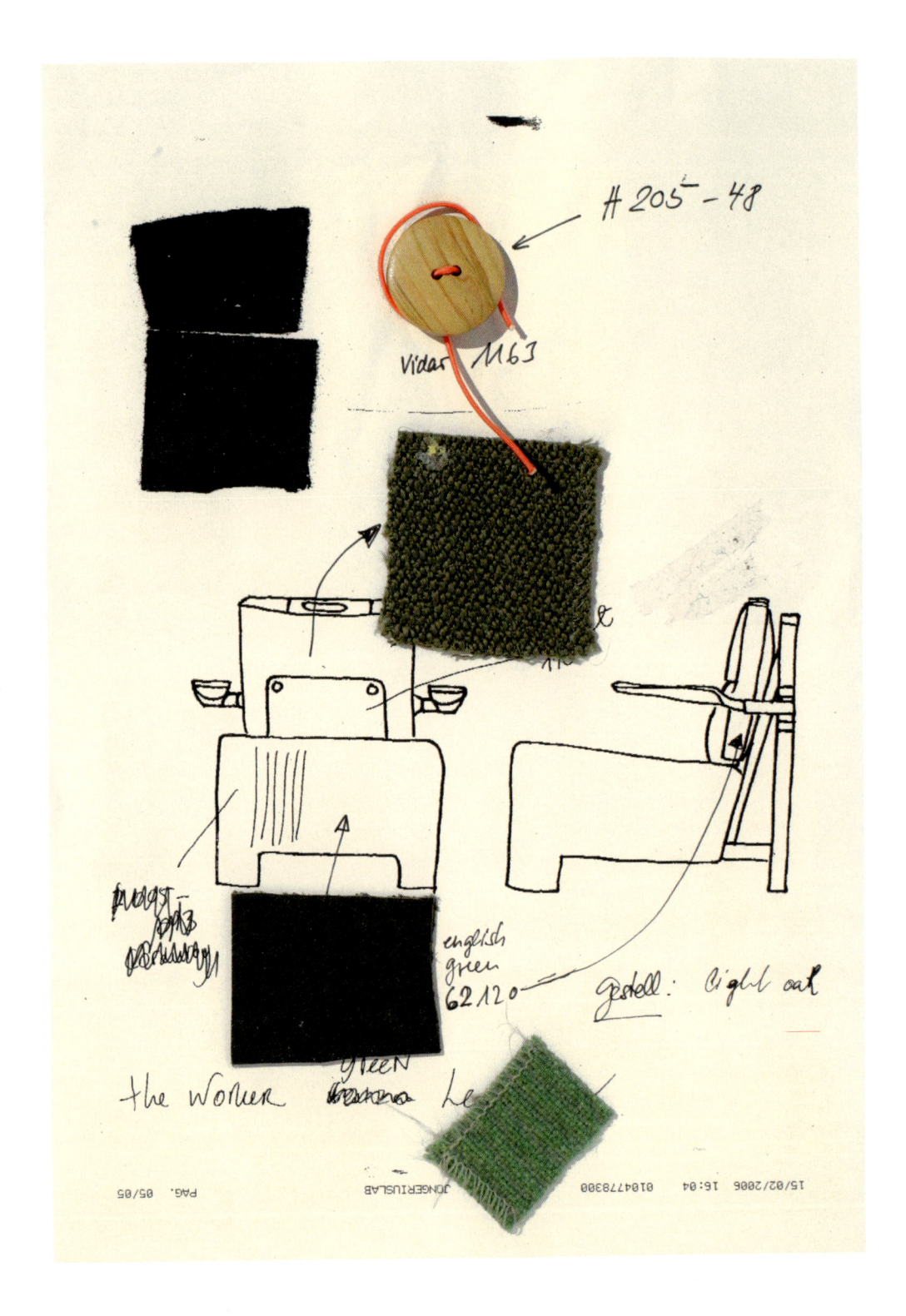

Hella Jongerius — The Polder Sofa (2005) and The Worker armchair (2006) are among Jongerius' most important works. The photograph shows a sketch created during the design/prototyping process.

Hella Jongerius

Hella Jongerius discusses new design ideas for the Vitra Home Collection with Rolf Fehlbaum at the Vitra Center in Birsfelden (spring 2007).

| AUTHORS | Designers and architects | 186 |

Maarten Van Severen — Maarten Van Severen on the MVS Chaise developed for Vitra between 1998 and 2000. Van Severen established his own workshop in Ghent, Belgium, in 1987, where he designed and produced small batches of furniture.

```
26/03 02  DIN 16:08 FAX 092331988        maarten van Severen                    ☒001
```

> DEAR ROLF,
> WE HAD A VERY NICE WEEKEND
> I FOUND BACK THIS PICTURE
> OF ABOUT ONE YEAR AGO
> THINKING OF THAT,
> I CALL YOU SOON.
>
> M Maah

Maarten Van Severen — Van Severen's collaboration with Vitra, which began in 1996, marked a new phase in his career, giving him access to new materials and production techniques and helping him reach a much wider audience. The relationship was fruitful and stimulated many new ideas, as this sketch for Rolf Fehlbaum attests.

Maarten Van Severen

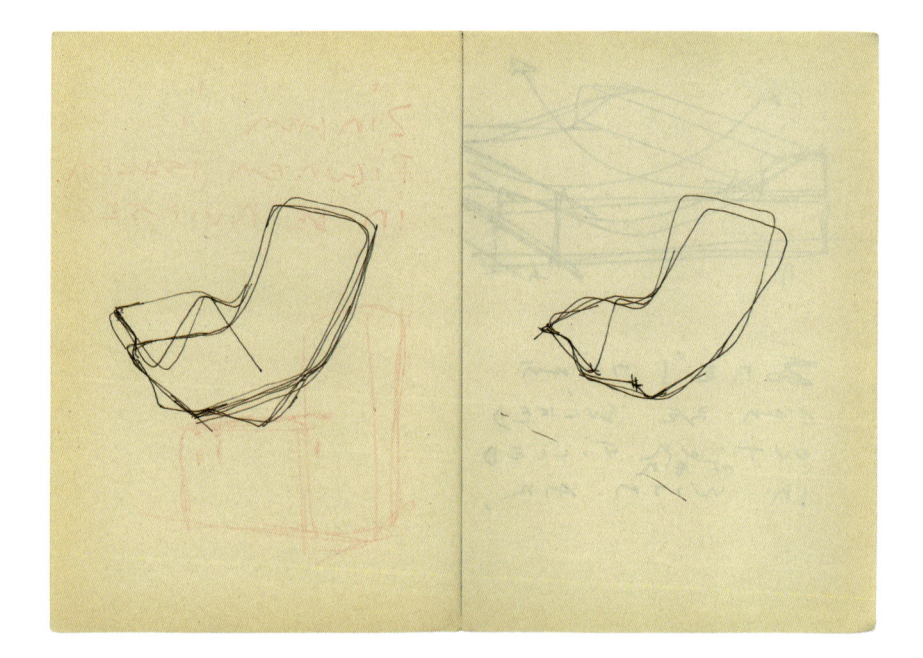

Maarten Van Severen's design drawings are almost as laconic and minimalist as his furniture: study for "Le plaisir d'être seul" by Willem Cole, 1991 (top left); drawing for the Blue Bench, 1992 (top right); undated sketches for a lounge chair (bottom).

AUTHORS — Designers and architects

Maarten Van Severen — Van Severen produced this steel table in his own workshop in 1993. He used steel profiles for the base frame and polyester resin for the top. The distinctive simplicity of this piece and its stylish proportions are trademarks of Van Severen's design.

Maarten Van Severen

Maarten Van Severen called this furniture prototype, developed in 1999, SOS (Short Office Sleep). The sequence of photographs illustrates the flexibility of this chaise longue. Users control the movement mechanism with the weight of various parts of their body.

Maarten Van Severen — Chair No. II, designed in 1994 and shown here in a photograph taken in Maarten Van Severen's workshop, consists of an aluminium frame and a seat made of thin-wall veneer. It is the immediate predecessor of the .03 (pronounced "point zero three") chair launched in 1999, which marked the beginning of Vitra's collaboration with Van Severen.

AUTHORS — Designers and architects — 192

Ronan & Erwan Bouroullec — The Bouroullec brothers, Ronan and Erwan, have worked with Vitra on both its Office and Home Collections since 2000. They are known for their conceptual approach to design, their fondness for experimentation and their strong interest in new technologies.

Ronan & Erwan Bouroullec — When building the Slow Chair, launched in 2006, the Bouroullec brothers used the latest developments in knitting technology to fit the upholstery around the steel-tube frame as snugly as possible. A few working models of this piece are shown here.

AUTHORS   Designers and architects   194

Ronan & Erwan Bouroullec — Development and test model of the Slow Chair (top). Custom-fit textile upholstery was also used in the swivel office chair Worknest (middle, an early prototype), presented in 2006. The Bouroullecs reworked the Rocs (bottom), launched in Milan in 2006, for the 2007 Vitra Edition.

AUTHORS   Designers and architects

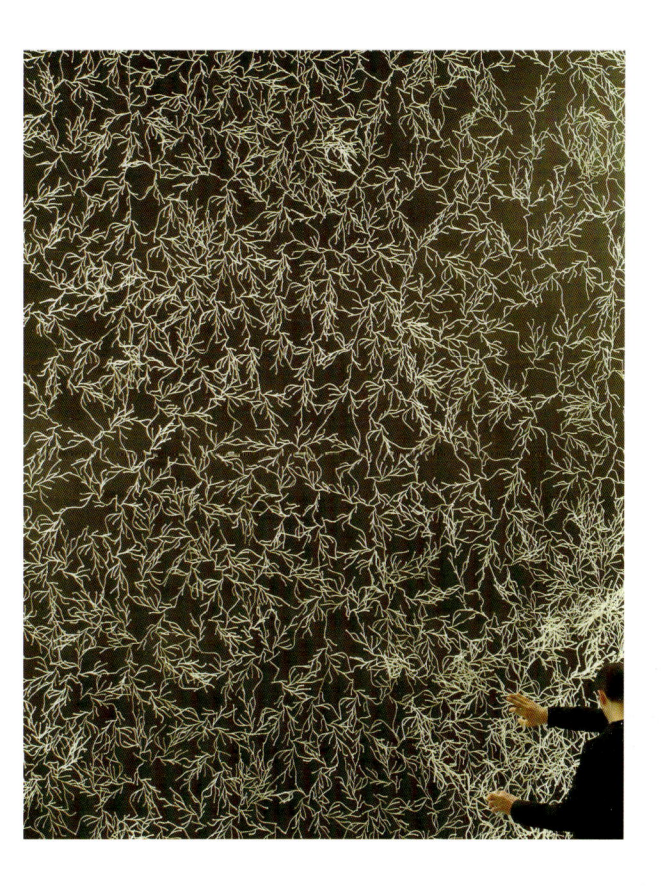

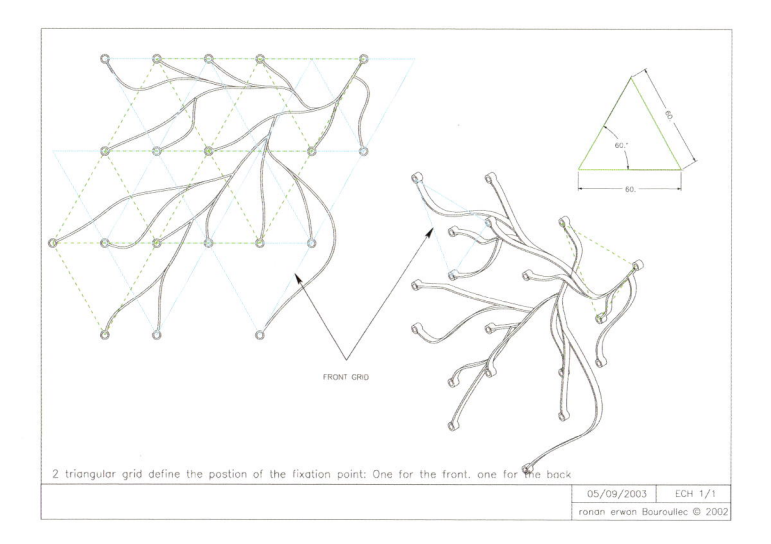

Ronan & Erwan Bouroullec

Algues, designed in 2004, illustrates the Bouroullecs' playful yet concept-driven approach. These delicate, organic, plastic structures, which can be configured into remarkably large, web-like forms, are decorative pieces and interior design units in one.

> Jean Prouvé est de la "Dynastie Nancy."
>
> 1900, l'Ecole de Nancy : Victor Prouvé (père de Jean), Gallé, Majorelle, Daume, etc ... : les créateurs et les artisans du "Nouveau Style".
>
> Un demi siècle a passé. Jean Prouvé est de même sang créateur, mais il exprime le temps présent. Il est ingénieur - architecte, - réunis en un seul homme, - ce qui est exceptionnel.
>
> Il a traversé toutes les intrigues, toutes les vicissitudes. Il est entré dans la réalité. Il construit et il conçoit. Un tel rôle est réservé à un caractère d'élite; c'est le rôle de l'abnégation, du courage, de la persévérance, de l'obstination .....
>
> Paris, le 7 Janvier 1964
>
> *Le Corbusier*
>
> LE CORBUSIER

Jean Prouvé

French architect and designer Jean Prouvé, born in Nancy in 1901, the son of a prominent Art Nouveau artist, always remained loyal to his home town. This photograph shows him in his studio in 1970. During his lifetime Prouvé was not widely known outside expert circles but was highly respected, as this letter from Le Corbusier illustrates.

Jean Prouvé

Table designs – this picture shows an installation by M/M (Paris) – are among the highlights of Prouvé's oeuvre. Working closely with the Prouvé family, Vitra started manufacturing them again in 2002.

74

Jean Prouvé — The Trapèze table, designed between 1950 and 1954, gets its name from its trapezoid legs. It has rounded feet and cantilevered table-top mountings. Its hollow body sections, made out of formed, welded sheet steel, resemble a human figure draped in a long, dark costume.

AUTHORS   Designers and architects   199

Jean Prouvé   Prouvé saw furniture first and foremost as an engineering challenge and was just as comfortable creating small-scale works as 300-metre towers. Wooden dining table from 1945/1946 (top). Metal base frame for a desk, c.1948 (bottom).

Jean Prouvé

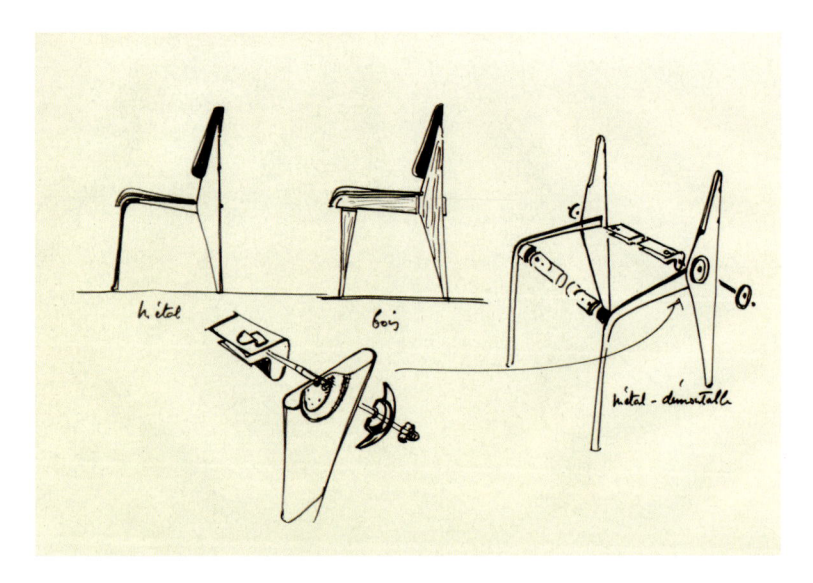

Prouvé redesigned his Standard chair (1934) more frequently than any of his other creations. He developed a dismantable wooden version in 1948 (photograph, top right; advertising flyer from 1951, top left). This sketch of the Dismantable Chair (below) was drawn while preparing for a lecture in 1965.

AUTHORS   Designers and architects

Jean Prouvé

A group of Cité easy chairs in the living room of the house Prouvé built for himself in Nancy in 1954 (top). He designed this chair (bottom) as early as 1930 for a student residence at the Cité Universitaire Monbois in Nancy.

Mario Bellini

Mario Bellini in his studio in Milan. Vitra has been working with Bellini since the end of the 1970s. The collaboration has produced numerous chairs, as well as storage and office furniture systems.

AUTHORS   Designers and architects   203

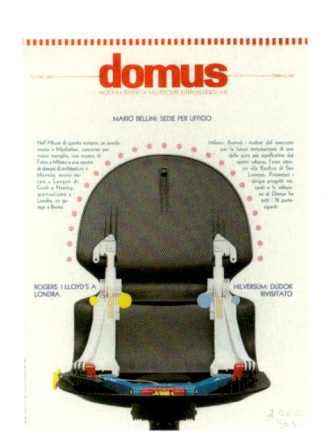

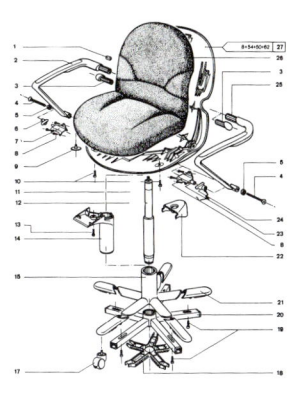

Disegno esploso di Persona / Exploded drawing of Persona.

Mario Bellini   The swivel office chair Persona was presented in 1984. The sketches, plans and photographs underscore this design's (largely invisible) complexity.

AUTHORS   Designers and architects   204

Mario Bellini

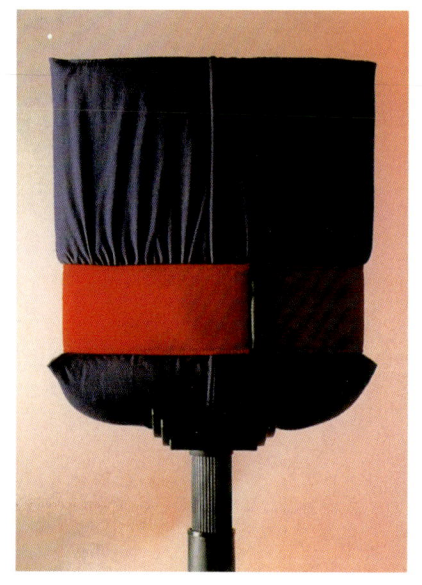

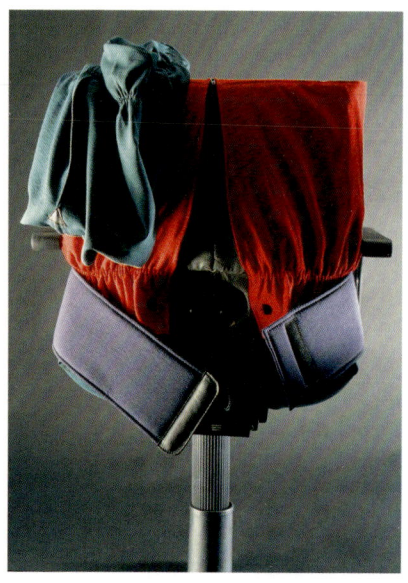

The continued success of Figura, which now graces the posteriors of Germany's members of parliament – among many others – is due in large part to its homely touch. The form of the cushions and colour of the upholstery play an important role here.

Mario Bellini

Renderings and photographs of the Headline chair designed by Mario Bellini and his son Claudio in 2005. A holistic approach to sitting and to office life lay at the heart of the development process.

| AUTHORS | Designers and architects |

Antonio Citterio

Vitra has had a very close relationship with Antonio Citterio since 1985. The Milan-based designer and architect – seen here developing the Ad Hoc office furniture system – designs the full range of office furniture.

Antonio Citterio

Important though the technical features and mechanics of an office chair are, the shape of the cushions, choice of upholstery and colour are equally significant for the end user. This long sequence of prototypes shows the care and dedication with which Citterio has tackled these issues.

Antonio Citterio

"Many people spend a large part of their lives in the office. My own office, where I spend ten hours a day working, is better furnished than my own home." This notion underlies all of Citterio's office furniture designs.

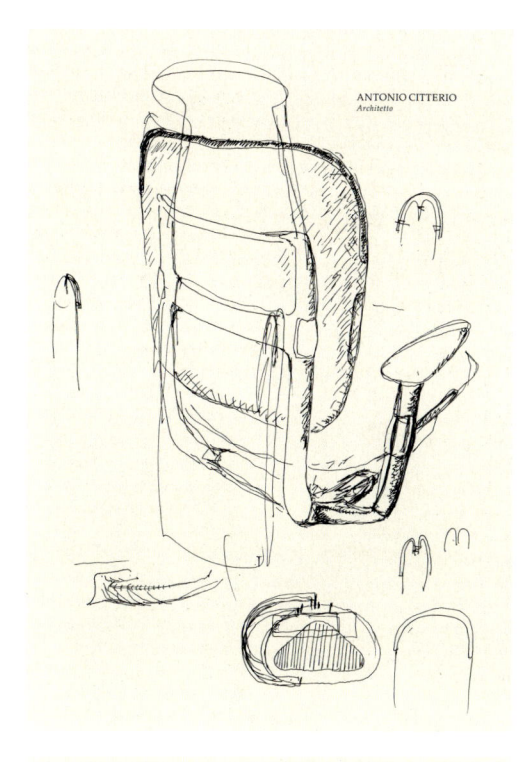

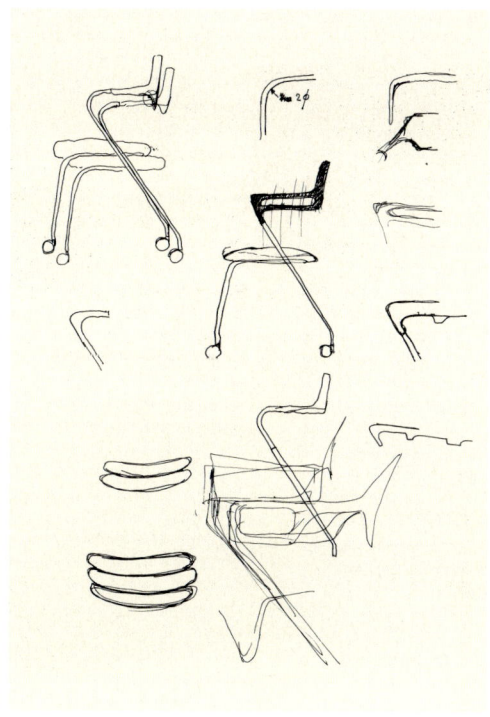

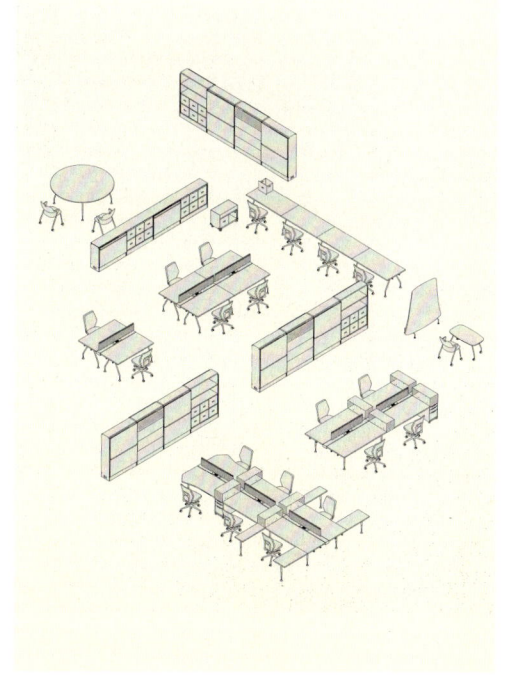

AUTHORS — Designers and architects

Antonio Citterio

Design drawings by Antonio Citterio for the swivel office chair Oson CE (top left), the meeting room chair ToniX (top right) and the office furniture system Ad Hoc (bottom left). Ad Hoc elements in a mock-up plan for a typical office (bottom right).

Alberto Meda

Technical and engineering issues are at the heart of Alberto Meda's design practice. He is pictured here in Vitra's product development unit in Birsfelden checking components for his MedaMorph base frame. Meda's approach is similar to that of Charles Eames and Jean Prouvé, both important role models.

| AUTHORS | Designers and architects | 211 |

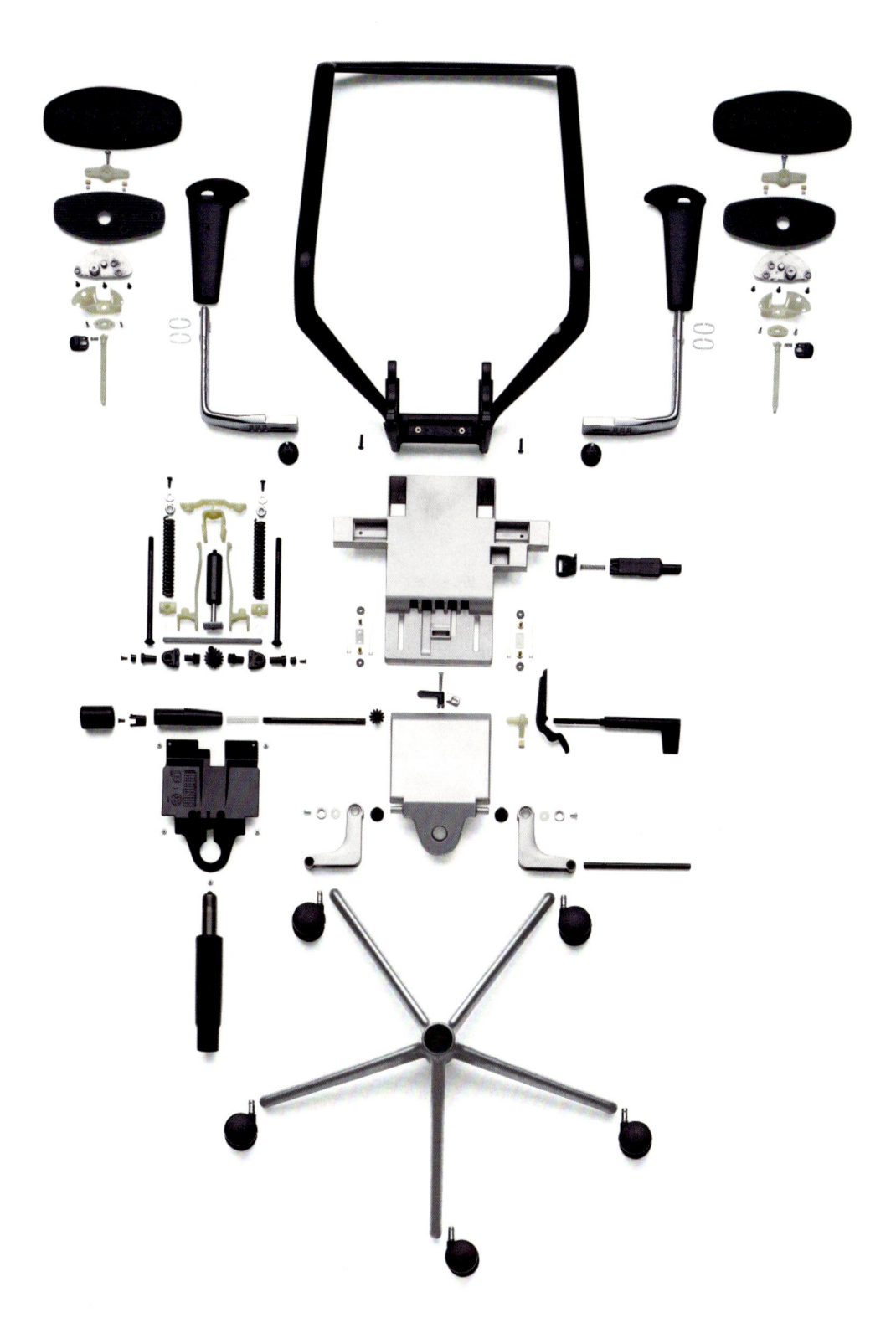

Alberto Meda

Meda, who like Bellini also works in Milan, has worked with Vitra since 1994. The first jointly developed product was the Meda Chair, which came onto the market in 1996 and soon became the progenitor of an entire 'tribe' of office chairs. The photograph shows a neatly dismantled member of this 'family'.

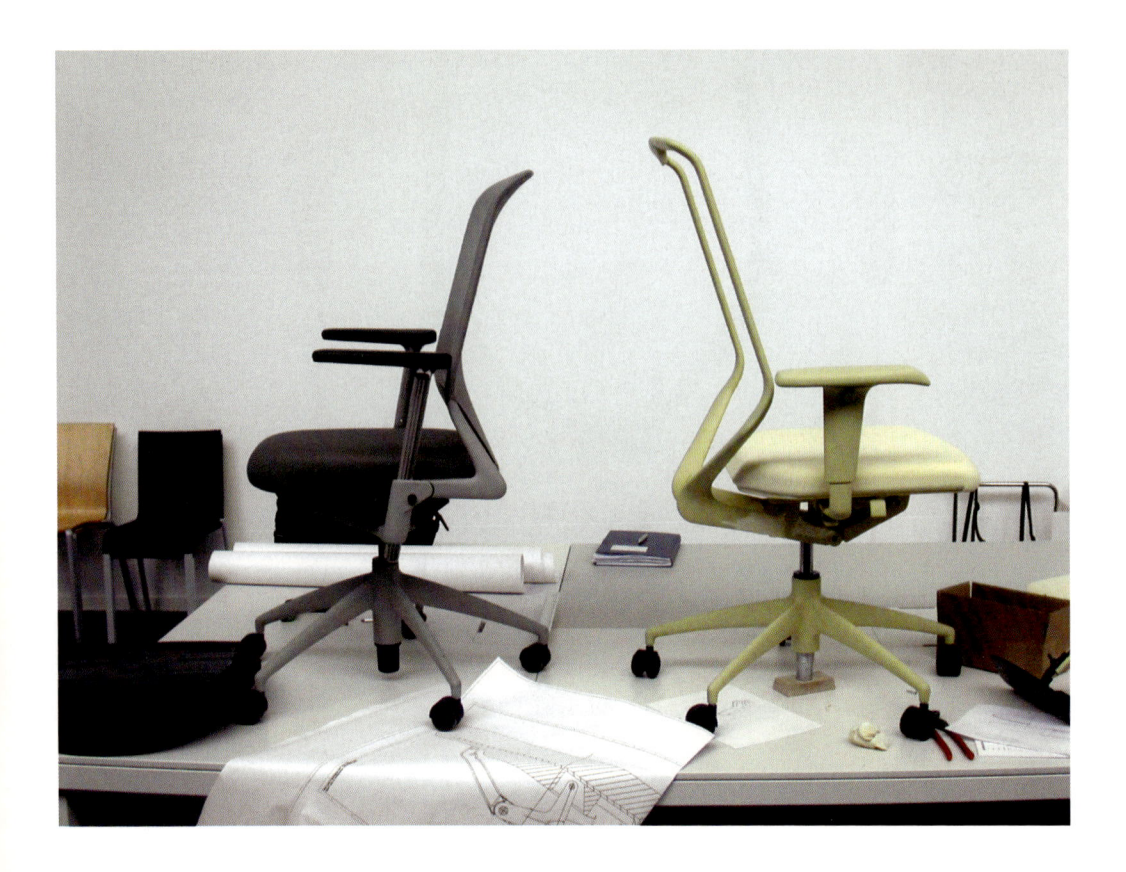

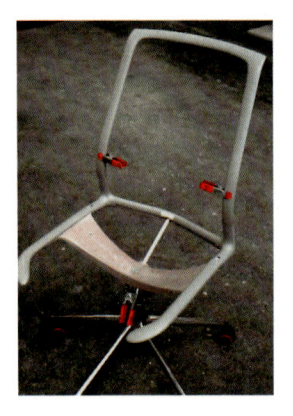

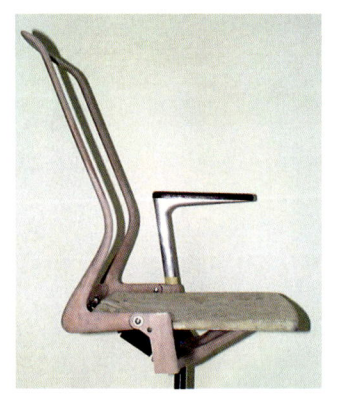

Alberto Meda — These prototypes give us an insight into the skeleton at the heart of the design. They also show a couple of variations on the mechanism.

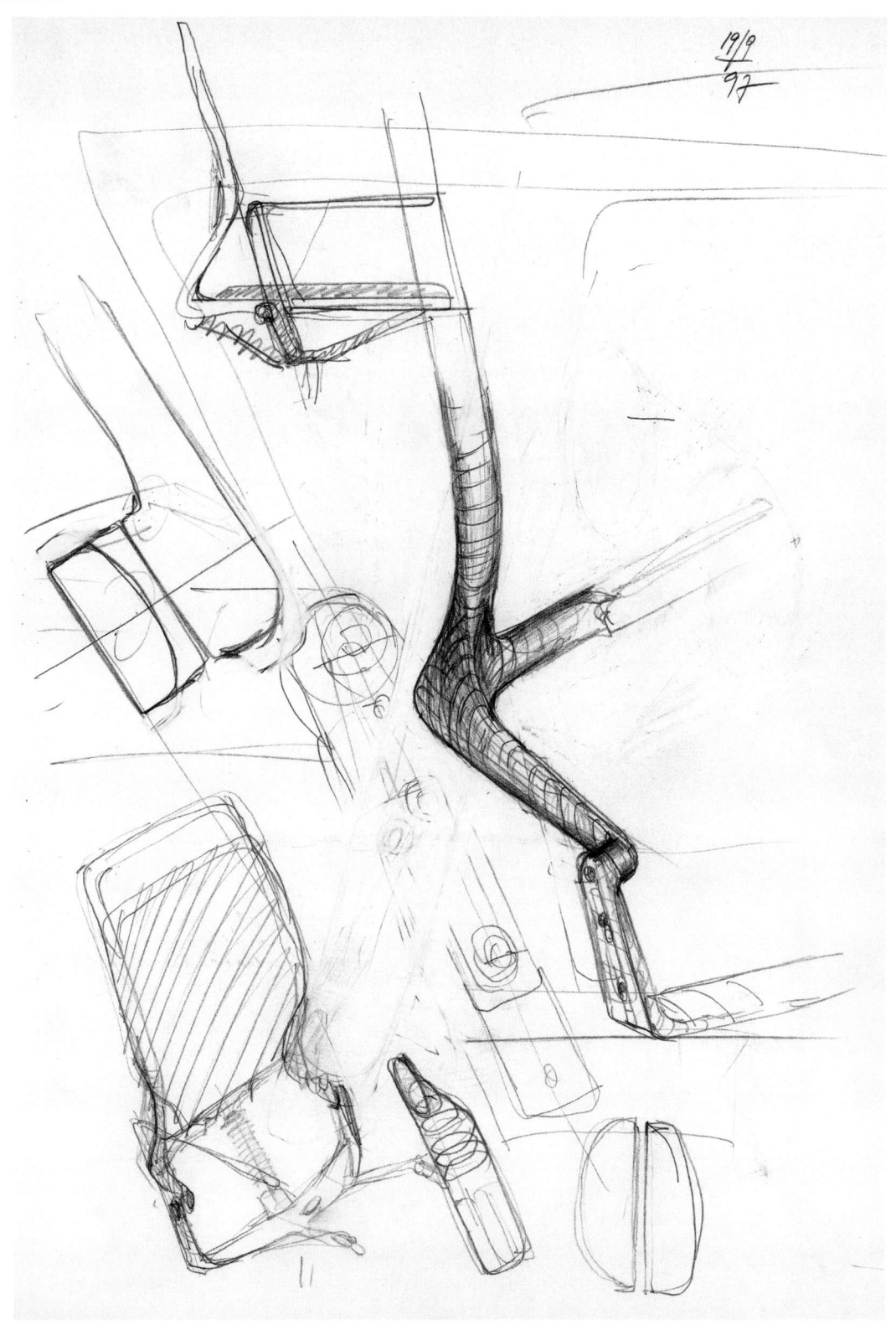

Alberto Meda

Charles Eames once said: "The detail is not the detail. The detail is the product." As the sketch (1997) illustrates, this statement could just as easily have come from Alberto Meda.

Verner Panton

Danish designer Verner Panton in his office in Basel around 1970. He came to Switzerland in the early 1970s looking for someone to manufacture his plastic chair. The Panton Chair was to become the first piece of furniture to be developed exclusively by Vitra.

Verner Panton

Panton's private residence, which he conceived as a kind of showroom-cum-laboratory, seemed just as revolutionary to contemporaries as his cantilevered, single-form, injection-moulded plastic chair. Panton used his home to test the viability of his ideas and give real-life demonstrations to potential clients. These pictures were taken at the beginning of the 1970s.

AUTHORS — Designers and architects — 216

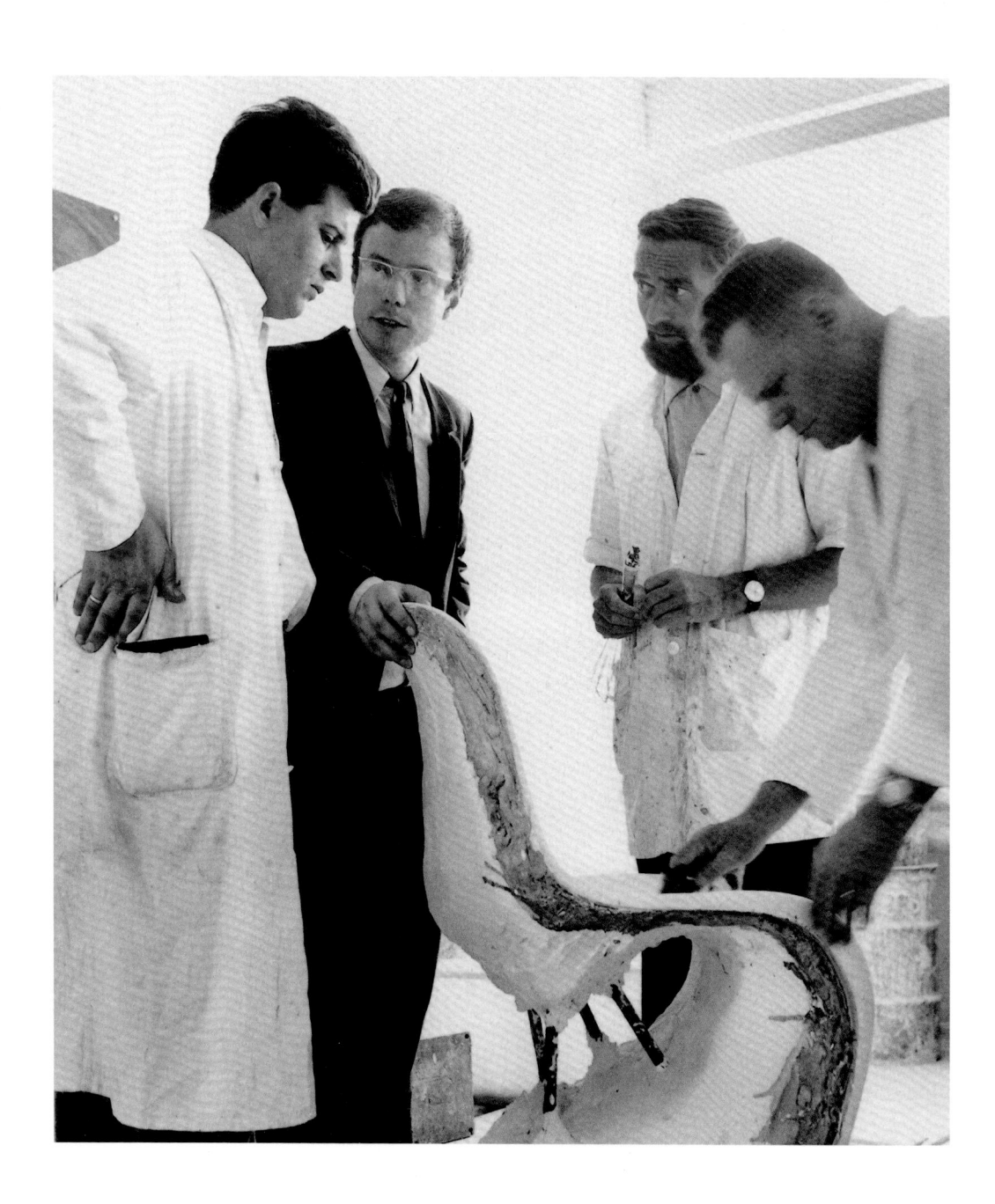

Verner Panton

Verner Panton and Vitra engineers worked hard on the Panton Chair between 1965 and 1967. The photograph shows Panton (right) with Rolf Fehlbaum (middle) and Manfred Diebold (product development) surveying a chair form in the Vitra workshop in Weil.

AUTHORS — Designers and architects

Verner Panton

The Panton Chair, with its daring, sensuous shape, soon became a media hit. The provocative photo sequence, entitled "How to undress in front of your husband", shows singer Amanda Lear stripping on, and next to, a red Panton Chair. She artfully avoids giving too much away. Shot in 1970.

Verner Panton

The photo shoot for the first report on the Panton Chair in the Danish design magazine "Mobilia" in 1967 was staged on the terrace and in the garden of Willi and Erika Fehlbaum in Riehen. Marianne Panton and Christine Fehlbaum were among the models.

AUTHORS   Designers and architects   219

Verner Panton

Panton's interiors also created a stir. In one exhibition he suspended the exhibits upside down from the ceiling (top left). "Fantasy Landscape", the centrepiece of the "Visiona 2" exhibition in Cologne (1970), is regarded as an icon of 1960s design (top right). Presentation of the Plus-Linje collection in a Zurich furniture store in 1960 (bottom).

AUTHORS   Designers and architects   220

Herzog & de Meuron — Jacques Herzog and Pierre de Meuron in conversation with Rolf Fehlbaum. VitraHaus is the first architectural project the company has undertaken with Herzog & de Meuron. Once completed in 2009 it will form the entrance to the Vitra Campus together with Gehry's Museum building.

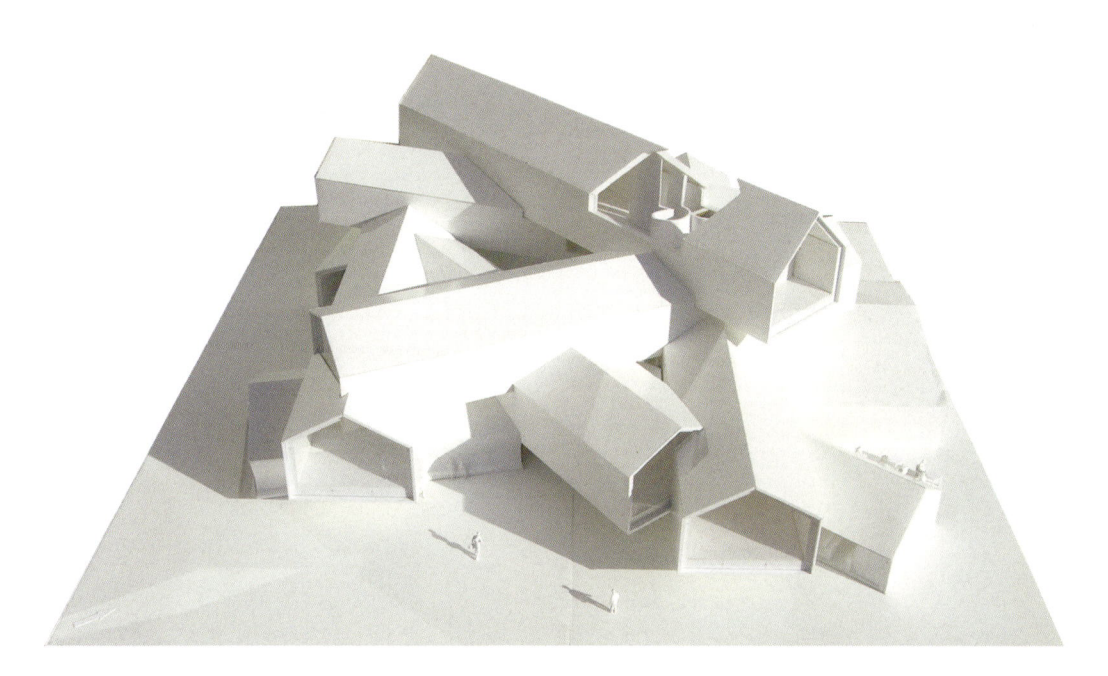

Herzog & de Meuron — A model and rendering of the planned VitraHaus whose complex, wedge-shaped structure will echo the Vitra Design Museum. Its gable roofs also reflect an architectural feature popular in the region.

Egon Bräuning

Egon Bräuning in the Vitra Center in Birsfelden inspecting Maarten Van Severen's SOS prototypes. Bräuning has managed Vitra's product development division since 1971. He is not only a formidable authority in this field but is the most important co-author of virtually every product Vitra brings to market.

DESIGN PROCESSES – INDIVIDUAL AUTHORSHIP AT VITRA

Vitra works with independent 'authors' – primarily with designers, but also with architects and graphic artists. What distinguishes the work of these people from that of other designers is the fact that their personal imprint and outlook is reflected in every one of their products. In contrast, designers who work for larger organisations must adapt their personal interpretation to the requirements of the client.

We do not define our roles in terms of client and contractor. Two business partners – the designer and Vitra – embark on a common quest for an optimal solution. Vitra's task is to provide a stimulating environment, technical support, conceptual input and constructive criticism. Yet even this is no guarantee for success. Sometimes a product just does not come together, making it necessary to start all over again. And the development process always takes a lot longer than anticipated. Sometimes the result is very different from what was originally planned. The product has to come into being, to find its identity. This understanding, and the ability to carefully channel it, is the art of design management.

The field of design covers a wide area: from the creation of edition pieces (which are close relatives of art objects) to design activity within the framework of mass production; from the collector's item to the anonymous utilitarian object; from the sensationally extreme to the suitably practical to the tritely mundane. Clearly, 'extreme'

Rolf Fehlbaum

manifestations are perceived differently from more functional or practical ones. The objects that typically find their way into collections and archives are extreme: they break with tradition; they present a brilliant solution to one aspect of a problem by ignoring other aspects. In short, they are spectacular individual works. But practical objects are quite different: they are absorbed into everyday use, serve their intended function, provide pleasure to the user, but rarely end up in a museum, even when they have made a significant contribution to the evolution of a genre.

However, there is another kind of newness – so practical and perfectly suited to its task that its reception is almost immediate, and it becomes established as a standard within a short period of time. This newness is typological. Even typologically novel objects are rarely shown in museums, in spite of the fact that they set new standards. One reason is that the quality of such objects is seldom demonstrative or spontaneously evident, in contrast to exciting, striking new designs. Paradoxically, much more basic research and development – time and effort, trial and error – is invested in the typologically new object than in the dramatic virtuoso piece. The introduction of Vitra Edition pieces in 1987 provided a vivid example of this: an object that was developed within just a few months attracted more attention than an office chair that had taken years to develop, offering novel mechanical features, innovative materials and a fresh appearance in conjunction with a new office concept. Both types of newness – the extreme and the practical – are important for design, but Vitra is primarily concerned with practical considerations – with designs that 'work'.

Rolf Fehlbaum

Sometimes a practical solution is remarkably striking at the same time. These are the great moments in design. Every discipline experiences such moments: literature, film, art. Something new is created and finds its definitive expression straightaway. When something is new in a climactic, epochal sense (and not just a hill in the mountain forelands), it determines the direction of subsequent developments for a long period of time. A pioneering work that began as a heresy becomes a classic. It remains relevant until the next epochal new development comes along, bringing with it a paradigm shift. The validity of this type of newness is not based on the fact that it is new, but on the establishment of a new equilibrium. This is especially true when innovative materials and technologies become accessible – as ultimately exemplified in the work of Charles & Ray Eames.

Vitra has worked with a number of designers for many years and with others from time to time. A sustained collaboration over a long period is possible and productive when it is both economically and creatively beneficial to the designer, while also bringing continuity to Vitra's pursuit of its central themes. Vitra's special relationships with certain designers will be described in more detail below.

The temperaments and working methods of some designers do not lend themselves to a continuous, long-term relationship with Vitra, yet project-oriented collaborations have produced groundbreaking results. The most important figures in this group include Frank Gehry, Philippe Starck and Ron Arad. In addition, the designers and artists of Vitra Edition during the 1980s deserve mention here: Ettore Sottsass, Alessandro Mendini, Borek Sipek, Gaetano Pesce, Denis Santachiara, Richard Artschwager.

Rolf Fehlbaum

Cooperative work with other designers has just begun. While the first results of these efforts can be seen, it is not yet apparent where these collaborations will ultimately lead: Christoph Ingenhoven, Alfredo Häberli, Hannes Wettstein, Arik Levy, Greg Lynn. There is also the new Vitra Edition, which among other things has brought the acquaintance of Konstantin Grcic, Naoto Fukasawa, Jürgen Mayer H., Jerszy Seymour and Jurgen Bey.

The twelve designers presented on the next pages – six of whom are still living – each embody in their own particular way what is typical about the relationship between Vitra and 'its' designers: a melange of pioneering spirit, interest in scientific research, unswerving determination, and the understanding of design as a "love investigation", as Charles Eames called the confluence of dedication and passion that leads to successful design solutions.

A CONTINENT OF DESIGN – CHARLES & RAY EAMES

For Vitra, Charles and Ray Eames are both a point of departure and a guiding star. In 1953, Willi Fehlbaum saw an Eames chair in New York City. He promptly decided to become a furniture manufacturer and successfully negotiated the licensing and production rights to Eames designs for the European market. Ever since, Charles and Ray Eames have been a ubiquitous presence at Vitra. Not a day goes by without reference to the Eameses' conceptual and philosophical approach in our discussions. In many different contexts, whether related to products, re-editions, exhibitions, anecdotes, recollections, acquisitions to the

Rolf Fehlbaum

collections, legal disputes with copyists, research, or important design decisions, one of the questions we most frequently ask ourselves is: "What would Charles say?" So it is hardly surprising that the Vitra Design Museum is located on Charles Eames Street, or that Charles's office has been reconstructed on the Vitra premises with original artefacts loaned by his daughter.

Like no one before or after, Charles and Ray Eames exploited the possibilities offered by industrialization in connection with new materials and technologies. But they were not merely technicians. Ray was a painter, Charles an architect. They were artists, even though they did not regard themselves as such. They used technology to solve specific problems and accepted the practical constraints of industrial production. They applied the principle of 'trial and error' – so strikingly demonstrated in their large accumulation of prototypes – with infinite patience to the task at hand. Not only did they work on something until a fully satisfactory result had been achieved, they also continued to improve their products when deficiencies became apparent with prolonged usage. Yet all of these things do not explain the unwaning attractiveness of Eames products. Their solutions were ultimately artistic in nature, and there is an undeniable genius (though Charles rejected this label) behind the almost magical allure of their designs. The currency and relevance of Eames products, even fifty or sixty years after their inception, is attested by the fact that they are still chosen to outfit the finest interiors – and also frequently copied by unauthorized manufacturers.

A number of Eames designs, however, have disappeared from the Vitra product line over the years. At some point they no longer seemed pertinent, either because of changes in production technology or due to the firm's emphasis on new marketing sectors. Yet such decisions should never be irrevocable: under altered circumstances, 'forgotten' products may suddenly appear in a new light. For instance, the La Fonda dining chair, which was designed by the Eameses for the La Fonda del Sol restaurant in New York City, fits perfectly in the new Vitra Home Collection. Consequently, it will be reintroduced in 2007. And occasionally a new approach – one that was not considered by the Eameses – makes it possible to produce a design that previously existed only as a prototype. The introduction of La Chaise (design by Charles & Ray Eames, 1948) by Vitra in 1989 and the first commercial edition of the Eames Elephant on the occasion of Charles's 100th birthday (2007) are examples.

DESIGN IS MORE THAN PRODUCT APPEARANCE – GEORGE NELSON

George Nelson (1908–1986) is another of those rare designers who demonstrate both aspects of innovative design: iconic and typological. Virtually everyone is familiar with the Marshmallow Sofa, the Coconut Chair and the Wall Clocks, which have entered many design collections as icons of the 1950s. More interesting and important for the evolution of design, however, were Nelson's typological innovations in the realm of the office world: Storage wall, the L-shaped desk (Executive Office Group) as a precursor of the workstation, his colourful metal desks and seminal storage concepts. While all of these things had a major effect on the development of design, they are seldom represented in museum collections. Nelson, who like the Eameses was a central figure in the early history of Vitra (he was director of design at Herman Miller, the company that sold licensing rights to Willi Fehlbaum for furniture production in Europe), greatly influenced me and contributed significantly to my understanding of design. No other prominent designer spoke as intelligently or wrote as coherently about design. Appropriately, the holdings of the Vitra Design Museum include George Nelson's personal archives.

EVERYTHING MUST CHANGE – VERNER PANTON

In contrast to the Eameses, whose pursuit of new materials and technologies was motivated by the inadequacy of traditional methods to solve specific problems, Verner Panton wanted to make everything different on principle. A new era should have new furniture and new interiors, different from everything that had preceded them. The heroic period of modernism had already become a thing of the past. Colour, Pop culture and 'Gesamtkunstwerk' would replace the sterility of modernism. Some things in the work of Panton will be (or already are) regarded as a curious aberration in the history of design, like the 'total environment' as a subsumption of all interior elements under a formal code. It eventually became clear that people did not want to live in a showroom. Yet there are also iconic pieces, objects that draw their power and longevity from the combination of a formal idea with new technology. A case in point is the Panton Chair. Panton's goal was to make a shape out of plastic that had never been seen before. His solution was both iconic and sensational. Even today, the Panton Chair inspires astonishment and enthusiasm by employing the cantilever principle, but in a more subtle way than cantilever chairs made of tubular steel. Panton's Cone Chair is more conventional, but it is also 'different': a basic geometric form, the cone, is transformed into a chair. The striking appearance of the Cone Chair is largely attributable to its anti-intuitive shape: it tapers sharply to a point at the centre of the cruciform base, right where the structural load is most highly concentrated.

In a small irony of history, most of the discussions between Verner Panton and myself, in our joint pursuit of ways to overcome the bourgeois fustiness of post-war domestic interiors during the 1960s, actually took place in the ground storey of a conventional apartment block in Basel. One product that resulted from those heady days was the Living Tower, which was produced in small numbers.

THE POETICS OF NECESSITY – JEAN PROUVÉ

There are significant similarities in the work of Jean Prouvé and the Eameses, for all three took a structural approach to design tasks. Yet in contrast to the American designer couple, Prouvé was also a manufacturer. His business was based on the production of building elements, as well as furniture commissions from universities and administrative authorities. While the Eameses essentially had access to the entire range of contemporary technology, Prouvé's designs were influenced by the equipment and production processes available in his factory. His matchless mastery of industrial metalwork resulted from the concentration of his attention to these specific conditions. Prouvé developed countless structural systems over the years, and it is one of the wonders of design that such technical solutions can simultaneously be so personal and poetical.

ESSENTIAL DESIGN – MAARTEN VAN SEVEREN

Maarten Van Severen is a special case among designers. Usually two parties are involved in the development of a product: the designer and the manufacturer. Sometimes one person assumes both of these roles. This was the case with Jean Prouvé – and also with Maarten Van Severen. During a significant phase of their careers, both Prouvé and Van Severen worked simultaneously as designers and manufacturers. While Prouvé devoted his efforts to specific commissions from independent clients, Maarten Van Severen worked like an artist on self-assigned tasks. Before coming into contact with Vitra, he had developed a distinctive idiom in furniture with tables, chairs, frames and containers, which he produced in small series with the help of a few assistants. The exciting thing about his collaboration with Vitra was that it presented an opportunity to adapt his previous work, which was based on handcraftsmanship, to industrial production methods. The fusion of these two approaches was a stroke of good fortune for both Vitra and Van Severen, for it culminated in a group of unique furnishings that lifted his creative abilities to a new level.

Rolf Fehlbaum

DESIGN AS TEAMWORK – ANTONIO CITTERIO

> "I have been working with Vitra for twenty-four years. There was never a pause in this cooperation. Many products were conceived during this time, but by no means all of them reached the market. Quite a few never went beyond the drawing stage. Recently I assembled all of these 'missed opportunities' in a booklet for Rolf Fehlbaum. We looked through it together. It was quite amusing, but also enlightening. We discovered that most of the designs were not missed opportunities after all, but proposals with some kind of inner contradiction which were therefore abandoned. Other 'missed opportunities' underwent a transformation and became successful products."

Antonio Citterio is known for the statement that every project has a father and a mother. This is also how Citterio defines his relationship with the manufacturers of his designs. The product is a cooperative effort. Vitra has worked together with Citterio consistently over a long period of time than with any other designer. Their step-by-step approach is characterized by immense patience and mutual understanding. It involves a level of conceptual communication and personal identification that transcends the individual product. There is no better example that design is not an ego trip, but a deliberate, collaborative quest to achieve an optimal solution by taking multiple factors into account: technology, pricing, ecology, perceptual psychology, economics, distribution, and of course aesthetic appearance. Enormous effort has gone into the projects developed during the twenty-four years of this partnership – but the products appear so natural and easy that one does not suspect this investment of labour.

Similar to George Nelson, Citterio has produced several iconic designs. But also like Nelson, his status as one of today's most influential designers is based on his typological innovations. Almost every

Rolf Fehlbaum

office furniture manufacturer in the world has something in their product line that harks back to Citterio's Ad Hoc system, and one can no longer imagine the realm of contemporary home living without his products for B&B Italia. 'Insiders' – competitors and other designers – recognize the significance of Citterio's typological innovations more quickly and thoroughly than press and media representatives, who are predisposed to take an interest in objects that lend themselves to visual illustration and description. Because technological or typological innovations require deeper comprehension, they receive less media attention.

SUPERNORMAL – JASPER MORRISON

> "The extent [to which] Rolf [Fehlbaum] still prioritizes design in production [is a hallmark of Vitra], and it is very hard to think of anyone else who thinks and breathes design as much as he does. I do not mean design in the magazine sense of glossy images, but in the fundamental sense of what it can achieve and how best to use it as a focus for what Vitra does. Since [becoming acquainted in 1988] we've had a continuous dialogue and almost always some ongoing project, whether it be a chair or a bus stop."

Our interest in working with Jasper Morrison was not initiated by a product, but by the slide show "A World Without Words", which I saw in Vienna. The show was a compilation of anonymous items and everyday objects, but also included eccentric and subtle images. The first opportunity for a collaboration between Vitra and Morrison was offered by the installation "Some New Items for the Home", which was exhibited at the DAAD gallery in Berlin.

What has been said here about George Nelson is probably equally true of Jasper Morrison: his work has profoundly effected the evolution of design, yet the extent of his influence cannot be measured.

Rolf Fehlbaum

More important than any individual product was the basic attitude from which it emerged. This attitude has been adopted by many younger designers. It proclaims 'the unimportance of form' – but in the sense of restraint rather than neglect.

The strong distinctiveness of Morrison's products proves the hypothesis that reduction can be as powerful as expressiveness. For Vitra, Jasper Morrison is more than a product designer. We often seek his opinion on new ideas. The question that has served us so well, "What would Charles say?", is now supplemented by an additional question: "What would Jasper say?" The advantage to the latter question is that it can be answered directly and specifically. The reciprocality of the relationship is evident in this forthright comment by Jasper Morrison: "Rolf seemed to me [at the outset of our acquaintance in 1988] the personification of an industrial entrepreneur, combining high design ideals with industrial production, which he still is and does, and which was then exceptionally rare. [...] You could say that Rolf is my design dad; going to see him has all the ingredients of a family meeting and the dialogue has always been an essential part of the attitude I bring to new work."

Rolf Fehlbaum

THE PLEASURES OF TECHNOLOGY – ALBERTO MEDA

"During the twelve years of our collaboration, I have been very fortunate: I have been able to complete many successful projects – very few fragmentary ideas are still lying in a drawer somewhere. At the same time, I have become acquainted with 'Swiss-German culture' – not by means of language, but through the working process. I have been able to observe how a model is changed without losing sight of the original intention. I am impressed by the care and precision that is part of the production process. I also had to get used to strict criteria regarding the compatibility of form and construction, and the extreme rigour of durability and safety tests, which occasionally made it necessary to increase the size of components."

Technicians and engineers are good at solving clearly defined problems. Alberto Meda, the only engineer among the designers who work with Vitra, has an expert knowledge of materials and technologies. Yet his design solutions are more than correct answers to specific problems. They respond to the desire for greater simplicity in an increasingly complex world. Alberto Meda has used aluminium and plastics to develop products whose technical lucidity is a source of pleasure in and of itself. This pleasure derives from the surprising simplicity that is achieved by a lengthy process of trial and error. There is a strong demand for the reduction of visual (and technical) complexity in modern society – but no one wants to relinquish the advantages of sophisticated technology. This is why people put up with so many poorly designed high-tech products. Not only is the technological performance of Alberto Meda's products unassailable; the enjoyment of the user stems from the fact that their technical features are easy to understand. In a way that is similar to the objects made by Charles & Ray Eames, this kind of simplicity is perceived as a gift.

Rolf Fehlbaum

TYPOLOGICAL CONCEPTS
FOR A NEW WORLD OF LIVING AND WORKING –
RONAN & ERWAN BOUROULLEC

"At Vitra, research and innovation are expected. At the same time, one is confronted with rigorous precision. We were lucky to start young and to do a lot of work for Vitra early on. The number of projects that we began is much larger than the number that has been brought to completion. Many of them had to be discontinued or rejected; in a demanding and competitive environment, occasional failures are an inevitable part of development work. Sometimes our collaboration with Vitra seems like an endless path, due to the fact that our step-by-step discoveries constantly expand the horizon of potential possibilities. Consequently, the meaning and excitement of every successful project is priceless to us."

The work of brothers Ronan and Erwan Bouroullec is one of the most amazing phenomena in contemporary design, because it unites two things that are seldom found together: a youthful, fresh mode of expression paired with conceptual maturity and technical competence – something typically acquired in a later phase (if at all) of a designer's development. The Bouroullecs' designs result from a collaboration between two very different personalities. The brothers maintain a constant dialogue, inspire one another with new ideas, and manage to transform conflicting perspectives into an enriching aspect of the creative process by maintaining a common goal and vision. Their success is based on an astute conceptual approach, paired with a penchant for experimentation, open-mindedness and a thorough understanding of technical aspects. Joyn, Algues, Slow Chair, Alcove Sofa are only the beginning. These products make one want to join forces with Ronan & Erwan Bouroullec in addressing the full range of problems posed by working and living in today's world. In addition to their strengths in the

Rolf Fehlbaum

areas of concept innovation and product development, their capabilities include a highly distinctive presentation of individual products and product groups. Examples include the Vitra booths for the Milan Furniture Fair, and photo installations for Joyn and Net 'n' Nest. And the relationship with Vitra is symbiotic, according to the Bouroullec brothers: "For us, Rolf Fehlbaum is an ally and an important source of energy."

REDISCOVERY OF THE SURFACE – HELLA JONGERIUS

> "As a designer you hope that a client will establish a framework, have its own opinion concerning the field in question and have a vision of the collection it is seeking to build up. Apart from that a client needs to have confidence in me as a designer, to provide me with room and respect at the ideas stage, to provide input during the actual design process and to provide support at the execution stage. And [...] a client must have the financial clout to turn a product into a commercial success. Vitra offers all of this. The corporate culture is aimed at allowing a designer to flourish."

The surface qualities of industrial products are subordinate to other criteria. The differentiation of surfaces is regarded as secondary, ornamental, even arbitrary, and is consequently most readily sacrificed to the constraints of production. This has led to uniformity and impoverishment, phenomena that are difficult to counteract. In this context, the person and design idiom of Alexander Girard were important for Vitra. Alongside the Eameses and George Nelson, Girard was an intriguing 'outsider' who added a new element to their modes of modernism. Textiles and colours from India and Mexico, folk art from around the world, patterns whose sole justification was the added pleasure of decorative forms – all of these things gave the products and interiors designed by Nelson and the Eameses a touch of magic, something that was missing in the stringent spaces of European modernism. Fabrics designed by Alexander Girard are still used on pillows and other products, and the Vitra Design Museum recently added a series of wooden doll figures by Girard to its product line.

Hella Jongerius brings with her the renewed chance to enrich the world of Vitra, which is dominated by industrial and technical concerns, by combining technology with colours, textiles and unusual objects. The first joint project was a spontaneous success: the Polder Sofa, introduced in 2005, immediately became a key product in the Vitra Home Collection. In addition to the development of new products for Vitra, Hella Jongerius is presently creating a guideline for colours and materials which should diversify and enhance our products and interiors. We hope for surprising results when this ability and knowledge can be applied to the office environment.

In the fifteen years of her work as a designer, Hella Jongerius has created an oeuvre that comprises mostly small objects, "things with a human dimension", as she says. Because she places great importance on the context and tradition in which such a 'thing' is rooted, she has a preference for traditional fabrication techniques and also likes to incorporate local references and customs. With Vitra, a new phase is beginning which introduces industrial processes to her work.

Rolf Fehlbaum

PROJECT VITRA

MUSEUM.
Premises and exhibitions —p. 242
The Vitra Design Museum. Collections and mission by Deyan Sudjic —p. 257

PROJECT VITRA

MUSEUM.

The Vitra Design Museum, designed by Frank Gehry, was opened at the Vitra Campus in Weil am Rhein in 1989. Since then it has been responsible for preserving the company's collections and promoting design-related issues to a broader public. The Museum features classics by the greats of architecture and design, as well as more functional, but no less fascinating, furniture models and artefacts. Thanks to its global network of partnerships, these exhibits are also displayed in countless other venues around the world.

Frank Gehry, 1989

Though its layout is relatively simple overall, the Vitra Design Museum's network of exhibition rooms, lit from above, is actually surprisingly complex. A rectangular opening in the roof of the main hall on the ground floor allows a view of the balustrade on the gallery floor and the framing of the roof light that straddles two halls.

MUSEUM   Exhibition spaces   243

Frank Gehry, 1989   Three of the four exhibition halls are connected via generous openings in the walls and ceilings, creating an ongoing spatial interplay between the rooms. The space is built in such a way that visitors encounter new views into other exhibition halls at every turn and have the sensation of moving within a single unified space rather than a collection of separate rooms.

MUSEUM   Exhibition spaces   244

Frank Gehry, 1989   The sculptural dynamism of the Vitra Design Museum's exterior is echoed in the complex ceiling structures of the upper exhibition hall's interior. In addition to the cross-shaped rib vaulting, another notable feature is the shaft of the large overhead roof light which juts down impressively into the space below.

MUSEUM Exhibition spaces 245

Frank Gehry, 1989 Two of the corners of the upper exhibition hall are cut off, allowing daylight to stream in from above and creating a highly original space where moods and light intensities are continually changing. The facade covers a triangular opening in the floor which allows daylight to filter down to the exhibition hall below.

Masterpieces, 1989

MUSEUM   Exhibitions   247

Floating Shapes, 1989

Europe and America: A Comparison, 1989

Erich Dieckmann. Practitioner of the Avantgarde 1921–1933, 1990

Ron Arad. Sticks and Stones, 1990

Plastic Furniture, 1990

Denis Santachiara. Goods and Animations, 1990

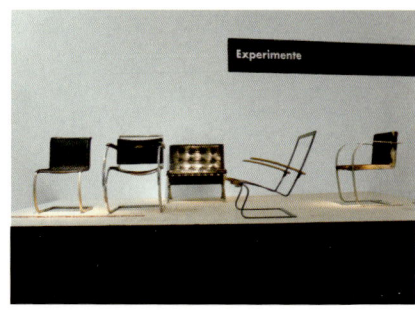

Tubular Steel Furniture, 1991

Czech Cubism. Architecture and Design 1910–1925, 1991

MUSEUM   Exhibitions   249

Stations of Modern Furniture, 1991

Borek Sipek. The Nearness of the Far, 1992

Citizen Office. Notes and Ideas for a New Office World, 1993

From the Industrial Product to Furniture Sculpture, 1993

African Seats, 1994

Thonet. Pioneer of Industrial Design 1830–1900, 1994

100 Masterpieces from the Vitra Design Museum Collection, 1995

Rooms in Time. Design from the 1950s, 1960s, 1970s and 1980s, 1996

The Work of Charles and Ray Eames, 1997

Kidsize. The Material World of Childhood, 1998

MUSEUM Exhibitions 251

Frank Lloyd Wright. The Living City, 1998

Mies van der Rohe. Architecture and Design in Stuttgart, Barcelona and Brno, 1999

A Hundred Years – A Hundred Chairs, 1999

Automobility. What Moves Us, 1999

Verner Panton. Collected Works, 2000

MUSEUM — Exhibitions — 252

Luis Barragán. The Quiet Revolution, 2000

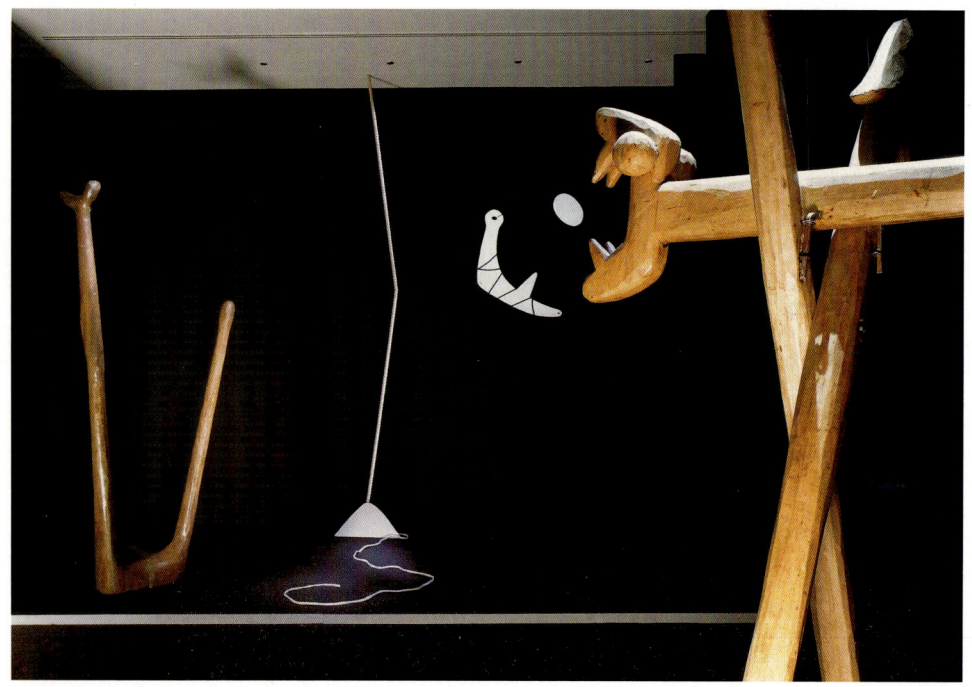

Isamu Noguchi. Sculptural Design, 2001

MUSEUM — Exhibitions — 253

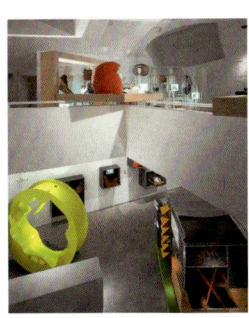

Living in Motion, 2002

Ingo Maurer. Light – Reaching for the Moon, 2002

Marcel Breuer. Design and Architecture, 2003

Airworld. Design and Architecture for Air Travel, 2004

Views of Modern Architecture. Photographs from the Sartoris Collection, 2005

Gaetano Pesce. Il rumore del tempo, 2005

Joe Colombo. Inventing the Future, 2006

MUSEUM   Exhibitions   254

Jean Prouvé. The Poetics of Technical Objects, 2006

The Destruction of 'Gemütlichkeit'?, 2007

MyHome, 2007

Le Corbusier. The Art of Architecture, 2007

Living under the Crescent Moon, 2008

… Carnegie Museum, Centro Cultural de Belém, Cooper Hewitt National Design Museum, Deutsches Architektur Museum, Design Museum London, Isamu Noguchi Foundation, Japanese American National Art Museum, Kunsthaus Graz, Louisiana Museum of Modern Art, MAK,

A selection of the Museum's international exhibition partners

MUSEUM

MARCO Monterrey, Museu Serralves, National Building Museum, National Museum of Singapore, Reina Sofia, Seattle Art Museum, Suntory Museum, TAMA, Thailand Creative and Design Center, The Montreal Museum of Fine Art, Triennale di Milano…

A selection of the Museum's international exhibition partners

THE VITRA DESIGN MUSEUM – COLLECTIONS AND MISSION

Imagine if Volkswagen were to open a museum of car design. A museum of car design that was based on bringing together all the archives of Henry Ford, Pierre Boulanger and Harley Earl, with a collection made up of the most significant cars in the development of automobile history from three continents, going back for a century, alongside a selection of the most intelligently designed engines ever produced. Or consider the likelihood of Chanel doing something similar with fashion not limited to the company's own output, or Boeing contemplating such an initiative with aircraft, and you have an idea of what Rolf Fehlbaum, its founder, and Alexander von Vegesack, its director, have achieved with the Vitra Design Museum in just twenty years. Of course neither Volkswagen nor Chanel, despite their generous cultural patronage across many fields, have attempted any such thing. Vision apart, there are simply too many questions of conflicting interests and ambitions at stake for them to try it.

    A less confident company than Vitra, or perhaps it is better to say, a company without the level of curiosity that drives Vitra, would be too busy asking itself why it should be investing in safeguarding and celebrating the heritage of what could be seen as commercial rivals, to invest so much time and effort in the enterprise. But moved by Fehlbaum's sense of curiosity about design, a curiosity and enthusiasm that go far beyond the boundaries of his own company's output, Vitra

Deyan Sudjic

has created one of the most remarkable collections of twentieth-century design anywhere. Much more than a corporate museum, it offers a perspective about what design can be in the contemporary world.

There are many design collections in the world now. Among the oldest of them is that of the Victoria and Albert Museum in London which established the idea of collecting design in the 1850s. Its purpose was not so much to entertain the public, as to educate it, and, above all, to provide the research and the reference material that the British government believed its manufacturers would need to help them make better products which in turn could better overseas imports. The Victoria and Albert was followed by a wave of similar institutions, from the Museum für Angewandte Kunst (the MAK) in Vienna, to the Neue Sammlung in Munich.

In time, of course, the Victoria and Albert became something else. It suffered mission creep, and turned into a museum of decorative art, where snuff boxes and Raphael cartoons, and collections from throughout Britain's colonial possessions accumulated apparently almost at random to fill up hall after hall. Now, it is a museum that is about a lot of things, but a focused idea of what design can offer a contemporary manufacturer is no longer one of them. It was followed in the 1920s by the Museum of Modern Art in New York, where industrial design was admitted to the collection on the basis of its aesthetic relevance to modernism in art. It was another definition of design, one which proved just as influential as that of the Victoria and Albert, and inspired as many other institutions to follow its lead. But the price

Deyan Sudjic

of admission for design into the art gallery was that it would be presented as if it were art: as large-scale sculpture in neutral white spaces, with no sense of context or process.

Vitra's collections have been assembled with an awareness of both these purposes in mind; they have learned from each of them and moved on. The company has a unique track record in manufacturing and conceiving new typologies for furniture. Studying the collections has played a real part in making that possible, in a way that the founders of the Victoria and Albert would recognize. In the early 1980s, before the Vitra Design Museum had been built, you could wander through the offices attached to the Vitra factory and find in between the desks the battered and faded survivors of the heroic days of the modern movement. They were a challenge to do better today, object lessons for a creative company, rather than trophies. And this collection is still there, in the midst of the company's production facilities, as a kind of reference encyclopaedia. It is also a reflection of Fehlbaum's world view; in which industrial design offers a crucial insight into the nature of the contemporary world, engaged both with the material, and the cerebral.

    Of course a collection like that of MoMA, or the Pompidou in Paris has a wider range. Vitra does not collect computers or cars, washing machines, or helicopters, or guns, or fashion. Its focus is on furniture in the context of architecture and interior design. And with the exception of a few classically styled pieces that demonstrate innovation in mass production, it limits itself to modernism and its descendants in its stylistic choices.

Deyan Sudjic

But in its chosen territory – and that now extends into lighting – of the modern period, Vitra has unmatched depth.

When Ray Eames died, there was no American museum with the resources ready to take on the bulk of the archives of what was perhaps the most brilliant mid-century design studio in the world. Vitra found the means to do it – and for its pains was presented for a moment as an unwelcome interloper, making off with a priceless piece of American heritage. Similarly, when the Barrágan papers in Mexico were in danger of dissolving into dust, it was Vitra that rescued them.

The Vitra collections include Sottsass and Memphis of course; they have pieces by Panton, Kuramata, Aalto and Arad, Pesce and Colombo. But they also go back to the dawn of industrial production, with items by Thonet, and even earlier.

The collections began with Rolf Fehlbaum's acquisition of a single chair designed and made by Jean Prouvé, the great, quintessentially French, engineer designer. What intrigued him was the combination of manufacturing skill and aesthetic sensibility that it represented. The collections took on their present form when Fehlbaum met Alexander von Vegesack. After a spell in theatre, and as an exhibition organizer, von Vegesack had knocked on Billy Wilder's door in Los Angeles to look at his collection of Bauhaus designs. Over the years, von Vegesack built up a substantial collection of his own, fuelled by the very special kind of knowledge that comes not from academic history but from the visceral insight into the evolution of production and technique that comes from the focus of a collector. Fehlbaum bought von Vegesack's holdings of bentwood and tubular steel furniture. As Fehlbaum says,

Workshops — Alexander von Vegesack and Robert Wilson attending a workshop in 1991. In the early years, these events were held in a marquee in front of the Vitra Design Museum. A decade later, in 2001, Robert Wilson was asked to produce the exhibition on Isamu Noguchi for the Vitra Design Museum.

he had no clear strategy about where to take the collections next. He has always taken pleasure in seeing where events will lead him.

No collection can be objective. It is in the nature of collecting that it is based on choices. What category of things to collect is one key choice. Which pieces to focus on is another. Unerringly, these choices will reveal the personality behind the collection.

Fehlbaum is inspired by how things are made. Standing by the Vitra production line, he becomes lyrical when he talks about the magic that accompanies the moment when a rubber disc closes up to connect the bent metal of a chair leg to the fibreglass shell of the seat. But he is as excited by the cultural significance of a chair and its ability to reflect an artistic moment, or a social development. He has a catholic, but coherent, taste that informs the choice of every object acquired for the collections and it is that taste, as much as anything, which makes the collections so impressive.

The idea of building a museum to show the collections was not part of the original plan. Fehlbaum had thought about buying a villa to house them. But then, as part of the wider expansion of the Weil am Rhein Campus of Vitra's industrial buildings, the possibility of a structure to show the collections came up.

There was a casual introduction to Frank Gehry from Claes Oldenburg, commissioned by Fehlbaum to produce a sculpture as a gift to his father for his seventieth birthday. Fehlbaum had already asked Gehry to think about furniture for the company, and somehow never managed to get a reply. The factory with museum attached, or possibly the other way around was Gehry's belated response.

Deyan Sudjic

The Museum and the collections have emerged as two distinct, and different, strands in Vitra's strategy. The collections allow Vitra to take a key place in the international museum circuit, to safeguard the historical legacy of the pioneers, and to collect newer work from contemporary designers. But the collections do not just sit on the shelves. The Vitra Design Museum has established itself as an equally important production house for exhibitions, both thematic and monographs, that push forwards the debate on architecture and design. It has been able to develop an important critical and curatorial voice, which is as important as acquiring and looking after objects.

Gehry's modest little building, such an unlikely curtain raiser to the age of iconic architecture that his later work made possible, has become a highly effective platform for the exhibitions programme that Vitra orchestrates, rather than a showcase and storeroom for the collections themselves. On a modest scale, and with restricted means – there is not a titanium fish scale to be seen anywhere in the building – Gehry has created a characterful series of spaces that are the antithesis of bland neutral flexibility, but which still offer a distinctive frame for the exhibitions that they accommodate. This is the public face of Vitra, the visible cultural programme that has a story to tell about design.

What has made the Vitra Museum so distinctive is a mix of Fehlbaum's passion and his eye, which has shaped the parameters of the collections, with his cool insistence that the Museum does all it can to support itself. An insistence that has brought out the most in von Vegesack's shrewd ingenuity. Among many other things, it led to the creation of

Deyan Sudjic

the series of miniatures – tiny scale models of classic chairs – in a special factory, which have enjoyed remark-able sales and consequently play a large part in supporting the Museum. And it has driven the Museum's exhibitions policy, tailoring them to travel easily, allowing it to work with more traditional institutions around the world.

Vitra's work with the Barrágan and Eames archives have allowed the Museum to celebrate established reputations and to throw new light on them, as well as in some cases to overcome unjustified neglect. And it has shown the way in which such archives can have a future.

The collections have a different role. They have become too large to have a permanent presence on display and are carefully looked after on the apparently endless shelves of the Museum storerooms. They are available for loan to other institutions, and to form the basis of the exhibitions that Vitra mounts. Their significance, and it has to be said, their value, has changed almost beyond recognition in the twenty years since the Museum opened. The explosion of the market in design objects would make it impossible to replicate Vitra's collections now without massive investment. Design is not yet in the same state as the art market which has priced much new work out of the reach of so many art museums. But prices have moved upwards decisively. Prouvé has already become an 'old master'. It is an unsettling transformation for a category of objects ideologically conceived to be the very opposite. Contemporary design has its ideological underpinning in mass production, which offers perfection in numbers, and promises the democratization that industry can bring, by allowing

Deyan Sudjic

the many to aspire to the contemporary version of craftsmanship once only enjoyed by the few.

Vitra's collections manage to square the circle. They track the course of technical innovation and the development of industrial manufacture. But they also show the aesthetic intensity of design and what it has to offer to the art galleries.

In the end it is the two sides of the Museum, its collections andits exhibitions, that give it the power to shift the conversation on design, to focus attention on the areas that it sees as important, to explore achievements and innovations and to help make new ones possible.

Deyan Sudjic — studied architecture at Edinburgh University and is director of the Design Museum in London. Prior to joining the London Design Museum, Sudjic worked as editor-in-chief of "Domus" and founded the design magazine "Blueprint". He was also director of the Venice Architecture Biennale (2002) and director of 'Glasgow 1999: UK City of Architecture and Design'.

Miniatures — Michele de Lucchi with a miniature version of his chair First.

MUSEUM

Miniatures

The Vitra Design Museum's best known product – and a substantial source of income for the museum – are its 'miniatures'. These are sold around the world and have become design icons. The 90-strong collection of classic chair designs – true-to-detail models scaled down to 1:6 of their original size – is continually being expanded to accommodate new pieces.

VITRA DESIGN MUSEUM

HISTORY AND CONCEPT

- The foundation stone was laid at the beginning of the 1980s by Rolf Fehlbaum, whose vision to create an institution dedicated to the history of modern design was the driving force behind the collections, which now comprise some 6000 objects
- The museum's director, Alexander von Vegesack, devised and implemented a plan to develop it into an independent and international institution
- The museum researches a huge range of designs but focuses in particular on furniture and interior design and their relationship to architecture
- An average of 70,000 architecture and design enthusiasts visit the Vitra Design Museum every year

BUILDING

- Architect: Frank Gehry
- Beginning of design process: 1987
- Opening: 3 November 1989
- Exhibition space: 740 m² (570 m² on ground floor; 170 m² on first floor)
- Materials: roofs: titanium-zinc cladding; outside walls: white plaster; inside walls and ceilings: plastered, painted white; floor (ground floor): Duratex; floor (first floor): parquet

ACTIVITIES

- Plans and runs exhibitions on design and architecture (more than forty exhibitions since 1989)
- Publishes books, particularly exhibition catalogues
- Runs the restoration laboratory, archives and library and manages the collections
- Organizes workshops featuring leading designers
- Lends works from its permanent collections
- Supports research projects by allowing interested parties access to its library and archives
- Gives guided tours of the Vitra Campus (exhibitions and architecture)

FINANCING

Vitra grants a substantial annual contribution towards operational costs of the Vitra Design Museum. To cover the full cost of its activities, the museum is required to secure additional financing through:
- sale of products from the Vitra Design Museum Collection, the Miniatures Collection and publications
- revenue from touring exhibitions and sales to other museums
- revenue from lending collection exhibits to other organizations
- collaborations with other museums or universities which contribute to the cost of setting up an exhibition
- partnerships with sponsors who support specific exhibitions and/or training programmes

COLLECTIONS.
From Rietveld to Panton to Memphis, photographed by Bruns/Ueberschär/Wootton —p. 272

Origins and holdings of the Vitra Design Museum collections by Alexander von Vegesack —p. 299

PROJECT VITRA

COLLECTIONS.

Since the 1980s, Vitra has been building up an extensive collection of furniture. Originally focused on chairs, it now contains the full spectrum of industrially produced furnishings, including lamps and other lighting fixtures, from the mid nineteenth century to the present. Over the decades, this collection has been enriched with the estates, or partial estates, of a number of prominent designers with whom Vitra has had special relationships. The company is committed to cultivating and sharing with others these historic legacies which often set standards for its own creations.

COLLECTIONS   From the Rietveld / Bauhaus group   272

6 3

6 2

6 1

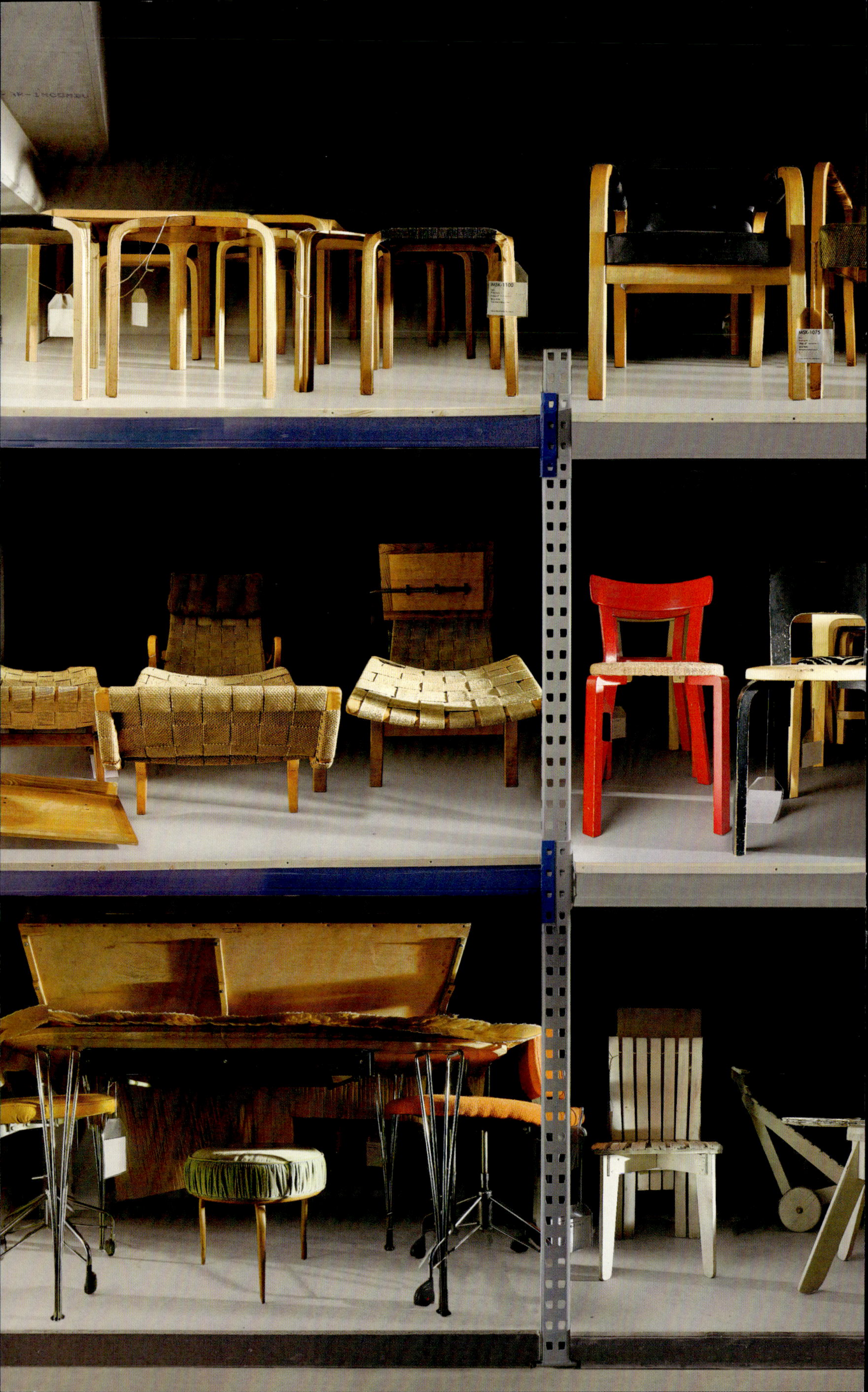

3 3

3 2

3 1

3 3

3 2

3 1

1 3

1 2

1 1

5 3

5 2

5 1

4 3

4 1

2 3

2 2

2 1

Gerrit Rietveld, Marcel Breuer, Ludwig Mies van der Rohe, Le Corbusier, et al

4 2

4 1

5 3

5 2

5 1

6 1

1 3

1 1

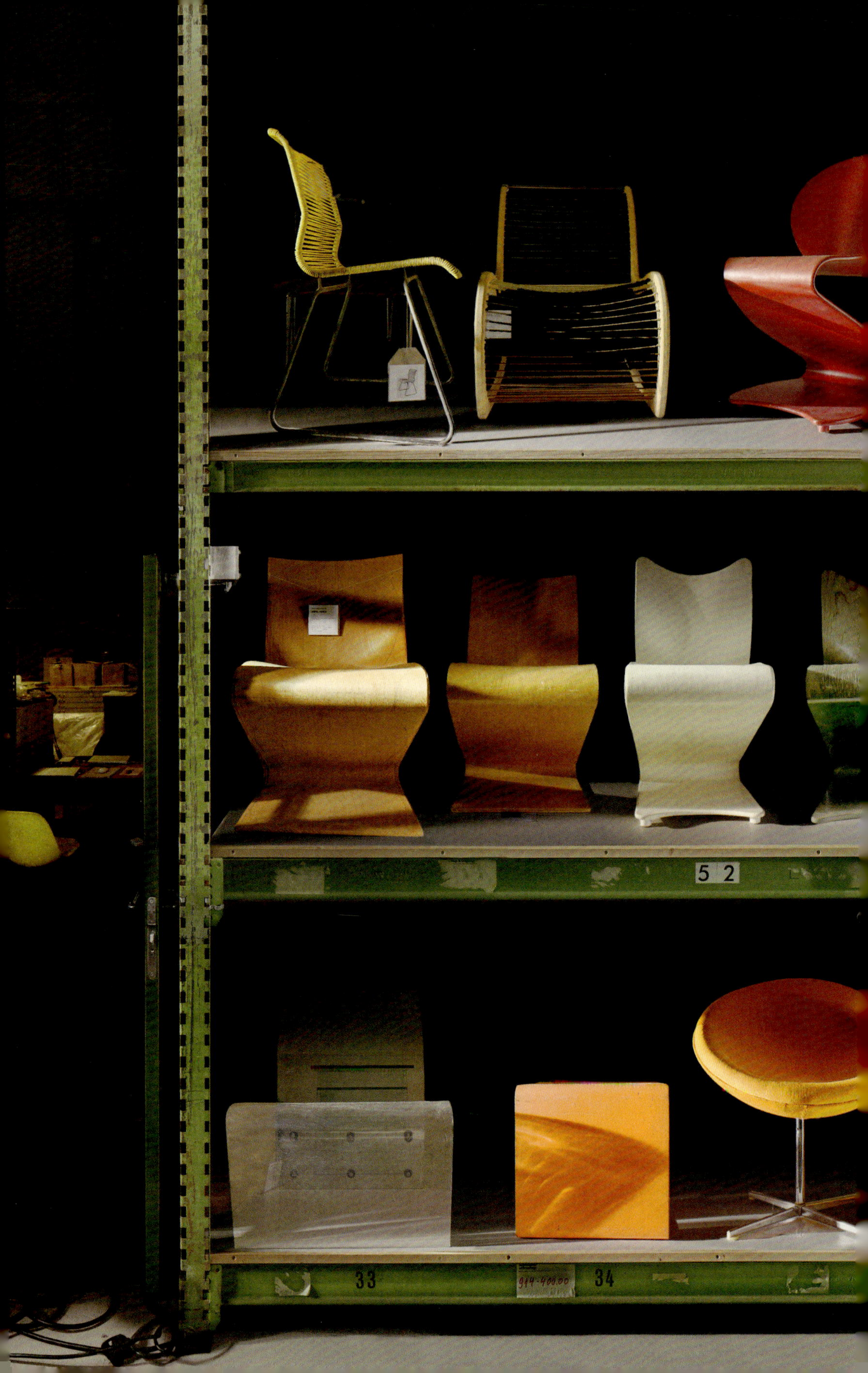
5 2
33
914-400.00
34

4 3

4 1

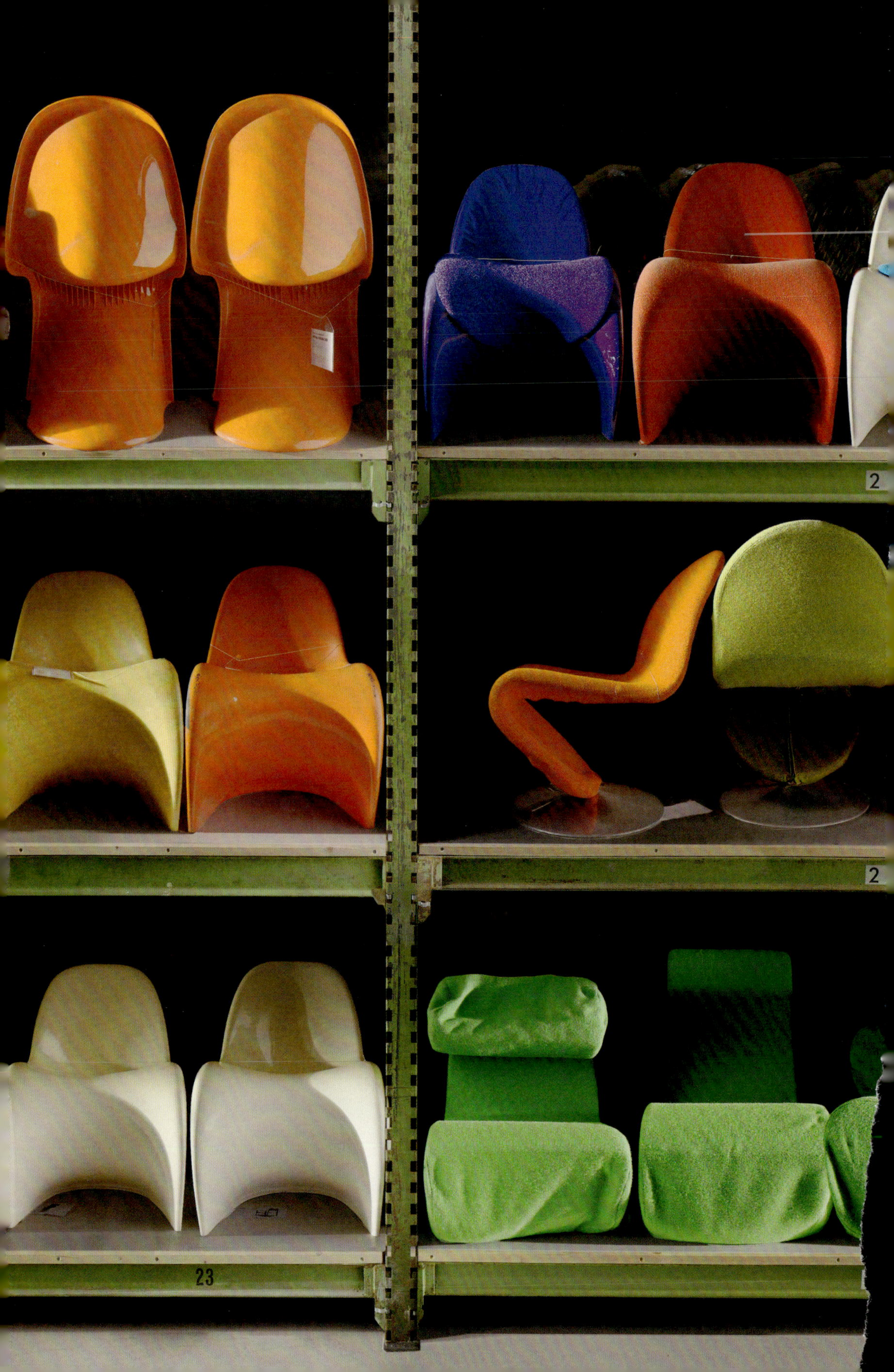
2
2
23

5 3

5 2

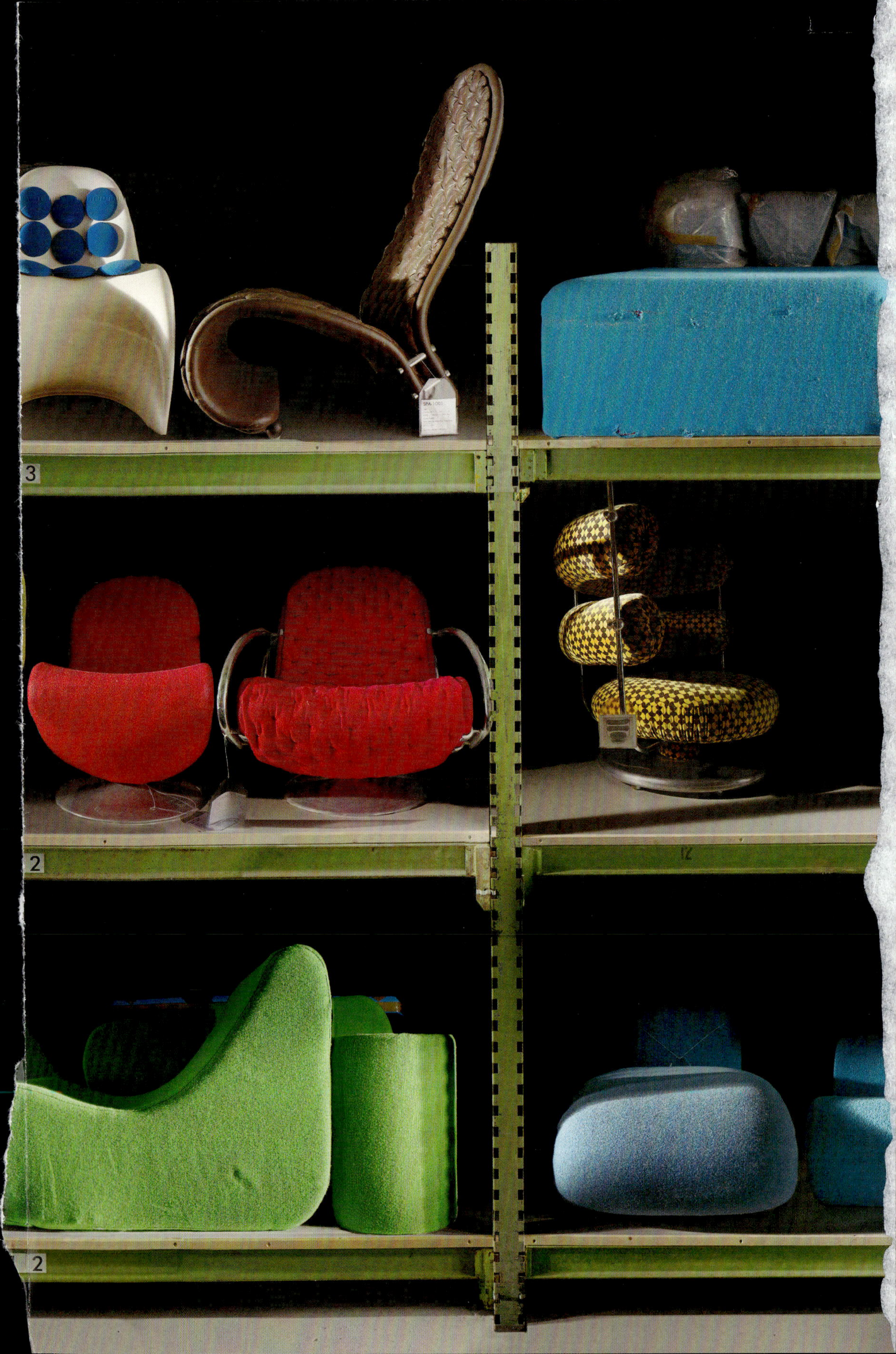
3
2
2

COLLECTIONS   From the 1960s–1990s group   296

COLLECTIONS
From the Verner Panton group

295

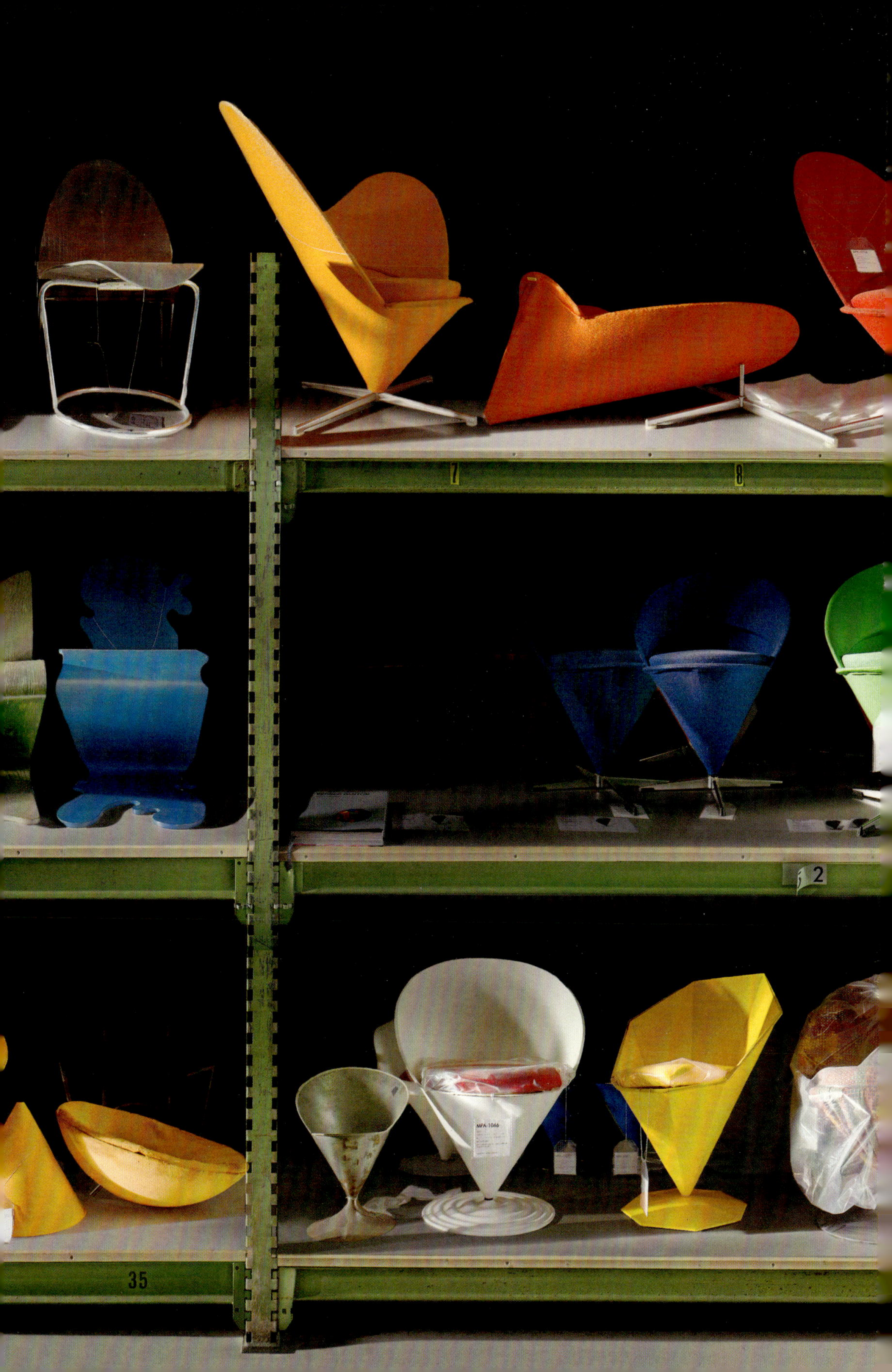
7
8
2
MPA-1066
35

2 3

2 2

2 1

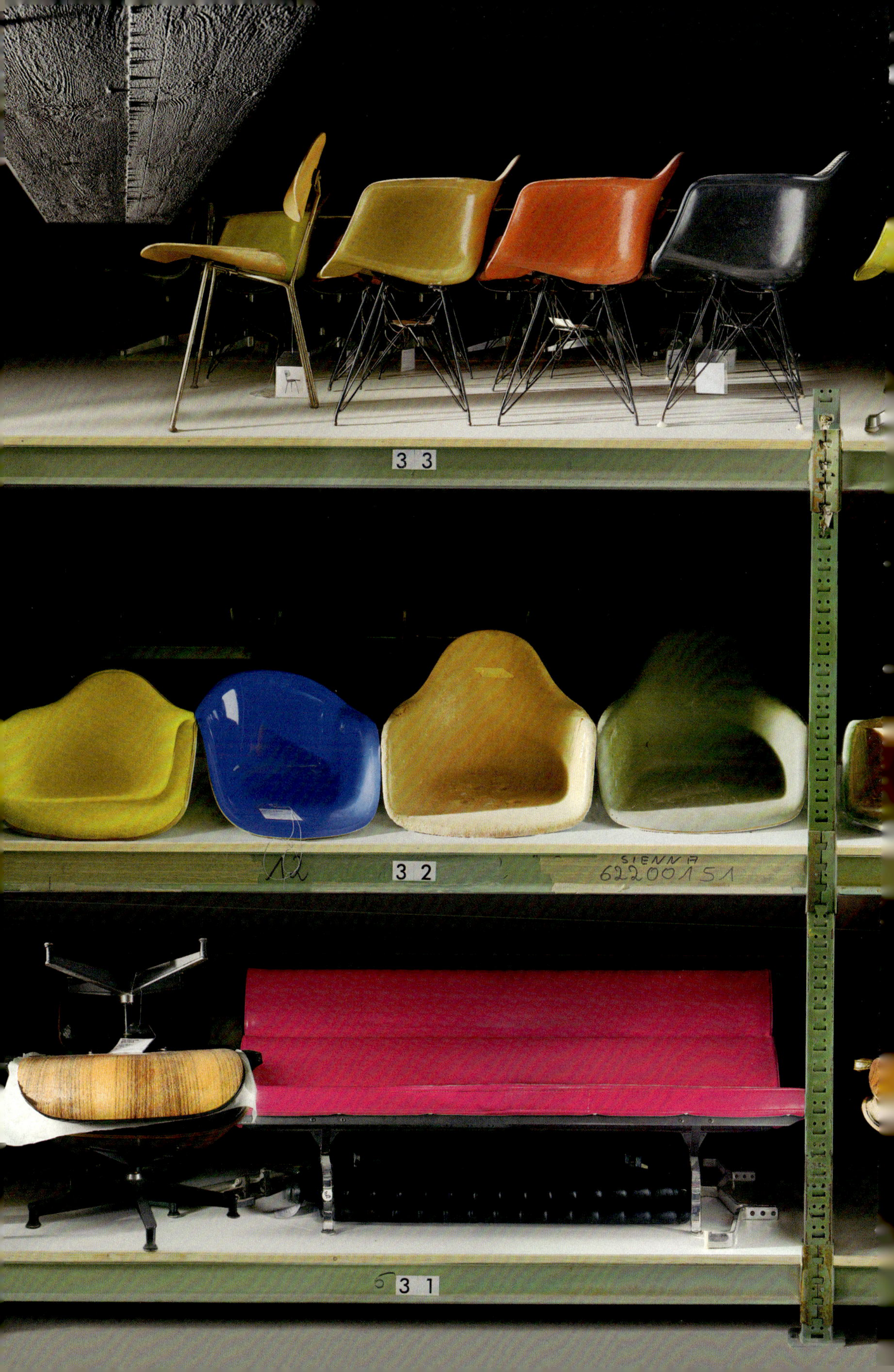
3 3
3 2
SIENNA
62200151
3 1

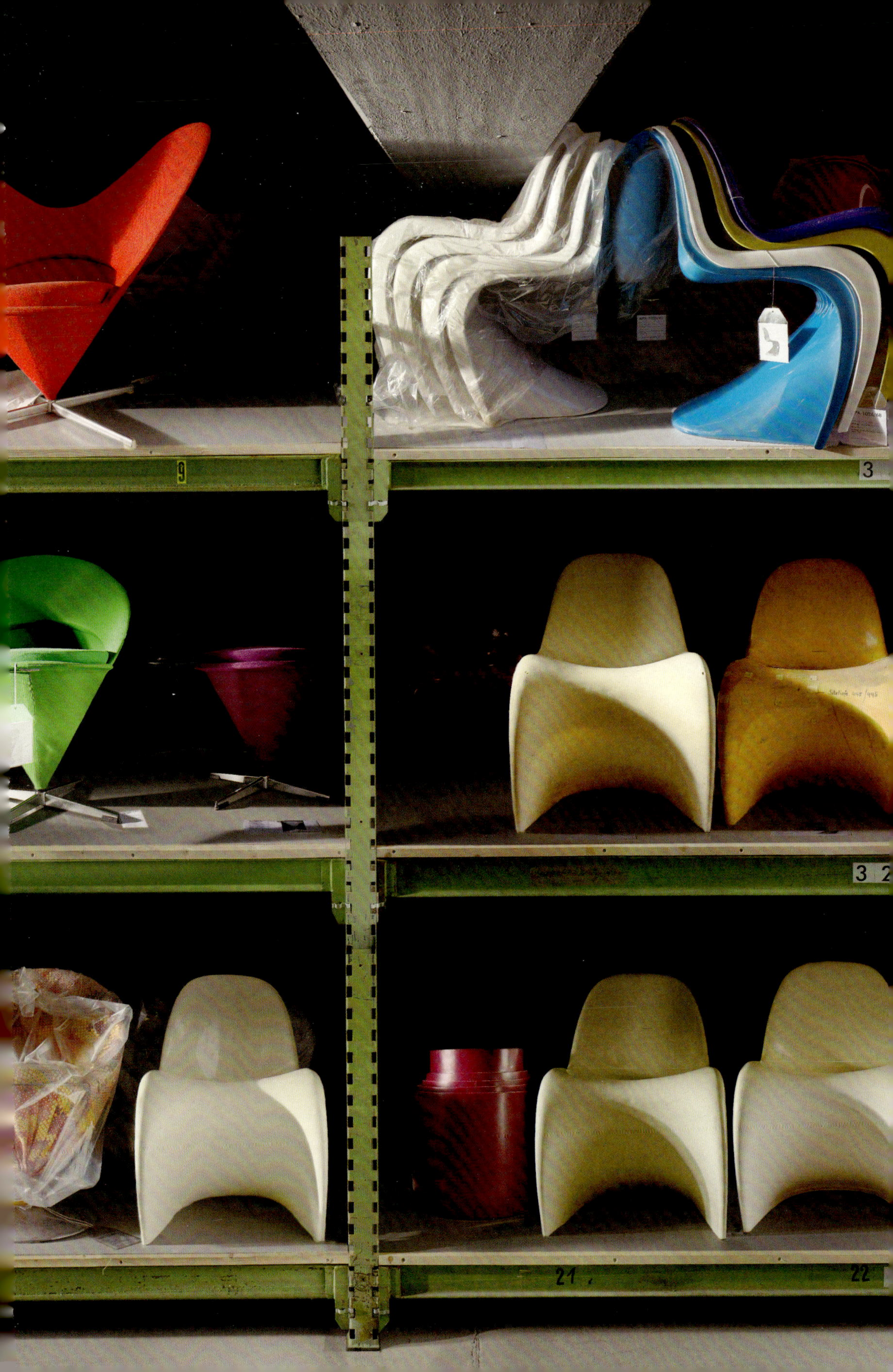
9
3
3 2
21
22

COLLECTIONS   Ettore Sottsass/Memphis, Shiro Kuramata, Marc Newson, et al   297

COLLECTIONS From the 1960s–1990s group 298

4 3

4 2

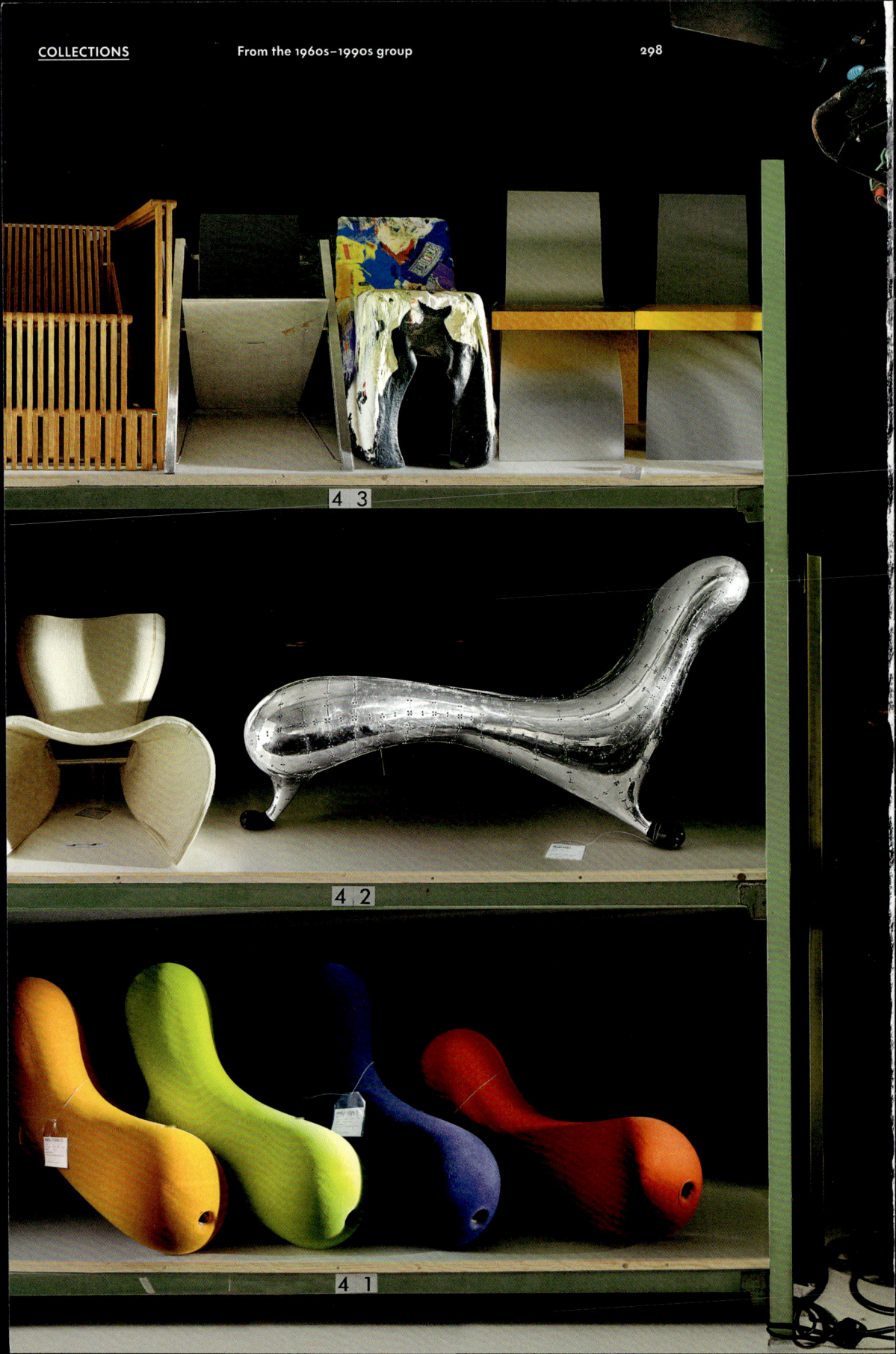

4 1

ORIGINS AND HOLDINGS OF
THE VITRA DESIGN MUSEUM COLLECTIONS

The Vitra Design Museum collections evolved from modest beginnings in the 1980s to become one of the world's most important collections of modern furniture. In 1989, the collections included some 1000 objects. In the years since, they have grown to encompass approximately 6000 pieces. Two furniture collections – one compiled by Rolf Fehlbaum for Vitra starting in the early 1980s, the other that I began as a personal initiative in the late 1960s – came together to form the foundation of the Vitra Design Museum collections.

My own collection arose from an interest in the earliest examples of industrially produced furniture, Michael Thonet's bentwood chairs. I was fascinated by the many variations of the designs, both functional and decorative, but even more so by Thonet's vision of industrial mass production, realized through innovations in technology, design and marketing. The collection documented the development of manufacturing techniques, materials and forms of modern furniture from the beginning of the nineteenth century through the mid twentieth century. The focus was on laminated plywood and bentwood pieces by Michael Thonet, Adolf Loos, Josef Hoffmann, Alvar Aalto and Charles & Ray Eames, as well as tubular steel furniture designed by Mart Stam, Marcel Breuer, Le Corbusier and Ludwig Mies van der Rohe. In addition, I had also acquired examples of furniture made from papier mâché, Bakelite and fibreglass – materials likewise used in mass

Alexander von Vegesack

production – as well as archival documentation including photos of working processes, sales catalogues, publications on historic exhibitions and corresponding trade literature.

Alongside important designs by the Eameses and George Nelson – both central pillars of Vitra's furniture production – Rolf Fehlbaum's collection also encompassed works by European designers such as Alvar Aalto, Jean Prouvé and Gerrit Rietveld. A sampling of some 150 pieces from the collection was exhibited on platforms in a large office space at Vitra as a historic model and inspiration for employees and customers.

Our joint collaboration began in 1987. Following his acquisition of a portion of my collection in 1988, Rolf Fehlbaum charged me with the task of systematically building up and expanding the combined holdings. To provide the objects with a dedicated venue, Fehlbaum had asked the architect Frank Gehry in 1986 to create plans for a small museum building. The building – originally conceived as a place to house the collections and show the holdings to friends, customers and business partners – became the present-day Vitra Design Museum, as well as Gehry's first built project on European soil.

My own proposals went beyond the original idea of merely displaying the collections to embrace the concept of a publicly accessible museum that would operate independently from the company. In addition to its own programme of exhibitions based on the collections, it would also show alternating temporary exhibitions. As founding director, I opened Vitra Design Museum in 1989 and have watched it grow into an important international facility with a diverse yet distinctive profile.

Alexander von Vegesack

In the two decades of our collaboration, Rolf Fehlbaum and I have worked with the Museum's head of collections, Serge Mauduit, to find and obtain the best examples of industrially produced furniture through individual purchases, auctions or the acquisition of complete estates. By far the most important acquisition was a substantial part of the three-dimensional estate of Charles & Ray Eames, which we obtained in 1988. In addition to designs that went into production, this estate also contains studies and prototypes that are of inestimable value in documenting and examining the creative processes underpinning the couple's work. No doubt the pre-eminent highlight of the collections, this estate is particularly remarkable in light of the fact that it made its way from Venice, California, to Weil am Rhein.

The other important estate holdings in the collections include furniture, drawings, manuscripts and photos from the office of George Nelson; the patents and correspondence of Anton Lorenz, the 'éminence grise' of the international tubular steel furniture industry; and the artefacts and documents collected by Alexander Girard, who accumulated samples of textiles, paper and other objects from all over the world and initiated an influential dialogue in the 1950s between the fields of design and folk art. The works of Harry Bertoia, Verner Panton and Eero Saarinen are also represented with extensive holdings in the Museum's collections, with the Panton estate containing many of his iconic fabric designs.

Surveying the collections as a whole, the following areas emerge as focal points: the period from the 1850s to the turn of the century shows a focus on bentwood furniture, the designs of Viennese architects and pieces by Charles Rennie Mackintosh and Frank Lloyd Wright.

Alexander von Vegesack

The first three decades of the twentieth century are most prominently represented by the work of Gerrit Rietveld, Marcel Breuer, Ludwig Mies van der Rohe and the Bauhaus, as well as Le Corbusier, Charlotte Perriand and Pierre Jeanneret. Along with the sizeable holdings from American sources, particularly Charles & Ray Eames, Eero Saarinen and Harry Bertoia, the period up to the Second World War is also defined by the French 'constructeur' Jean Prouvé, whose work is superbly documented with his most significant furniture designs, as well as many of his facade elements. From Scandinavia, there are designs by such figures as Alvar Aalto, Arne Jacobsen, Hans Wegner, Poul Kjaerholm and Verner Panton and, from Italy, pieces by Gio Ponti, Carlo Mollino, Achille Castiglioni, Studio Memphis and Alchimia. Furnishings from the Arts and Crafts movement along with Art Deco and Art Nouveau are represented, albeit with relatively few examples. Taking the position that subsequent developments in modern furniture can only be fully understood as the ideological and stylistic heirs of these late nineteenth- and early twentieth-century movements, the earlier periods would presumably be the mostly likely candidates for expansion within the collections.

    The collections cover nearly all areas of furniture for everyday use: seating for the home, children's furniture, interior concepts for cooperative living, office furnishings and, finally, modern forms of nomadic living. For the period starting in the 1960s, there are also numerous examples of furniture that reflect contemporary art and then, from the 1980s onwards, an increasing number of objects produced as one-off pieces or in limited editions from designers who emphasize the concept of individual authorship in their work. By no

Alexander von Vegesack

means exclusively limited to industrial furniture, the collections also include quite a few models that were produced individually or in small series. They too have their rightful place at Vitra Design Museum in recognition of their formal, structural, technological or functional contributions to the development of industrial furniture design.

In addition to a minor section on consumer electronics – principally consisting of a collection of Braun electronic devices – a group of industrially produced lighting is being developed under the direction of Raymond Fehlbaum that allows the Museum's exhibitions to more aptly portray the design history of the home environment. The selection criteria here correspond to those in the area of furniture. A key difference lies in the time frame for the different areas, as the period of industrially manufactured electric lighting does not begin until the later years of the nineteenth century with the inventions of Thomas Alva Edison. The collection starts with Peter Behrens followed by the Bauhaus designers Christian Dell, Marianne Brandt and Wilhelm Wagenfeld. Scandinavian designers like Poul Henningsen and Verner Panton, the latter of whom made significant contributions in this area, are likewise represented. There are also numerous Italian works, such as those by Gino Sarfatti or Angelo Lelli, along with creations by Serge Mouille. Notable among the important figures from more recent years is Ingo Maurer with his poetic light sculptures.

As a source of information, the library and archives are as important to the work of the Museum as the furniture collection itself. Extensive holdings of the 250 most important journals and magazines and some 9500 book titles on furniture design, architecture and related disciplines,

Alexander von Vegesack

as well as archives with company catalogues, photos, films, drawings and written documents form the basis for our scholarly research and writings.

A collection that extends up to the present will always be incomplete. The more recent an object, the more difficult it is to assess its historic significance. With the veritable flood of designs over the last twenty years – including many one-off pieces and limited editions that by their very nature have attained tremendous publicity – collectors must exercise particular caution when considering acquisitions of current products. It is precisely in this sensitive area, however, that the expertise and visual judgment of Rolf Fehlbaum has always played an essential role. In regard to the collections' gaps in the truly historic decades of design history, these will become smaller over time, even if some can no longer be entirely eliminated – either because the missing objects are extremely rare and the few that do exist are firmly rooted in other collections, or because they simply no longer exist at all. The picture the Vitra Design Museum collections sketch of the history of modern furniture design may be incomplete, but precisely because of its deliberately restricted focus, it is considerably more distinct and coherent than many of the leading collections of publicly operated institutions.

Alexander von Vegesack has been founding director of the Vitra Design Museum since 1989. Since taking up this position, von Vegesack has established a highly diverse and international programme of design and architecture exhibitions, issued numerous publications, initiated an annual international museum conference and launched an internationally renowned seminar series.

OBJECT COLLECTIONS

AUSTRIA

Thonet Brothers, J. & J. Kohn, Otto Wagner, Adolf Loos, Josef Hoffmann, Josef Frank

FRANCE

Pierre Chareau, Le Corbusier, Pierre Jeanneret, Charlotte Perriand, Eileen Gray, René Herbst, Robert Mallet-Stevens, Jean Prouvé, Louis Sognot, Olivier Mourgue, Pierre Paulin, Quasar, Philippe Starck

GERMANY

Karl Friedrich Schinkel, Michael Thonet, Peter Behrens, Richard Riemerschmid, Marcel Breuer, Erich Dieckmann, Egon Eiermann, Walter Gropius, Herbert Hirche, Ludwig Mies van der Rohe, Ferdinand Kramer, Anton Lorenz, Hans & Wassili Luckhardt, Erich Mendelsohn, Heinz & Bodo Rasch, Dieter Rams, Hans Gugelot, Luigi Colani, Stiletto/ Pentagon, Ginbande, Werner Aisslinger

ITALY

Chiavari chairs, Carlo Bugatti, Franco Albini, Carlo Mollino, Gio Ponti, Gae Aulenti, Mario Bellini, Cini Boeri, Osvaldo Borsani, Pier Giacomo & Achille Castiglioni, Ceretti/ Derossi/Rosso, Joe Colombo, De Pas/D'Urbino/Lomazzi/ Scolari, Piero Fornasetti, Gatti/Paolini/Teodoro, Vico Magistretti, Enzo Mari, Sergio Mazza, Giancarlo Piretti, Marco Zanuso, Archizoom, Alessandro Mendini, Gaetano Pesce, Michele De Lucchi, Ettore Sottsass, Andrea Branzi, Denis Santachiara, among others

JAPAN

Sori Yanagi, Toshiyuki Kita, Shiro Kuramata, Tokujin Yoshioka

NETHERLANDS/BELGIUM

Gerrit Rietveld, Wim Rietveld, Mart Stam, Henry Van de Velde, Maarten Van Severen, Droog Design

SCANDINAVIA

Alvar and Aino Aalto, Eero Aarnio, Arne Jacobsen, Grete Jalk, Finn Juhl, Poul Kjaerholm, Hans J. Wegner, Verner Panton

SWITZERLAND

Jürg Bally, Hans Bellmann, Max Bill, Mario Botta, Andreas Christen, Hans Coray, Hans Eichenberger, H.R. Giger, Battista & Gino Giudici, Max Ernst Haefeli, Wilhelm Kienzle, Gian Franco Legler, Berta Rahm, Bruno Rey, Alfred Roth, Flora Steiger, Kurt Thut, Peter Wenger, Hannes Wettstein, Armin Wirth, Pierre Zoelly

UNITED KINGDOM / AUSTRALIA

Windsor chair, Charles Rennie Mackintosh, Gerald Summers, Ron Arad, Jasper Morrison, Marc Newson

UNITED STATES

Windsor chair, Shaker furniture, Frank Lloyd Wright, Norman Bel Geddes, Paul Frankl, Charles & Ray Eames, Harry Bertoia, Vladimir Kagan, Warren McArthur, George Nakashima, George Nelson, Richard Neutra, Isamu Noguchi, Gilbert Rohde, Eero Saarinen, Rudolph Schindler, Kem Weber, Frank Gehry, Robert Venturi, Scott Burton, Robert Wilson

LIGHTING AND OBJECT COLLECTIONS

Peter Behrens, Marianne Brandt/Hin Bredendieck, Christian Dell, Wilhelm Wagenfeld, Pierre Guariche, Serge Mouille, Archizoom, Gae Aulenti, Gino Sarfatti, Vittorio Vigano, Angelo Lelli, Angelo Mangiarotti, Memphis (Sottsass, De Lucchi, Bedin), Ingo Maurer, Verner Panton, Dieter Rams/Hans Gugelot/Herbert Hirche, among others

ESTATE COLLECTIONS

CHARLES & RAY EAMES
(1907–1978 / 1912–1988)

Furniture and other objects from the estate and some archival records (material studies, prototypes, furniture models, tools, serial products, photographs, printed matter).
Period: 1940–1978, c. 1000 items.
The Vitra Design Museum archives possess a variety of documents: vintage photos, magazines and journals, promotional materials, films from the 1940s on. The main body of the Eames estate is held by the Library of Congress.

GEORGE NELSON
(1908–1986)

Records from the estate (library holdings, plans, drawings, photographs, slides).
Period: 1924–1984, c. 7400 items.
Nelson's estate encompasses the areas of product design (especially furniture design), graphic design, industrial design, interior design and exhibition design; extensive coverage is given to his involvement with the "American National Exhibition" in Moscow in 1959. The George Nelson estate is the body of material most frequently consulted by outside users at Vitra Design Museum.

ALEXANDER GIRARD
(1907–1983)

Textiles, objects and records from the estate.
Period: 1929–1985, c. 750 items.
The holdings focus on his major exhibitions and corporate designs at the interface between design and folk art. The documents were carefully maintained by Girard and his assistants. In addition to professional activities such as his association with Herman Miller and furniture design, the estate also covers Girard's folk art collection that later went to the Museum of International Folk Art in Santa Fe.

VERNER PANTON
(1926–1998)

Objects, records and textiles from the estate.
Period: c. 1949–1998, c. 600 items.
Many projects from the fields of furniture and product design and other areas (including many that were never realized) are documented with numerous large-format drawings.

ANTON LORENZ
(1891–1966)

Pioneer and co-inventor of cantilevered tubular steel furniture records, including case files on the functional principle of the cantilevered chair.
Period: 1927–1974, c. 45 linear metres of files, c. 370 items.
Inventor of the 'movement chair', Lorenz lived and worked in Berlin, and then in the United States from the 1940s. Worldwide, this is the most significant estate on the history of tubular steel furniture, containing correspondence with Le Corbusier, Charlotte Perriand, Laszlo Moholy-Nagy, Marcel Breuer and Ludwig Mies van der Rohe.

HARRY BERTOIA
(1915–1976)

Correspondence, photographs.
Period: 1943–1979, c. 600 items.
The bulk of the holdings concerns Bertoia's work as a sculptor and metal artist.

COLLECTIONS 307

Charles Eames's study

Photographs of the interior of Charles Eames's study which is now on permanent loan to the Vitra Showroom in Weil am Rhein. The ensemble, meticulously reconstructed to the original plans, shows the kind of objects Eames surrounded himself with and gives us an insight into the way he worked.

COLLECTIONS

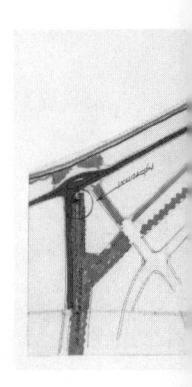

Barragán Archives

Luis Barragán (1902–1988) is one of the most important architects of the twentieth century. The Mexican was awarded the Pritzker Prize in 1980 for his oeuvre in which the International Style and continually evolving local traditions converge. Barragán's explorations into his own culture and his active dialogue with peers, engineers, artists and photographers led him

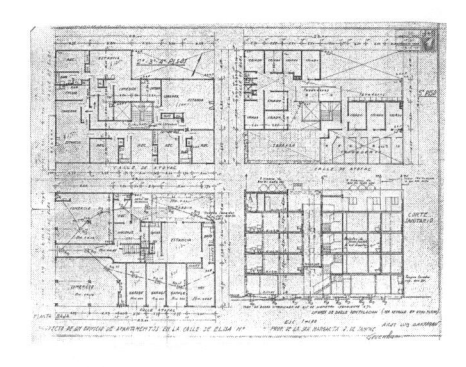

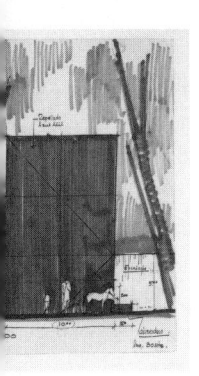

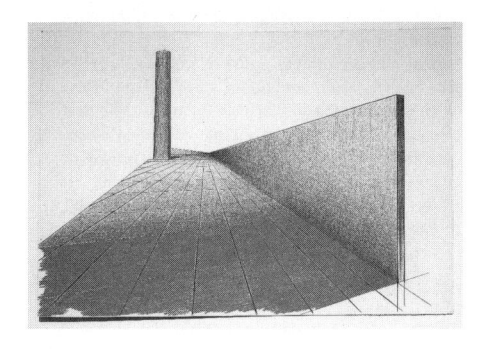

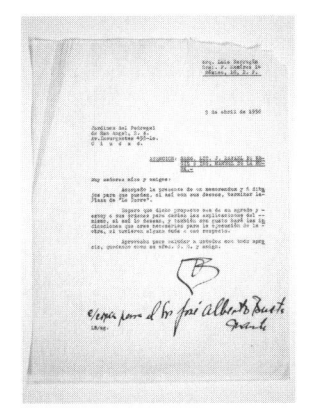

COLLECTIONS

to create a unique iconography. This is reflected in the single buildings, landscape architecture and entire urban developments he designed.

BARRAGAN FOUNDATION

HISTORY AND CONCEPT

The Barragan Foundation was established in 1996 after the acquisition of the Barragán archives. The collections were enriched in 1997 with selected material from the estate of the photographer Armando Salas Portugal. A range of Barragán's furniture and objects, as well as other documentation directly or indirectly related to Barragán's work and its context (recent publications, correspondence, photographic documentation, reproductions of material belonging to other collections, etc.) were also acquired.

As a form of bibliographic support to future research the Barragan Foundation is continuously collecting publications and documentation related to the artistic and architectural production of twentieth-century Mexico. Since its inception, the Barragan Foundation has been headed by Federica Zanco. At present, the work of the foundation is concentrating on the preparation of a comprehensive publication about the archive.

BARRAGÁN ARCHIVES

13,500 drawings; 7500 photographic prints (b/w, col.); 82 photographic panels; 3500 negatives; 7800 transparencies/slides; 290 publications concerning Barragán's work; 54 publications collected by Barragán, not related to his work; 7 files of clippings related to Barragán's work (newspapers, magazines, etc.); 7 models; several files of manuscripts, notes, lists and correspondence are also included.

ARMANDO SALAS PORTUGAL COLLECTION

2342 negatives (b/w, col.); 283 transparencies; 481 photographic prints; 8 photographic panels.

PROJECT VITRA

SIGNS.
Vitra as time goes by. Treasures from the art world, the media and Vitra's archives — p. 314
DesignArt. The kernel of product design by Alex Coles — p. 357

PROJECT VITRA

SIGNS.

Chairs, furniture, design objects – even office furniture and seating systems – are more than just physical artefacts: they are signifiers. This is true whether they appear in public or private settings; whether they occur randomly or are consciously deployed in art or fashion, film or TV, advertising or communications. For fifty years now, Vitra has been creating such distinctive symbols and making its mark on everyday life and the media – sometimes intentionally, sometimes unintentionally; sometimes seriously, sometimes with a touch of irony. This is particularly true of the Vitra Editions, which explicitly blur the lines between art and design.

G8 Summit, 1999

The participants of the 1999 G8 Summit, held in the Ludwig Museum in Cologne, sat on Eames Soft Pad Chairs during the talks. At the table are Boris Yeltsin (Russia), Jean Chrétien (Canada), Jacques Chirac (France), Bill Clinton (United States), Tony Blair (Great Britain), Gerhard Schröder (Germany), Keizo Obuchi (Japan), Massimo D'Alema (Italy) and Jacques Santer (European Commission).

SIGNS   From the Vitra archives   315

SIGNS

From the Vitra archives

316

SIGNS
From the Vitra archives

317

SIGNS   From the Vitra archives   318

Andreas Gursky — "Bundestag", 1998, c-print, 284 × 207 cm
(Figura, design by Mario Bellini).

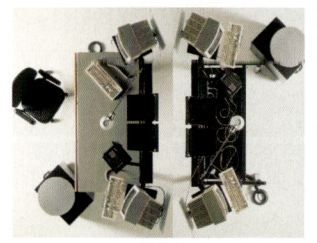

SIGNS

From the Vitra archives

World Chess Championship, 1972

Held in Reykjavik, Iceland, this photo shows Bobby Fischer from the United States (right) and Boris Spassky from the Soviet Union (left) play for the title while seated on Eames Lobby Chairs, apparently requested specifically for the championship by the winning Fischer. Against the backdrop of the Cold War, it had been billed the "Tournament of the Century".

"Das Aktuelle Sportstudio", 1975, 1982

Top: Muhammad Ali in 1975 on an Eames Lobby Chair being interviewed on the popular German sports programme "Das Aktuelle Sportstudio" with Hanns-Joachim Friedrichs.
Bottom: Franz Beckenbauer on an Eames Aluminium Chair in 1982 in an interview with Harry Valérien.

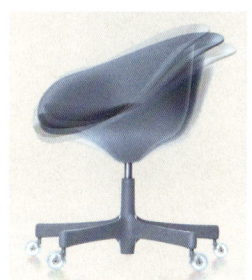

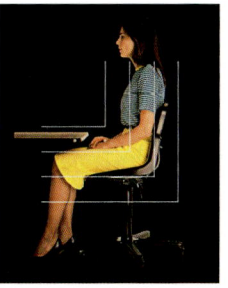

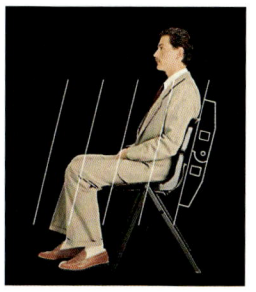

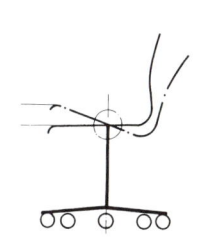

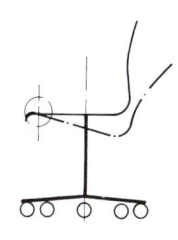

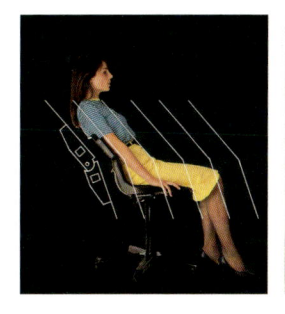

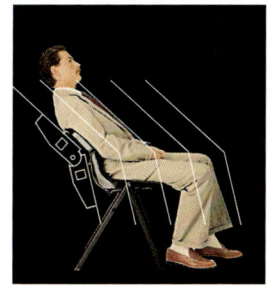

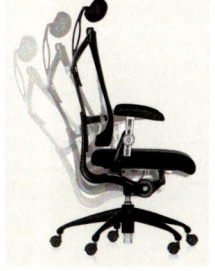

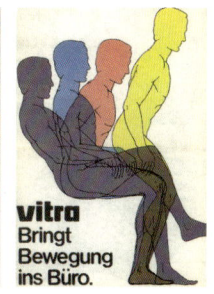

SIGNS   From the Vitra archives   323

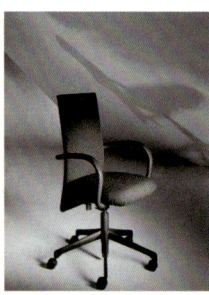

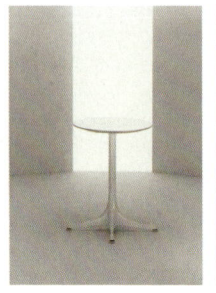

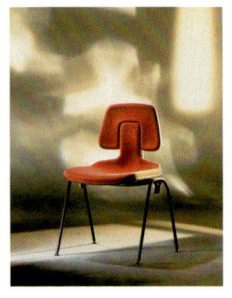

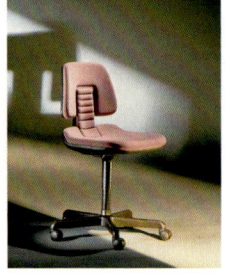

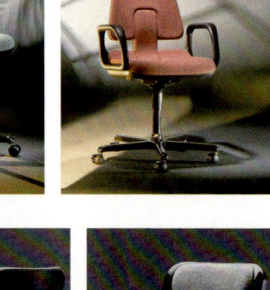

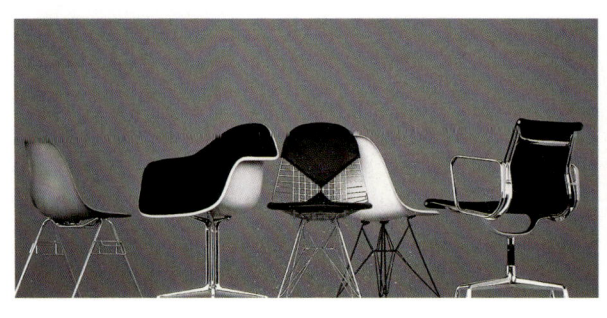

SIGNS From the Vitra archives 324

Papal visit, 1996

Pope John Paul II during his visit to Croatia in 1996. A pale cream leather version of Antonio Citterio's AC 2 office chair was the basis for the papal 'throne', especially designed by architect Robert Somek.

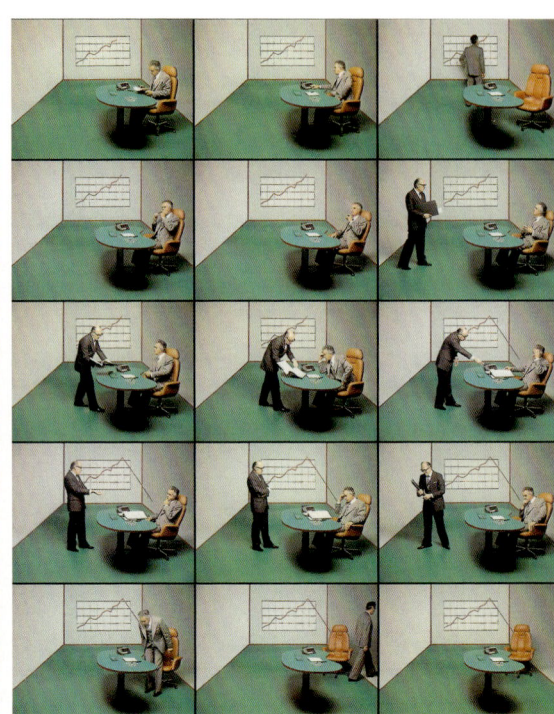

SIGNS From the Vitra archives 326

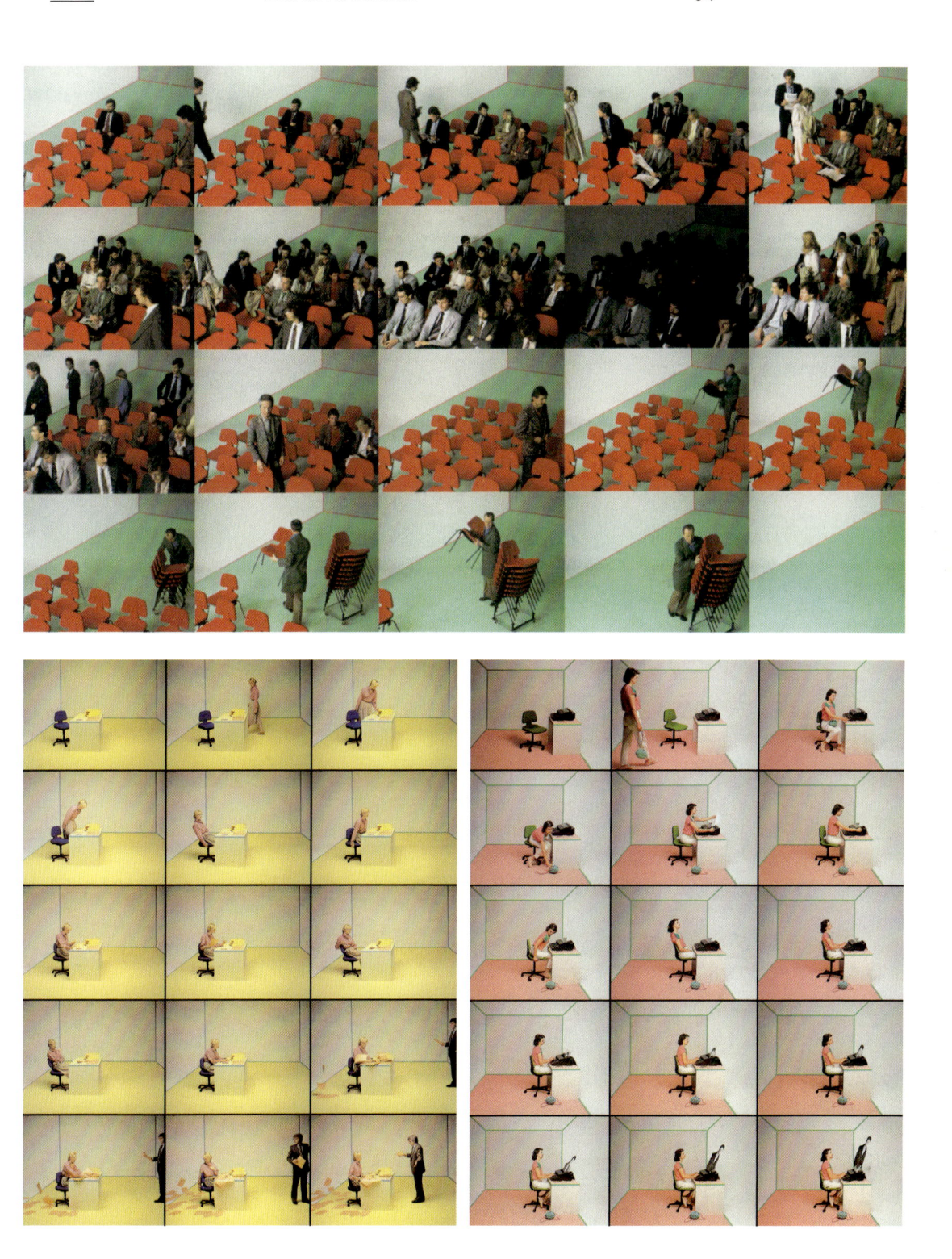

SIGNS   From the Vitra archives

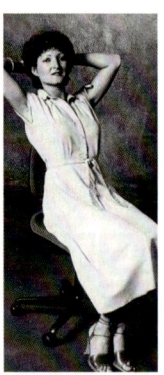

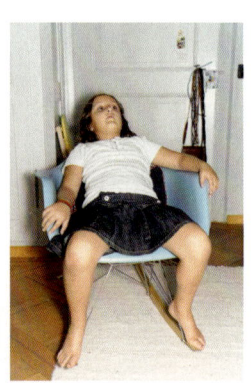

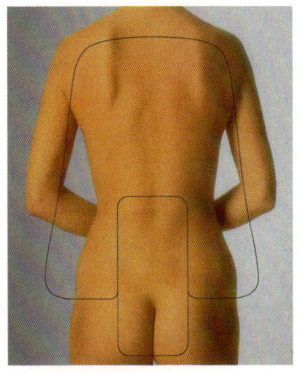

SIGNS

From the Vitra archives

328

SIGNS   From the Vitra archives   329

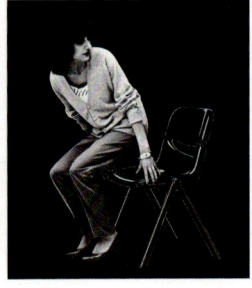

SIGNS

From the Vitra archives

SIGNS From the Vitra archives 331

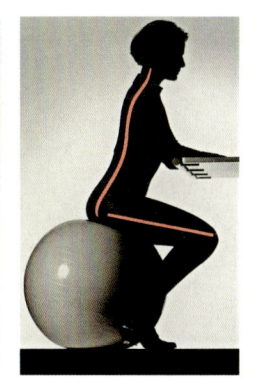

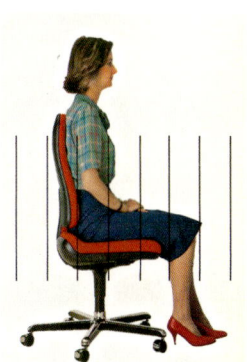

"Girls Like Us", 04.2006 — Caron Geary photographed by Liz Fletcher (Panton Chair, design by Verner Panton).

"Vogue UK", 01.1995 — Kate Moss photographed by Nick Knight
(Panton Chair Classic, design by Verner Panton).

Fashion advertising

Top: an advertisement for Tod's, photographed by Mikael Jansson, in "Vogue USA", 03.2006 (Eames Plywood Table CTW, design by Charles & Ray Eames).
Bottom: advertisement for Blumarine, photographed by Inez van Lamsweerde & Vinoodh Matadin, in "Vogue Italia", 10.2004 (Eames Lounge Chair, design by Charles & Ray Eames).

Issey Miyake, Modeschöpfer, auf How High The Moon Design: Shiro Kuramata. Stühle, Sessel, Tische und Einrichtungs-Systeme von Vitra, Basel-Birsfelden (CH), Telefon 061/315 15 18, Telefax 061/315 15 10. Weil am Rhein (D), Telefon 07621/70 20, Telefax 07621/70 22 42.

vitra.

'Personalities' campaign — Between 1987 and 1997 Christian Coigny photographed well-known personalities from the art and cultural scene for an ad campaign. The project aimed to feature individuals who are not normally associated with advertising.

SIGNS   Vitra in the media   336

Spike Lee, Regisseur, auf Axion. Design: Antonio Citterio mit Glen Oliver Löw. Stühle, Sessel, Tische und Einrichtungs-Systeme von Vitra, Basel-Birsfelden (CH), Telefon 061/315 15 18, Telefax 061/315 15 10. Weil am Rhein (D), Telefon 07621/70 20, Telefax 07621/70 22 42.

vitra.

'Personalities' campaign   In the course of the ten-year 'Personalities' campaign well over one hundred figures from the visual arts, literature, film, music, dance, fashion, design and architecture posed on virtually every chair in the Vitra collection.

Louise Bourgeois, Künstlerin, auf Louis 20. Design: Philippe Starck. Stühle, Sessel, Tische und Einrichtungs-Systeme von Vitra, Basel-Birsfelden (CH), Telefon 061/315 15 18, Telefax 061/315 15 10. Weil am Rhein (D), Telefon 07621/70 20, Telefax 07621/70 22 42.

vitra.

'Personalities' campaign

'Personalities' campaign

From top left to bottom right: Roy Lichtenstein, Patricia Highsmith, Jean-Luc Godard, Jasper Johns, Merce Cunningham, Philip Johnson, Miles Davis, Charles Bukowski, Jörg Immendorff.

Juergen Teller — "Bruce Nauman, New Mexico", 2001, c-print, 40.6 × 30.4 cm
(Eames Soft Pad Chair, design by Charles & Ray Eames).

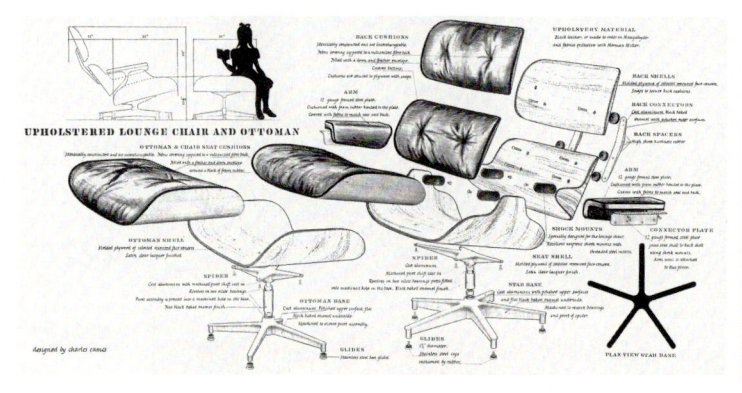

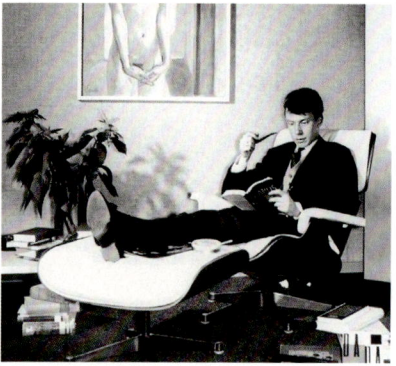

SIGNS

From the Vitra archives

340

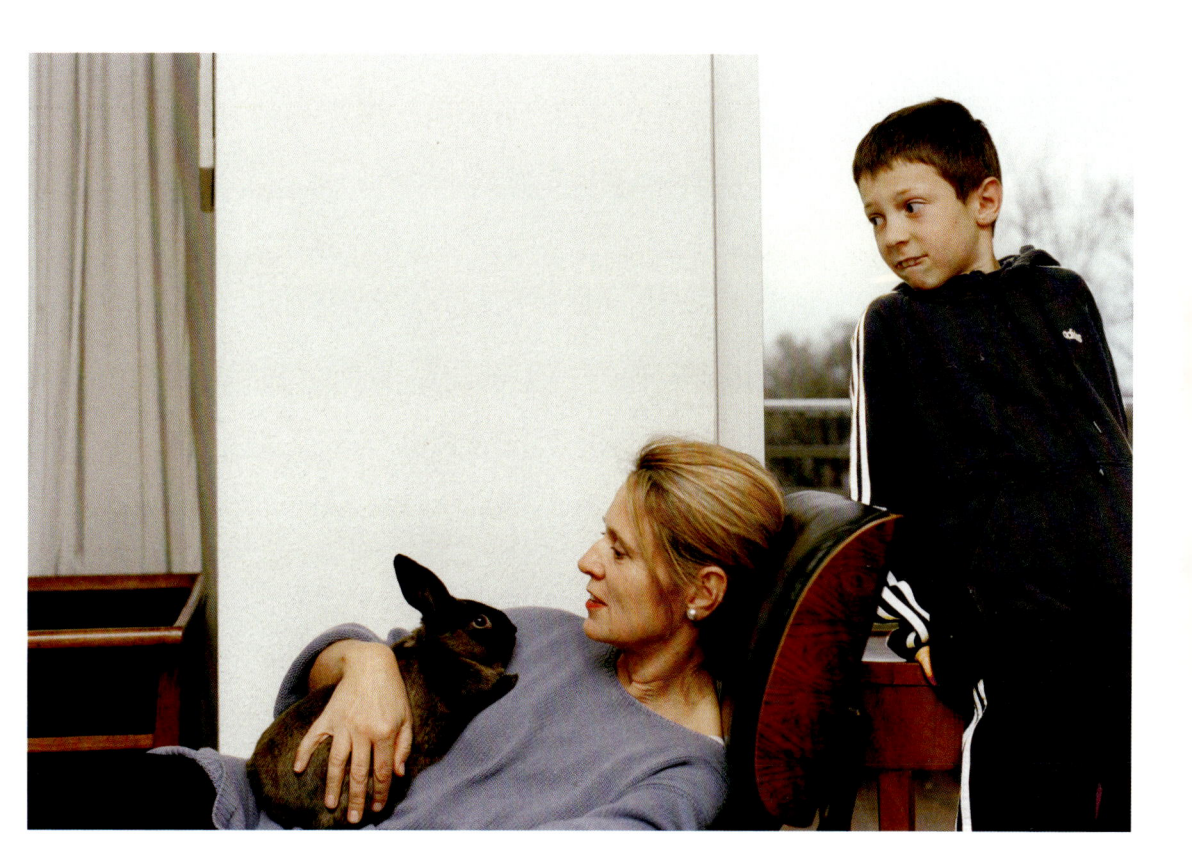

Wolfgang Tillmans "Monika and Vito", 1997, c-print, various dimensions
(Eames Lounge Chair, design by Charles & Ray Eames).

SIGNS From the Vitra archives

SIGNS   Vitra in art   343

Barbara Visser   "EACH19991012/ST/L/c", from the series "Detitled", 2000, c-print, different sizes
(Eames Lounge Chair, design by Charles & Ray Eames).

Erik Steinbrecher — From "GUTE FORM VERY GOOD (aluminium, leather, glass)", 2006, photocollage, 29.7 × 20.9 cm (Eames Lobby Chair, Eames Soft Pad Chair, Eames Aluminium Chair, design by Charles & Ray Eames).

Clino Castellis Farben beim vitramat.
Dazu neue Ausführungen.

vitra Bringt Bewegung ins Sitzen.

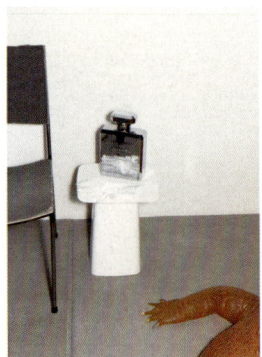

SIGNS

From the Vitra archives

Richard Hamilton   "Interior II", 1964, oil, cellulose, paint and collage on board, 121 × 162 cm
(La Fonda Chair, design by Charles & Ray Eames).

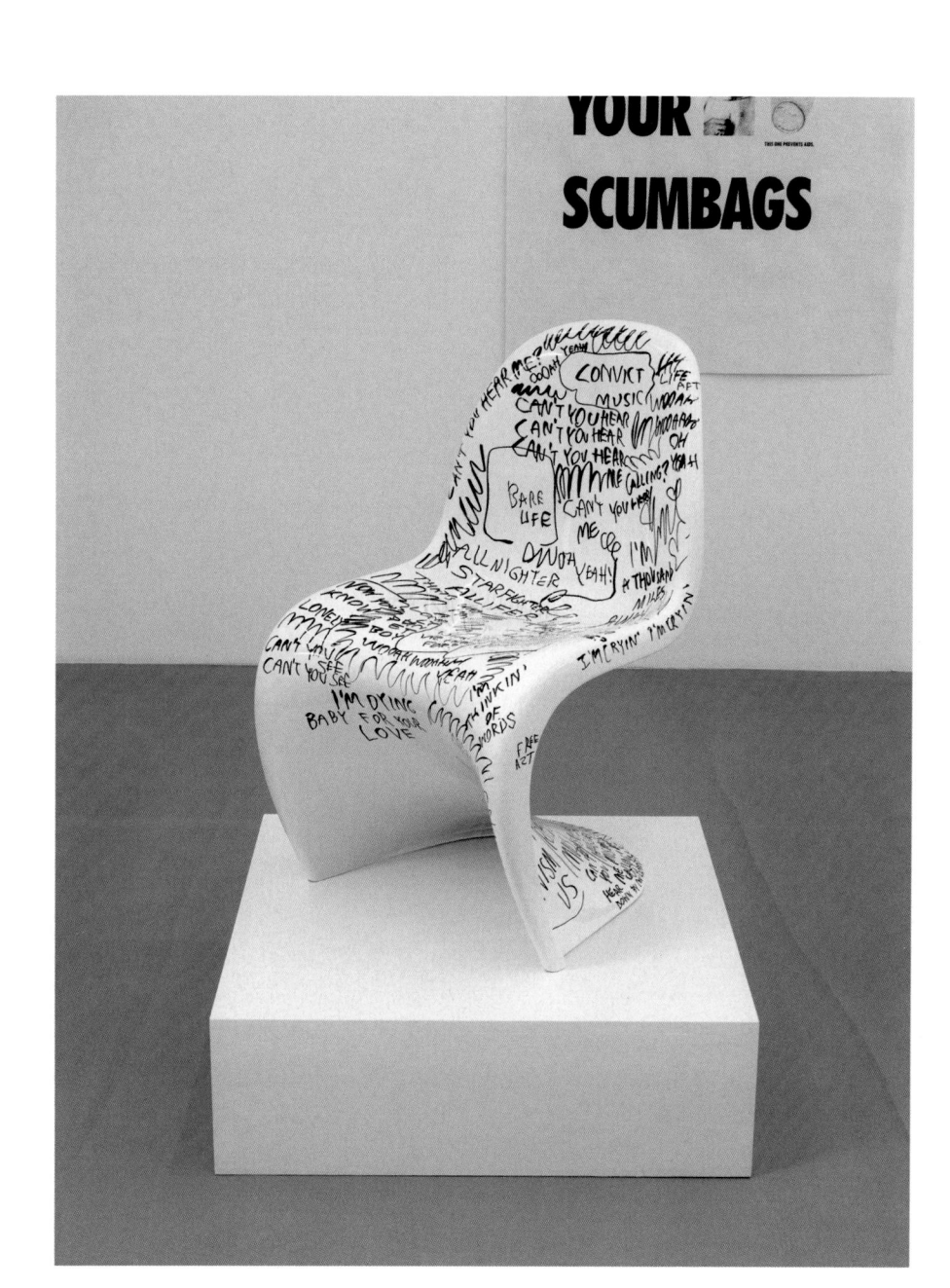

SIGNS Vitra in art 348

Karl Holmqvist "Lonely Planet Panton", 2006, magic marker on Panton Chair
(Panton Chair, design by Verner Panton).

SIGNS From the Vitra archives 349

SIGNS From the Vitra archives 350

Erwin Wurm

Top: "Eames", 2005, c-print, 69 × 81 cm
(Eames Plastic Armchair DAW, design by Charles & Ray Eames).
Bottom: "Use the Chair, follow the instructions and think about Sigmund Freud", 2003
(Panton Chair, design by Verner Panton).

| SIGNS | Vitra Edition |

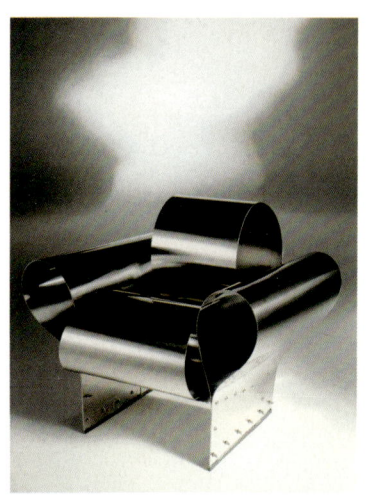

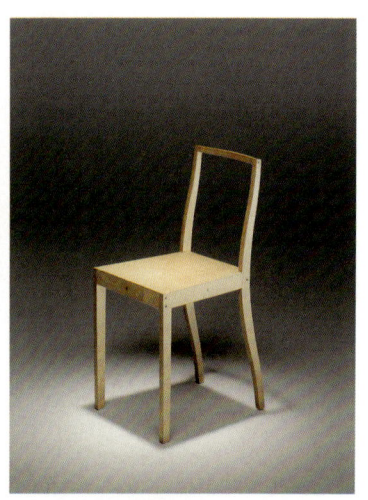

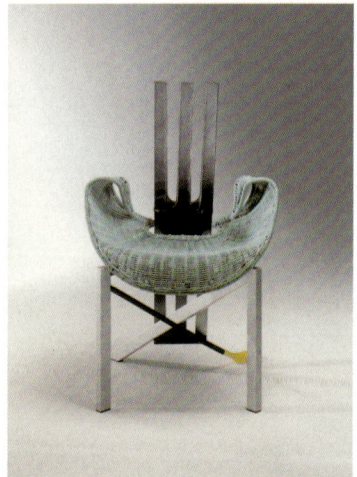

Vitra Edition 1987

From top left to bottom right: Greene Street Chair by Gaetano Pesce; Schizzo by Ron Arad; Well-Tempered Chair by Ron Arad; Ota Otanek by Borek Sipek; How High The Moon by Shiro Kuramata; Ply-Chair by Jasper Morrison; Little Beaver by Frank Gehry; Documenta Chair by Paolo Deganello; Maracuta by Alessandro Mendini. Next page: Vodöl by Coop Himmelb(l)au.

| SIGNS | Vitra Edition | 353 |

Vitra Edition 1987

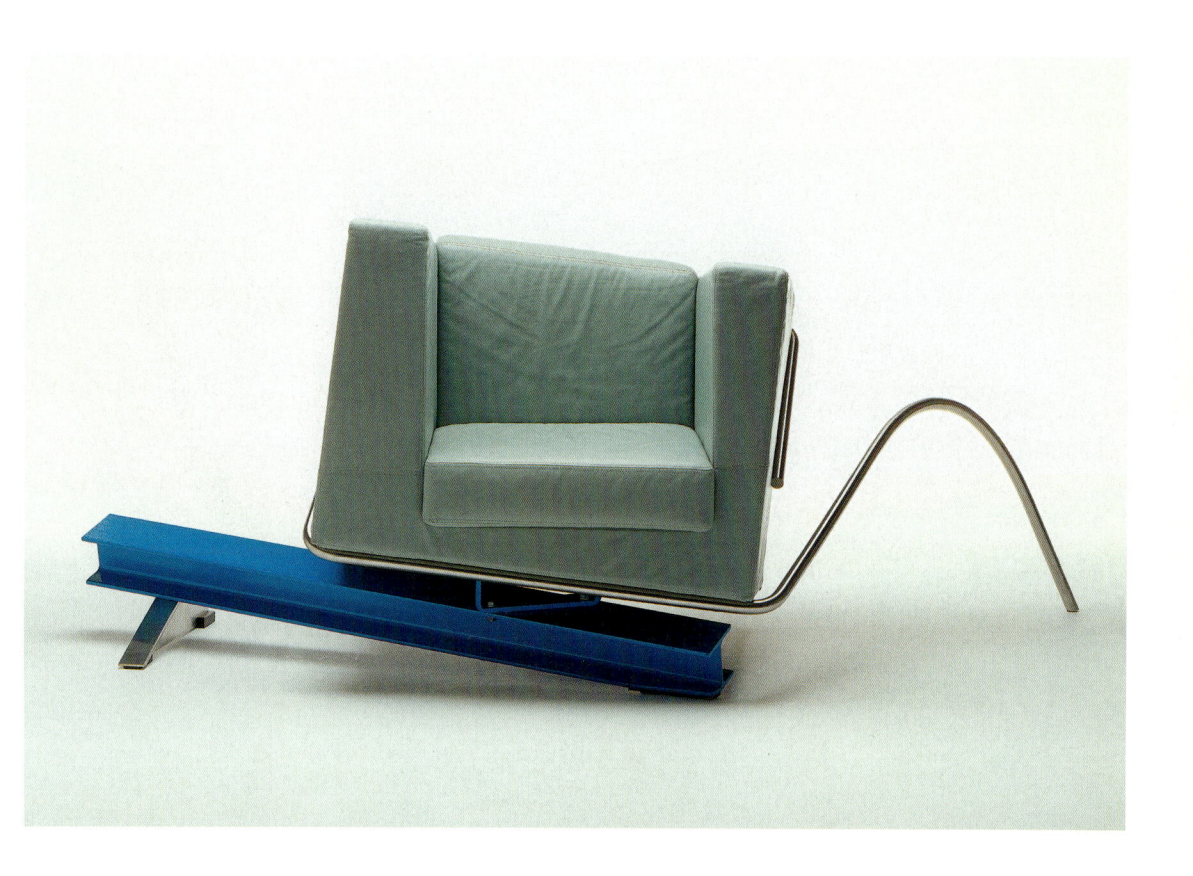

Vitra Edition is a kind of laboratory in which architects, designers and artists are given free rein to develop experimental works. The initiative allows selected authors to take a fresh look at design by liberating them from market and production-related pressures. The first Vitra Edition was presented at the Musée Rath in Geneva in 1987.

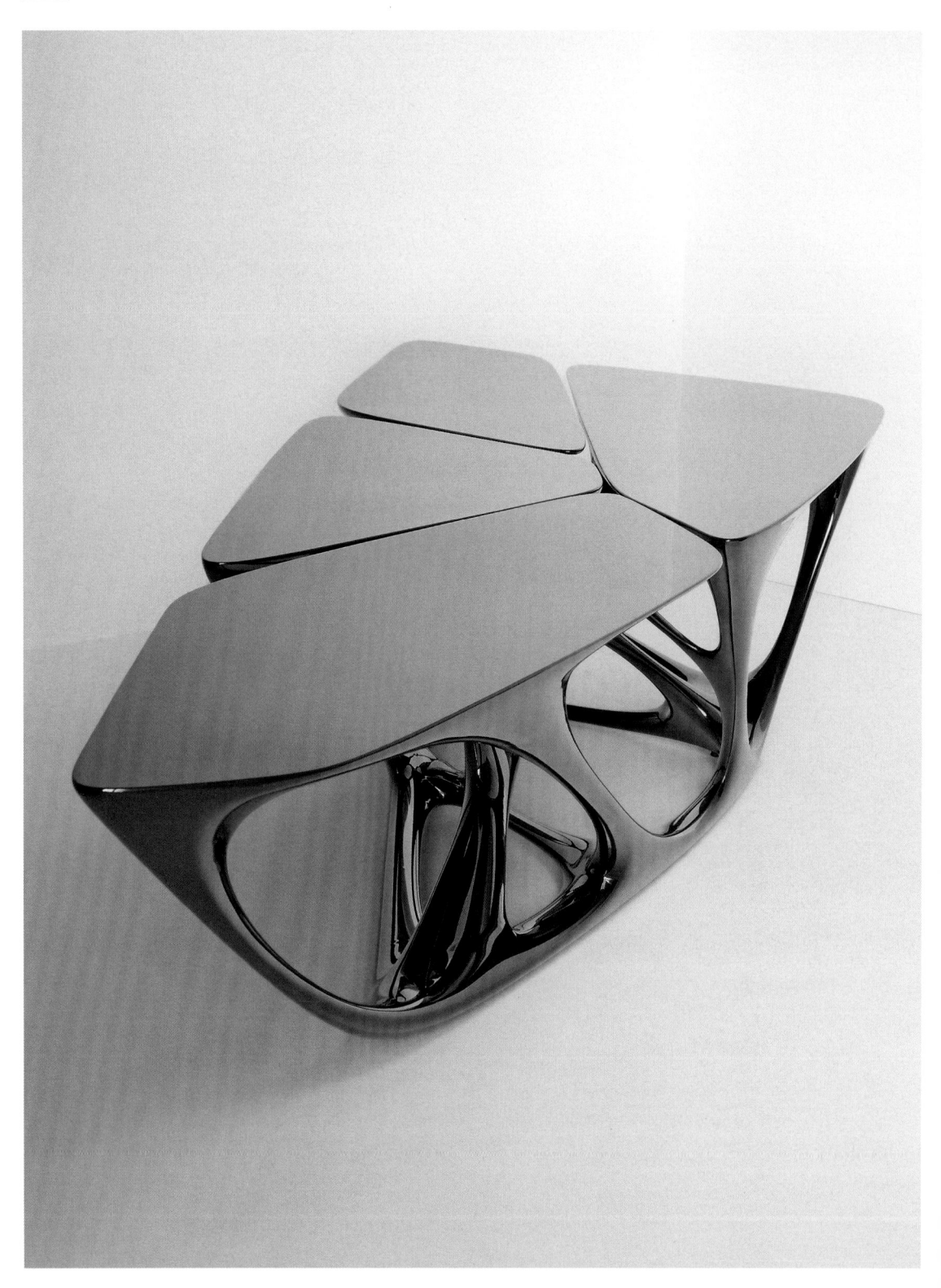

SIGNS	Vitra Edition

Vitra Edition 2007	During Vitra Edition 2007 designers and architects were once again free to choose their materials, techniques and formal concepts. The resulting works are therefore as diverse as their authors and reflect the depth and breadth of interest for which Vitra has become known.

SIGNS   Vitra Edition   355

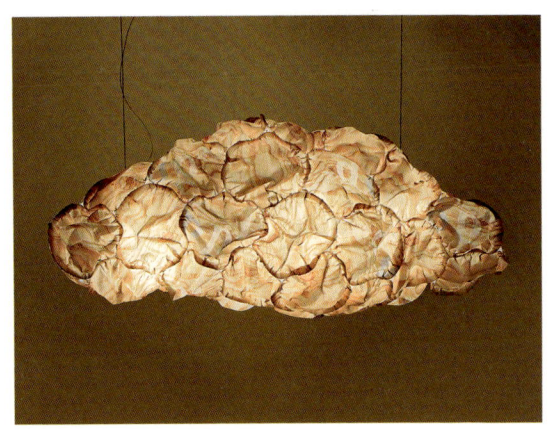

Vitra Edition 2007   From top left to bottom right: Landen by Konstantin Grcic; Rocs by Ronan & Erwan Bouroullec; Mamma Cloud P by Frank Gehry; Chair by Naoto Fukasawa; The Duke & The Duchess by Greg Lynn; Lo Glo by Jürgen Mayer H. Previous page: Mesa by Zaha Hadid.

Vitra Edition 2007 — Office Pets by Hella Jongerius.

DESIGNART – THE KERNEL OF PRODUCT DESIGN

The expansive design philosophy nurtured by Vitra provides a fresh opportunity to think through the relationship between art and design. In some instances in Vitra's back catalogues there is an overt play-off between the two disciplines; at others, the point at which they meet is inherent to the very approach of the particular designer. In different ways, the output of the classic mid-century designers – the Eameses, George Nelson and Isamu Noguchi –, followed by Verner Panton, demonstrates this. So, too, do the relatively recent works by Ron Arad, Jasper Morrison and Maarten Van Severen, and the even more recent ones by Ronan and Erwan Bouroullec or Hella Jongerius.

Each of the Vitra products by these designers is based on a conceptual ingenuity that in part comes from their observation of qualities more conventionally associated with art. Since these designers do not conceive of the notion of the conceptual as being a supplement to the object being designed there is no danger of their running into superficial styling. For each of them, form is derived from their conceptual hold on the character of the function for which the object they are designing is intended (which is different to the binding 'form follows function' orthodoxy since it admits subjectivity). These designers choose not to parry with the context of art, but rather to ensure that its conceptual premise is tightly wound into the kernel of the method by which they approach the design of their products. In this sense Vitra has created a place in which to nurture the meeting point, or interface, between design and art.

The Eameses mark the beginning of the time frame under consideration here. Their early experiments moved between the contexts of art and design: a moulded plywood splint they produced was closely related to a series of contemporaneous laminated plywood sculptures they were experimenting with and also the ingenious LCW chair. The open-ended and playful nature of the Eameses' design methodology generated a meta-level of discourse on design – partly visible in their products and exhibition designs, partly visible in their films – that distinguishes them from many of their contemporaries. This meta-level of discourse is what lent their practice its conceptual acuity and keeps it feeling current today. The same thing is true of George Nelson, albeit in an entirely different way. Nelson's iconic designs from the 1950s – the Marshmallow Sofa, the Coconut Chair – foresee the work of the Pop artists in the next decade. In parallel with his product designs, Nelson generated a considerable discourse on design for which he chose the medium of writing – both short articles and extended essays – as the means to communicate. In one article devoted to the subject of 'good design' from 1957 Nelson ruminated: "Good design, like good painting, cooking, architecture, or whatever you like, is a manifestation of the capacity of the human spirit to transcend its limitations. It enriches its maker through the experience of creating, and it can enrich the viewer or user who is equipped to respond to what it has to say." Nelson provided an expanded textual commentary on the context for

Alex Coles

design in his time – one that is yet to be equalled by a contemporary product designer – and many of his texts encouraged in the reader both a broader understanding of design and a sharper awareness of its role in the modern world. The designs of Verner Panton follow on from those of both the Eameses and Nelson (despite their being in creative tension at the time) in terms of the way they generate a meta-discourse on the discipline in the form of a dialogue on the parallel developments that art and design were experiencing then. Starting off with his one-piece moulded Panton Chair, through to his Living Towers, Panton eventually went on to create entire environments, a development that paralleled the contemporaneous move in the art world away from the autonomous art object and towards the fully integrated interior environment. In this sense, Panton was a part of the development of installation art and particularly crucial to artists like Claes Oldenburg and Dan Graham.

Today, this notion of concept-based furniture piloted by the post-war generation of designers is developed in the work of Jasper Morrison, Ronan and Erwan Bouroullec and Hella Jongerius. Morrison is particularly important amongst the present generation of product designers since much of his output stems from a critique of the present trend in the design world for over-designed objects. Morrison's designs are sparse and pared back in tone and no excessive designing has gone into any of his products. His minimalism is not the result of styling but of a clear vision of the symbiotic relationship between form and function. The Bouroullecs, in particular, have drawn on Morrison's work and two of their most recent products are especially pertinent here.

Alex Coles

The first of these, Joyn, is an open office system that incorporates numerous approaches to the workplace within its structure; Joyn actively promotes interaction and communication between individuals sharing a space and also encourages the user to reconfigure the parts the system is composed of according to their requirements. The second example is the Bouroullecs' contribution to the 2007 Vitra Edition. Titled Rocs, the product is a variously sized movable surface that can function as a dividing wall or simply as a patterned surface to be leant against a wall. Rocs is abstract to an extreme degree – in the sense that it reveals nothing about its function from its appearance, as if its function were always in a mode of suspension. In its very muteness, Rocs thwarts the overt functionality of much furniture and in so doing is firmly an example of designart.

The notion of 'designart' is only really engaging when it is part of a process of questioning – a continual pushing of the boundaries between art and design. Any attempt to completely erase these boundaries runs the risk of losing the tension between the two disciplines, a tension which is crucial because the energy that drives design's interface with art derives from it. The desire on behalf of designers to bring art into play – through its critical and conceptual methods and various site-specific and gallery bound contexts – cannot be downplayed. Likewise, many artists, such as Andrea Zittel, Tobias Rehberger and Jorge Pardo, engage design because it is a vehicle for questioning art by injecting it into utilitarian scenarios that lend the practitioner a critical hold on autonomous forms of art. There is also the issue of collaboration: when the designer and architect Kjetil Thorsen works on a joint commission with the artist Olafur Elliasson, the resulting hybrid object and the experience that object triggers in the viewer is beyond anything either of them could have realized alone. The notion of designart finds its precedents within modernism: the historical avant-gardes – the Soviet Constructivists, De Stijl and the Bauhaus – were all structured on the model of interdisciplinary collaboration and, although they dropped the strict adherence to an interdisciplinary programme, the practitioners who followed, including Donald Judd and Andy Warhol, based their work on principles of layout and production inherited from product and graphic design respectively. So a creative dialogue with design has been crucial to the unfolding of avant-garde art since its very inception and continues to be so today.

Vitra Edition provides a special opportunity for the dialogue between art and design to flourish. Contributors to the first edition in the series, in 1987, included Richard Artschwager, Frank Gehry, Shiro Kuramata, Gaetano Pesce, Scott Burton and Ron Arad. The 2007 Edition brings the trajectory up to date: besides the Bouroullecs' contribution, it includes works by Zaha Hadid, Naoto Fukasawa and Constantin Grcic. The philosophy underlying the project is clearly laid out in the following statement: "Vitra Edition is a laboratory that gives designers, artists and architects the freedom to create experimental furniture objects and interior installations. Their choices of materials, technologies, appli-cations and formal concepts are not limited. Working without the constraints of market and production logic has a liberating effect and results in surprising solutions and new ways of seeing design." The question that needs to be posed in relation to Vitra Edition is this: what is the precise nature of the objects included

Alex Coles

in the series? Is design no longer design when it presents us with something we can look at but no longer use? Is the logical resting place of these objects a museum or gallery display rather than a home or office? If the answer to any one of these questions is affirmative – or even if the receiver of the questions wavers in their response to them – then perhaps it is the case that the notion of what both design and art are has to be re-examined. Even more than the objects in Vitra's main collection, those produced for Vitra Edition provide an opportunity for precisely such a process of re-examination.

One thing that links the otherwise diverse set of designers discussed above is the way that at first glance their output is awkward to look at and take in; there is something 'other' about it since it challenges preconceived notions of what a piece of furniture should look like and what it should do. The reason behind this is clear: the furniture is concept-based rather than style-based. Styling is merely a way of making something that is familiar appear slightly different and thereby attractive without losing the conservatism of the basic form and function that are its traditional attributes. Instead, these designers are distinguished by their desire to escape the traps set by styling, emphasizing a firm conceptual grip on function and the siting of a design object in the world: even in Vitra Edition where the objects play with the very notion of both function – by occasionally thwarting it – and site – by questioning the correct location of the object being produced. All of them treat the meeting point between art and design as a conceptual methodology, as if in the knowledge of the fact that only in this way can engaging designs be generated. They enable a more

Alex Coles

speculative approach towards the dialogue between art and design in the form of product design. The speculative is crucial here because this is exactly how the future of both art and design and designart should be thought of: namely, as open.

Alex Coles studied at Goldsmiths College in London and went on to become a writer, publisher, critic and guest professor at universities in England and the United States. Today, he is professor of visual arts at Otis College of Art and Design, Los Angeles. He authored "DesignArt" (Tate Publishing, 2005) and published "Design and Art" (Whitechapel/MIT Press, 2007).

CHRONOLOGY.
—p. 367

GLOSSARY.
Keywords, people
—pp. 371, 379

CHRONOLOGY, GLOSSARY.

CHRONOLOGY

1953–2007

1953

The entrepreneur Willi Fehlbaum, who runs a shopfitting company together with his wife Erika Fehlbaum in Basel and Weil am Rhein, discovers the furniture of Charles & Ray Eames in a New York store during his first trip to the United States. Immediately taken with the designs, his enduring enthusiasm leads to the decision to become a furniture manufacturer. Back in Switzerland, Fehlbaum gets in contact with the Herman Miller furniture company in Zeeland, Michigan, the manufacturer of Eames furniture.

1957

After several years of negotiations, Willi Fehlbaum's company begins with the licensed production of the Herman Miller Collection. In addition to the furniture of Charles & Ray Eames, the collections also include designs by George Nelson, Alexander Girard and Isamu Noguchi. In the following years, the Fehlbaum family (Willi Fehlbaum and his wife Erika, as well as their eldest son Rolf) comes into contact with the designers Charles and Ray Eames, George Nelson and Alexander Girard on numerous occasions. For Rolf Fehlbaum, these encounters number among his most formative experiences.

1967

In the early 1960s, Willi Fehlbaum makes the acquaintance of the Danish designer Verner Panton, who is seeking a manufacturer for his design of a plastic chair. Vitra's expertise in the processing of plastics gives Fehlbaum the confidence to develop the chair for mass production together with Panton. After several years of collaborative effort, Panton's sculpture-like chair comes onto the market in 1967 – the first cantilever-based plastic chair moulded in one piece and the first product developed directly by Vitra. After the success with the Panton Chair, Willi Fehlbaum seeks collaboration with further designers.

1976

Around 1970, Willi Fehlbaum recognizes the growth potential of the office furniture market and the opportunities it holds for Vitra. The application of ergonomic aspects in the development of office chairs and other office furniture is common practice in German-speaking countries at the time. Design expertise, by contrast, is lacking in this market segment. The combination of ergonomics with ambitious design sets Vitra apart. At the first-ever Orgatec office furniture fair in Cologne in 1976, Vitra presents the Vitramat by Wolfgang Müller Deisig – a meticulously designed office chair with an integrated mechanism for synchronous movement.

1977

Willi and Erika Fehlbaum, the founders of Vitra, turn over management of the company to their sons Rolf, Raymond and Peter. Peter Fehlbaum leaves the company in 1992.

1979

A new collaboration with the designer Mario Bellini marks an increased orientation towards Italian design in the following years, which holds a leading role at the time in terms of conceptual and formal aspects.

1981

A major fire, sparked by a lightning strike, destroys large sections of Vitra's production facilities in Weil am Rhein. New factory buildings need to be constructed within a short period of time. Rolf Fehlbaum recognizes these construction projects as an opportunity to reshape the company's architectural identity. Working with the architect Nicholas Grimshaw, he develops the concept of a defining corporate architecture for Vitra.
The first factory buildings based on Nicholas Grimshaw's plans are completed, marking the new beginning of the architectural site in Weil am Rhein and laying the foundation for the future Vitra Campus.

1983

Rolf Fehlbaum begins to establish a collection of industrial furniture design. The burgeoning collection is systematically built up in the following years and forms the core of the Vitra Design Museum.
Work on the development of furniture leads to the initial contact with Frank Gehry.

1984

The sculpture "Balancing Tools", designed by Claes Oldenburg and Coosje van Bruggen, is erected in front of the Vitra premises in a meadow planted with cherry trees – a present for Willi Fehlbaum on his seventieth birthday from his sons.
Work on this project results in further meetings with Frank Gehry and discussion of potential building projects, which soon begin to take shape.
Rolf Fehlbaum abandons the idea of a uniform corporate architecture for Vitra and embraces the pluralistic development of the Vitra grounds in Weil am Rhein.
Vitra launches the first office chairs designed by Mario Bellini and Dieter Thiel. The partnership with Herman Miller, which has existed since 1957, is terminated by mutual consent. Vitra acquires

CHRONOLOGY 1953–2007

all rights for the production of furniture designs by Charles & Ray Eames and George Nelson, as well as Alexander Girard's textiles for Europe and the Middle East. Now able to sell these products under its own label, Vitra operates as an independent brand from this point forwards. The internationalization of the company continues apace as it also markets its new products in countries outside Europe.

1985

Beginning of the exceptionally intensive and productive collaboration with the Italian designer Antonio Citterio.

1987

The launch of the experimental Vitra Edition series causes a sensation in the international design community. A number of the designers involved in this project go on to enjoy a long-term work-ing relationship with Vitra. The 'Personalities' campaign begins: the advertising series with black-and-white photographs of prominent cultural figures on Vitra chairs runs through 1997 and helps raise awareness of the brand outside professional circles.

1988

After the death of Ray Eames, the Eames Office at 901 Washington Boulevard in Venice, California, is disbanded. Vitra acquires the three-dimensional estate of Charles & Ray Eames, which encompasses a considerable portion of the surviving experimental models and prototypes from their office.
Beginning of the collaboration with the British designer Jasper Morrison.
At Orgatec, the Metropol office furniture system designed by Mario Bellini is launched – the first office furnishing system from Vitra.

1989

The Vitra Design Museum opens in a new building designed by Frank Gehry. Under the leadership of its founding director Alexander von Vegesack, a multitude of activities are initiated. Thanks in large part to the production of internationally circulating exhibitions on design and architecture themes, the young Museum manages to establish itself within just a few years as a widely esteemed cultural institution that generates most of its own funding. A key basis for the work of the Museum is constituted by the furniture collection, which is one of the largest and most significant of its kind worldwide.

1990

The Vitra Design Museum launches a design workshop programme. Led by renowned designers, the workshops are first held in Weil am Rhein and move in 1996 to the present-day location of Domaine de Boisbuchet in France.
AC 1, the first office swivel chair designed by Antonio Citterio, comes onto the market. In the following years, Vitra develops further office swivel chairs with Citterio.

1991–1993

The exhibition project "Citizen Office" explores the future of the office. The discussion process associated with the project leads to intensified reflections on the office work environment at Vitra. The impact of technological developments on the design of the office is addressed, as well as the emotional messages of office furnishings.

1991

The Vitra company is the first recipient of the Design Prize Switzerland.

1992

The Ad Hoc office system, developed in collaboration with Antonio Citterio, is launched and sets new standards in the office furniture market.

1993

The Fire Station designed by Zaha Hadid and the Conference Pavilion by Tadao Ando are officially opened. The Vitra Campus in Weil am Rhein attracts a growing number of architecture enthusiasts from all over the world.
Beginning of the collaboration with the graphic designer Tibor Kalman.

1994

The Vitra Campus in Weil am Rhein sees the completion of a new factory building by Álvaro Siza. The same year, the Vitra Center designed by Frank Gehry opens in Birsfelden as the new administrative headquarters.
Beginning of the collaboration with the Italian designer Alberto Meda.
Beginning of the collaboration with the Belgian designer Maarten Van Severen.
Rolf Fehlbaum receives the Lucky Strike Design Award from the Raymond Loewy Foundation.

1996

The Meda Chair, the first office chair conceived with Alberto Meda, comes onto the market. In the following years, Vitra's collaboration with this designer produces a whole family of office chairs.

1997

The German Design Council and the German Federal Ministry of Economics and Technology bestow the Federal Prize for Design Promotion on Rolf Fehlbaum. In conjunction with the award, the book "Chairman Rolf Fehlbaum", designed by Tibor Kalman, is published in 1998.

1999

Market launch of the chair .03 by Maarten Van Severen. It is his first design intended for industrial production. Until his death in 2005, Van Severen works extensively on numerous designs for Vitra.

2000

Beginning of the collaboration with the young French designers Ronan & Erwan Bouroullec. The first joint project is an innovative new office furniture system.

2002

Introduction of re-editions of designs by the French 'constructeur' Jean Prouvé in close cooperation with the Prouvé family.
Joyn, an office furniture system conceived by the Bouroullec brothers, is presented. Discussions with Jasper Morrison and the Bouroullec brothers lead to the concept for the new Vitra Home Collection.

CHRONOLOGY 1953–2007

2004

Vitra Home is launched. The collection encompasses Vitra classics, a number of re-editions, as well as contemporary designs by Jasper Morrison, the Bouroullecs and Maarten Van Severen.
Beginning of the collaboration with the Dutch designer Hella Jongerius, who soon makes important contributions to the rapidly expanding Vitra Home Collection.

2005

The manager Hanns-Peter Cohn becomes chief executive officer of Vitra and Manfred Meier assumes the position of chief operating officer. As Chairman of the Board, Rolf Fehlbaum remains responsible for the orientation of the company and also works in the areas of product development and corporate communication.
Rolf Fehlbaum is recognized for his service to the field of design with the Design Prize Switzerland.

2006

At Orgatec, Vitra presents its new Net 'n' Nest concept.
Among the products introduced is Worknest, the first office swivel chair designed by Ronan & Erwan Bouroullec.
The office swivel chair Headline, designed by Mario and Claudio Bellini, sets new ergonomic standards.
Plans are announced for the expansion of the Vitra Campus in Weil am Rhein with buildings by the architects Herzog & de Meuron as well as the Japanese firm SANAA.

2007

To mark the centennial of Charles Eames's birth, the exhibition "The Furniture of Charles and Ray Eames" is staged in the Fire Station on the Vitra Campus in Weil am Rhein.
The Vitra project celebrates its fiftieth anniversary.
During Art Basel, the new Vitra Edition is presented.
Construction of the VitraHaus, designed by Herzog & de Meuron, commences in Weil am Rhein.

CHRONOLOGY Logotype development

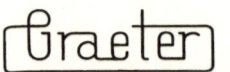

Graeter

1934 Willi Fehlbaum takes over the shopfitting company Graeter

vitra

1950 The first "vitra" sign

herman miller international collection

1957 Licensing agreement with Herman Miller

vitra Wir bauen die herman miller collection, das vitra programm und das action office.

vitra

1974 (Designer unknown)

1974 "vitra Shop + Display"

vitra
vitra
vitra

1982 (Design concept: Karl Gerstner)

1982 "vitrashop"

1984 Termination of the partnership with Herman Miller

vitra.

1990 (Design: Pierre Mendell)

KEYWORDS

ARCHIVES

In addition to its collections, the Vitra Design Museum maintains archives of two-dimensional documents on the history of industrial furniture design and related fields. Among the most important items held in the archives are the estates, or partial estates, of designers like → George Nelson, → Alexander Girard, → Verner Panton, Anton Lorenz and Harry Bertoia. The archived material is complemented by a comprehensive technical library of books and periodicals on the history of furniture, design, architecture and art. Although the archives and library are primarily intended for internal use, they are also available to external researchers.

BARRAGAN FOUNDATION

A cultural foundation under the auspices of Vitra. It conserves and researches the estate of the Mexican architect Luis Barragán and promotes academic study and discussion of his work. Luis Barragán (1902–1988), who was awarded the Pritzker Prize in 1980, is one of the greatest figures of the modernist movement. Seven years after his death, Vitra was able to acquire parts of his estate, thereby preventing this cultural heritage from being dispersed. Since it was established in 1996, the Barragan Foundation (based in → Birsfelden near Basel) has examined and classified the estate (which includes some 13,500 drawings and plans and over 20,000 photographs) and has ensured that it is stored in accordance with good archiving practice. The Foundation (headed by Federica Zanco) first achieved public prominence with its exhibition entitled "Luis Barragán. The Quiet Revolution" which was on show at major museums in Europe, Japan and Mexico from 2000 until 2003, together with the accompanying catalogue. A comprehensive publication on the Barragan Foundation's archives is currently being compiled.

BIRSFELDEN

Vitra's headquarters are located in Birsfelden near Basel. → Willi Fehlbaum acquired the site after selling the cramped building which housed the original shopfitting business to the City of Basel. The first factory building was constructed in Birsfelden in 1957, with an office wing built to the plans of Beck and Baur, the Basel architects. This building is still standing, and it houses Vitra's → product development division and the → Barragan Foundation. The new administrative building by → Frank Gehry (the Vitra Center) at the same location was occupied in 1994. This building houses Vitra's headquarters with the management and the controlling, marketing and international divisions.

CHAIRMAN ROLF FEHLBAUM

The title of an illustrated book by → Tibor Kalman, published in 1998 by Lars Müller Publishers, about → Rolf Fehlbaum and Vitra. The book was published to mark the award of the Federal Prize for Design Promotion to Rolf Fehlbaum in 1997 by the German Design Council and the German Ministry of Economics. The poetic yet playful tone of the book is already evident in the double meaning of its title: "chairman" not only refers to the head of a company but also alludes to Fehlbaum's long-standing preoccupation with chairs.

CITIZEN OFFICE

The title of a touring exhibition presented for the first time at the Vitra Design Museum in 1993, and of the accompanying publication containing suggestions on the contemporary organization and design of office workplaces. Based on the thesis that an office is a living space for people as well as their workplace, the designers → Andrea Branzi, Michele De Lucchi and → Ettore Sottsass developed three alternatives to the uniformly hierarchical and inflexible office style which was prevalent at the time. Specimen solutions of an experimental and pioneering nature were developed after a consultation process coordinated by James Irvine and supported by Vitra. Although none of the suggestions in the exhibition actually went into production, the "Citizen Office" project prompted thoughts about how the design of the office world could be made more people-friendly and effective, and it provided stimulus for future developments.

CLASSICS

Vitra regards as classics the products that are still up to date even though they were created in a previous era. Such pieces are revolutionary and signal the birth of a new concept of design. In subsequent decades, the design proves to be resilient in the face of its successors and imitators. It outlives them and becomes a classic. This does not mean that it is now 'tamed': its revolutionary origins live on and it seems to remain eternally fresh. A classic appears to be timeless, and only becomes dated when a new era begins. Vitra classics include designs by → Charles & Ray Eames, → George Nelson, → Jean Prouvé and → Verner Panton.

COLLAGE

A design philosophy for indoor spaces which aims to create a practical and inspiring interior that can be used for work as well as relaxation and entertainment. Instead of using integrated, stylistically pure and uniform solutions, collage advocates a mixture of elements which are selected and arranged so as to reflect the individual personality of the occupants. Collage does not aim for a design that will be valid once and for all, but views the interior and its composition as 'work in progress' that remains open to reconfigurations and additions. One inspirational example of collage is the house by → Charles & Ray Eames, with an interior design that offers a varied, vivacious and often surprising mix of old and new, handicrafts and industrial products, technology and art, the simple and the complex, and of decorative and practical, natural and artificial elements.

COLOUR WORLDS

Colour is highly important in terms of the emotional and atmospheric effect created by furniture and interiors. During its history, Vitra has been inspired by the colour worlds of different designers. Like the perception of form, preferences for certain colours and colour worlds depends on passing fashions, and is thus subject to change. At the outset, the use of colour at Vitra was dominated by the bright and cheerful colour palette of → Alexander Girard, influenced by traditional Central American folk art, but from the mid 1960s onwards → Verner Panton increasingly gained the upper hand with his powerful colour shades. In the 1980s, Vitra cooperated closely with the Italian colour designer Clino Castelli in this field. → Hella Jongerius is currently developing a new colour world for Vitra.

DESIGN

Vitra views design as a complex and often lengthy process of integrating function, aesthetics, → ergonomics, production logic, ecology and symbolic messages, all of which ultimately culminates in a product (if the outcome is positive). The greatest challenge during this process is to reconcile the various, and sometimes conflicting, objectives and claims. Vitra works exclusively with freelance author-designers. They contribute their ideas to the process. As a producer and client, Vitra contributes its technical know-how, its knowledge of materials and markets, and its critical eye for design. On this basis, a → trial-and-error process gradually results in a product that should be regarded as a collective achievement. Design is a method of solving problems, not only of making an object more aesthetic.

ERGONOMICS

A branch of occupational science which adopts a multidisciplinary approach to research and defines rules for the design of working equipment and workplaces. Vitra has viewed ergonomics as an important subject since the early 1970s.

EXHIBITIONS

Conceptual and organizational work for design and architecture exhibitions is an important part of the Vitra Design Museum's activities. The Museum usually produces travelling exhibitions, which go on tour for several years thanks to an extensive international network of partner museums. Exhibition sales make a major contribution towards financing the high costs of production. An average of ten exhibitions will be 'on the road' at any given time, and they will be shown at twenty-five to thirty venues each year. The Vitra Design Museum in → Weil am Rhein welcomes about 70,000 visitors each year. (This figure includes guided architectural tours of the → Vitra Campus.)

GUEST-HOST RELATIONSHIP

→ Charles Eames once said that every time a designer produced a design, he should act like a good host to accommodate his guests' wishes and needs in an obliging manner. Vitra adopted this 'guest-host' philosophy for its own work, but with one modification: Vitra believes we can only work and act as a good host for target groups if we are also able to identify with them. Vitra views its role of host at several levels: it must be evident in the → quality of products, in the cultural activities (the Vitra Design Museum, → Vitra Campus), in the way the company presents itself (→ showrooms and appearances at fairs) and in its corporate communication.

HERMAN MILLER

The Herman Miller Furniture Company, based in the city of Zeeland, Michigan (USA), was founded in 1923 by Dirk Jan DePree (1891–1990), who named the company in honour of his father-in-law and benefactor, Herman Miller. The company enjoyed limited success into the 1930s, producing a highly traditional range of furniture. The Great Depression forced DePree to rethink his business model. Following the advice of designer Gilbert Rhode, the furniture-maker began focusing on more modern, contemporary designs. In 1946, DePree hired → George Nelson as design director, precipitating the rise of the furniture-maker to a global player and one of the most important representatives of American mid-century modernism. It was Nelson, who held this position until 1972, who brought in such important designers as → Charles & Ray Eames, → Alexander Girard and → Isamu Noguchi, who jointly shaped the company's output and culture for many years. In the 1960s, Hugh and Max DePree took over the business from their father. It was under their leadership that Robert Propst developed the modular Action Office, which revolutionized office furniture and coincided with a period of rapid expansion for Herman Miller during which the company became increasingly focused on office furniture and objects, rather than home furniture. Today, Herman Miller is one of the largest furniture manufacturers in the United States, but the founding family is no longer active in the company. While Vitra holds licenses to manufacture the furniture of Charles & Ray Eames and George Nelson in Europe and the Middle East, Herman Miller holds these rights for the rest of the world. As licensee between 1957 and 1984, Vitra had a close working relationship with Herman Miller.

LOVE INVESTIGATION

This phrase was used by → Charles Eames to express his conviction that valid design solutions can only be successfully developed if the work is undertaken with passion (as if it were a love affair) and dedication, for its own sake. Vitra shares this conviction and regards dedication to any cultural and commercial project as an essential requirement for success.

METROBASEL

The short name for the metropolitan area around Basel, which is home to Vitra and most of the company's employees. The catch-name was introduced in 2005 and describes not just the geographical area but a wider social project designed to revitalize and develop the region. The roughly 900,000 people who currently live in Metrobasel come from three countries: Switzerland (large parts of the north-west, including the cantons Basel-Stadt and Basel-Landschaft, as well as parts of Aargau, Jura and Solothurn), France (the Pays de St Louis) and Germany (Lörrach region). The Metrobasel initiative, a partnership between state institutions, private companies and the public, seeks to overcome political fragmentation in the region by defining a common identity, and aims to develop the region into one of the world's leading life-science hubs.

MINIATURES

True-to-detail models of historically important chair and armchair designs, scaled down to 1:6 of their original size. Originally conceived by the Vitra Design Museum as exhibition pieces, the miniatures have become one of Vitra's most important products and a major source of income for the museum. Miniatures are sold mainly as collector's items or souvenirs, but are also suitable for study purposes as their detailing is extremely fine. The collection is continually being expanded and currently comprises around ninety models which are sold in furniture stores and museum shops around the world.

NET'N'NEST

An office design concept unique to Vitra specially developed to balance communication and teamwork with the simple human need for individual space and the desire to withdraw into one's private sphere. The open-plan office – the predominant interior design for offices today – allows flexibility, eases communication and encourages teamwork, thereby helping employees to solve complex problems quickly and efficiently. This aspect of office work is called "networking" or "netting". However the obvious advantages of the open-plan office conflict with the legitimate desire for privacy. After all, many office workers spend a significant portion of their working lives working in these environments. The individual's urge to retreat ("nesting") is fundamental, and failure to respect it can be highly detrimental to productivity. The Net 'n' Nest concept developed by Vitra addresses the dialectic interrelationship between 'netting' and 'nesting' by adding structures to the fundamentally network-oriented open-plan office that allow 'nesting' to take place.

NETWORK OFFICE

A concept for the interior design and organization of office space developed by Vitra around the turn of the millennium. The catch-phrase "break the walls" spread the idea that efficient teamwork would only come about by abolishing physical and mental barriers. The network office was based on the view of the office as a forum for exchanging knowledge and ideas. With this in mind, its central goal was to create physical spaces in which employees could communicate openly and directly with one another. The office furniture system Joyn, devised and designed by the → Bouroullec brothers, is the physical manifestation of the network office concept. The → Net 'n' Nest concept is essentially a continuation of network office.

ORGATEC

The world's largest trade fair for office furniture and objects has been held in Cologne bi-annually since 1976. Vitra has a tradition of using Orgatec as its forum for presenting new products and launching → "Workspirit". Vitra's presence at the fair has been designed by → Dieter Thiel since 1986, most recently in co-operation with → Sevil Peach and the → Bouroullec brothers.

PRODUCT DEVELOPMENT

All new Vitra products are the fruit of close collaboration between the company and author-designers. Vitra's own research and development team is responsible for a large portion of the success of any new product. With decades of experience, the team has built up unparalleled expertise in materials and → ergonomics, and most of Vitra's patents are registered by this unit. Developing a new product is often a complex and time-consuming process of → trial and error that involves both the designer and the Vitra team in equal measure. Vitra's research and development divisions have been led by → Egon Bräuning since 1971 and are located in → Birsfelden.

QUALITY

A complex phenomenon and not always easy to define, but it is central to everything Vitra does. It manifests itself first and foremost in the → design of its products and the company's cultural activities. Naturally, the physical quality of the materials – which Vitra itself has subjected to rigorous testing in its laboratory in → Weil am Rhein since 1988 – is the only thing that is actually measurable. With the help of computer-controlled testing equipment, all of Vitra's products are exposed to a variety of mechanical stresses in order to determine the durability and other physical properties of the materials. Vitra's own testing regime is more stringent than any government quality standards or test certificates and the results are fed into → product development and maintenance guides.

RE-EDITION

A furniture design that has not been produced for a long time but is then re-released and brought on to the market. Vitra only re-releases designs that are indisputable → classics, solve a specific design problem and have an enduring value.

RESTORATION LABORATORY

In addition to collecting, museums have traditionally also been responsible for researching, exhibiting and maintaining cultural treasures. To this end, the Vitra Design Museum has set up its own restoration laboratory known as the Conservation Lab. In its work it follows the international code of ethics set by the European Confederation of Conservator-Restorers' Organizations, according to which the principal aim of restoration is to preserve the object rather than focus myopically on maintaining its original appearance. Museums face huge challenges when attempting to preserve nineteenth- and twentieth-century works in particular, for many of them are deteriorating rapidly, despite the fact that they were created relatively recently. This is due primarily to the widespread use of new materials at the time that have turned out to be less durable than originally thought. Many of the plastics that were deployed in art and design during the twentieth century are particularly problematic. The Vitra Design Museum's restorers have thus put a lot of energy and resources into researching plastics restoration in recent years.

SHOWROOMS

Vitra has its own showrooms in many parts of the world: Melbourne and Sydney (Australia), Vienna (Austria), Brussels (Belgium), Shanghai (China), Prague (Czech Republic), Paris (France), → Weil am Rhein and Frankfurt a. M. (Germany), Budapest (Hungary), Bangalore, Delhi and Mumbai (India), Mexico City (Mexico), Amsterdam (Netherlands), Oslo (Norway), Warsaw (Poland), Singapore (Singapore), Madrid and Barcelona (Spain), Zurich (Switzerland), London (United Kingdom) and Chicago, New York, San Francisco and Los Angeles (United States).

STUDENT WORKSHOPS

In addition to its regular → workshops, the Vitra Design Museum in → Weil am Rhein has organized workshops for school parties since 1994. The events are usually related thematically to current exhibitions in the Vitra Design Museum or the architecture of the → Vitra Campus. The workshops are attended by around 2000 students a year from throughout Baden-Württemberg, northwestern Switzerland and the Alsace region.

TRANSVERSALITY

Vitra's broad interest in all aspects of furnishing and (interior) design, ranging from technically sophisticated office chairs to Alexander Girard's ornamental puppets, from sofas to office furniture systems, from furniture miniatures to buildings. More specifically, transversality refers to the wish to create furniture that is not destined exclusively for one of the three traditional design categories: office, public, home. Technological developments, the PC and Internet in particular, have broken down the boundaries between the office and the home in recent years. Two major trends may be observed: the home is once again becoming a workplace – even if only temporarily – for a growing number of people; and modern office designers are introducing more and more 'homely' elements into their interiors in the hope of creating a more familiar atmosphere and, ultimately, improving productivity. This blurring of the professional and private spheres has created a need for furniture that can be used in a variety of contexts (see → Net 'n' Nest). Many of → Charles & Ray Eames's designs already anticipated this trend – one thinks of their Aluminium Group series and Plastic Chairs, for instance – and many Vitra products are built around this notion today. The Worknest office chair, designed by the → Bouroullec brothers, is another good example of a model that features homely, emotionally appealing elements without compromising functionality.

TRIAL AND ERROR

In the design process, trial and error is a method of solving problems mainly through hands-on experimentation with 1:1 models as opposed to traditional sketch-and-drawing techniques or theoretical reflection. Naturally, as the term suggests, this kind of approach involves failures as well as successes. These failed experiments are vital steps on the long, and often bumpy, road towards a finished design. Notable exponents of the trial-and-error method include → Charles & Ray Eames and the French architect and designer → Jean Prouvé, who stopped producing furniture after losing his development workshop in 1954.

TÜLLINGER

An extension of the Black Forest. This distinctive ridge runs north-south right up to the Swiss border and separates the towns of → Weil am Rhein and Lörrach from one another. Seen from the → Vitra Campus, this ridge, with its grapevines, ancient fruit orchards, meadows and woods, is the region's dominant topographical feature. A climb to the highest point yields a stunning view of the Vitra buildings and the entire border triangle on the 'knee of the Rhine' (→ Metrobasel).

VINTAGE

In the design world, a piece is considered 'vintage' if it is one of the first products, or dates from an early phase, of a mass-produced series. Vintage objects are mainly attractive for collectors, museums and design historians. They tend to be rare, are generally second-hand, and are often an early form of a design or product that is later optimized in the course of production. It is precisely the flaws in vintage models that make them so desirable for design historians and collectors.

VITRA

The name "Vitra" was invented by → Willi Fehlbaum. It is derived from the French word 'vitrine' (glass display case) and harks back to the company's roots in the shopfitting business. The owners began consciously building up the Vitra brand in 1984 once the longstanding partnership with → Herman Miller, dating back to 1957, came to an end. → Pierre Mendell designed Vitra's logotype, complete with distinctive full stop, in 1990.

VITRA CAMPUS

The architectural ensemble at the Vitra headquarters in → Weil am Rhein. The term "campus" underscores the pluralistic coexistence of multiple buildings that, irrespective of their different purposes, construction dates and styles, reflect the company's design culture and shape the way its staff perceive their employer. The Vitra Campus features buildings by → Nicholas Grimshaw (two factories), → Frank Gehry (Vitra Design Museum and Vitra factory), → Zaha Hadid (Fire Station), → Álvaro Siza

Herman Miller Collection 1957, Panton Chair 1967, Vitramat 1976, Bellini Collection 1984, Vitra Edition 1987, Metropol 1988, AC 1 1990, Ad Hoc 1992, Meda Chair 1996, .03 1999, Jean Prouvé Re-Edition 2002, Joyn 2002, Home Collection 2004, Vitra Edition 2007

A selection of the main product launches since 1957

(factory) and → Tadao Ando (Conference Pavilion) and smaller structures the company has acquired over the years by → Richard Buckminster Fuller (geodesic "Dome", originally intended for automobile exhibitions) and → Jean Prouvé (petrol station). Directly in front of the Vitra Campus stands a bus stop designed by → Jasper Morrison. Two other buildings – a factory by Japanese architects → SANAA and the VitraHaus by → Herzog & de Meuron – are currently under construction and are due for completion in 2009.

VITRA EDITION

Contemporary experimental furniture manufactured in small numbers and marketed by Vitra. Vitra Edition, which was launched in 1987, was inspired by a wish to create a space in which designers could work more freely, liberated from the traditional constraints of industrial furniture production (safety standards, production techniques, marketing, sales mindset, etc). The programme invites selected authors and gives them a unique opportunity to exploit Vitra's technical know-how and experiment with shapes, materials and constructions of all kinds. Although enthusiasm for the idea has been muted in the furniture market, it has created a stir and triggered lively discussions in the design community. Vitra's aim was simply to push the boundaries of design. The programme has also catalyzed some valuable long-term relationships with new designers. A new Vitra Edition was presented in June 2007.

VITRA HOME

One of the company's business units dedicated to objects for the home, it was founded in 2004. In many respects the launch of Vitra Home was like a throwback to the business's roots in furniture manufacturing. When the company began producing the designs of → Charles & Ray Eames and → George Nelson in 1957, the home was the dominant theme. Although Vitra has always retained home furniture in its programme, from the early 1970s the emphasis shifted decidedly towards the office environment. In recent years, mainly due to technological and social changes, the pendulum has swung back and the home has once again become the focus of various activities. Inevitably, interior decoration requirements have also changed in line with this trend. Vitra thinks less in terms of monolithic solutions and more in terms of practical, inspiring arrangements of furniture, objects, lights, textiles and technical appliances that are customized to meet individual needs and preferences. Its role model here is → Charles & Ray Eames's "select and arrange" collage principle. Vitra Home offers such → collages: "good goods" that are both durable and stylish. The Vitra → classics form the foundation of the Home Collection, which is complemented by contemporary designs by → Jasper Morrison, the → Bouroullec brothers, → Hella Jongerius and others.

VITRA OFFICE

Office furnishing is one of Vitra's core competencies. In purely economic terms, it is also the company's most important business segment. Officeware and interior decoration have always been a key area for Vitra, as much of the furniture designed by the → Eameses and → George Nelson was also – or even primarily – intended for this environment. The company began producing office furniture (Vitramat) in earnest in the mid 1970s. This chair, the innovative synchronous mechanism of which was based on the very latest ergonomic research, set new standards in the sector. Initially focused on designing individual components for the office, especially chairs and tables, Vitra moved towards developing entire office systems and environments in the 1980s. At the very latest with the inception of the → "Citizen Office" project, Vitra began to explore the office world holistically and to question its traditional structures. The company has since developed its own office and furnishing concepts designed to maximize efficiency and make the workplace as human as possible.

VITRASHOP

The group name for the Vitra subsidiary specializing in showroom design and run by → Raymond Fehlbaum between 1977 and 2005. Since 2001 the Vitrashop Group has consisted of three business units: Visplay, Vizona and Ansorg. Visplay focuses on modular shopfitting solutions, Vizona on store concepts for retailers and manufacturers, and Ansorg on commercial lighting fixtures and concepts.

WEIL AM RHEIN

Vitra's first factory on German soil was built in Weil am Rhein in the 1950s, a mere seven kilometres from → Birsfelden, on the garden of some of → Erika Fehlbaum's relatives. Over the next fifty years, Erika Fehlbaum carefully acquired land in the surrounding area to accommodate the ever-expanding business. The original site is now home to the → Vitra Campus.

WORKSHOPS

Shortly after it opened, the Vitra Design Museum began organizing a workshop programme featuring renowned designers from around the globe. Between 1990 and 1992 these courses took place during the summer months in a tent next to the Design Museum in → Weil am Rhein. Since 1996 they have been held at the Domaine de Boisbuchet in southwestern France in cooperation with the Centre International de Recherche et d'Education Culturelle et Agricole (C.I.R.E.C.A.). The Centre Georges Pompidou in Paris has been a partner for the workshop programme since 1997. The topics under discussion are drawn from various design disciplines (furniture, product, graphic design, fashion, jewellery, lighting) and also include courses on architecture, exhibition design, photography and art. The workshops, which focus on practical, creative work, are a forum for debating experimental approaches and sharing skills. Lectures and discussions are also held. Between twenty-four and thirty workshops of six to twelve days each have been organized each year since 1996, and every summer around 220–300 people take part in the programmes. Over the years, approximately 2700 people from around sixty-five nations have participated in one of the Vitra Design Museum's workshops.

WORKSPIRIT

The name of a Vitra publication which has been produced every two years since 1998 to coincide with the → Orgatec fair. Image brochure and product catalogue in one, the "Workspirits" illustrate Vitra's furniture and office design solutions using both text and images. The series aims to document the latest thinking on office design and define what conditions an office interior needs to fulfil if it is to be humane, functional and multi-purpose. Internationally renowned graphic designers are commissioned to produce "Workspirits" series and are given considerable creative freedom in carrying out the assignment. Each edition is therefore visually unique. The following designers have been involved in "Workspirits" to date: → April Greiman (1988), → Mendell & Oberer (1990 and 1992), → Tibor Kalman (1994 and 1996), → Irma Boom (1998), → Bruce Mau (2000), → Michael Rock's 2x4 (2002 and 2004) and Cornelia Blatter and Marcel Herman's → COMA (2006).

ABC, AC 1, AC 2, AC 3, ATM, CTM, DAR, DAW, DAX, DCM, DCW, DKR, DKX, DSR, DSS, DSW, DSX, EA, EDU, EM, ES, ESU, ETR, ETS, H.A.T., IXIX, LCM, LCW, LTM, LTR, MEG, MVS, PACC, PSCC, RAR, SIM, W.W., ETC.

A selection of product names and abbreviations from the Vitra collections

PEOPLE

WERNER AISSLINGER
(*1964)

studied design at Berlin's University of the Arts and went on to acquire professional experience in the studios of → Jasper Morrison, → Ron Arad and Michele De Lucchi. He started his freelance career in 1993, establishing the Studio Aisslinger in Berlin which is actively involved in product development, design concepts and brand architecture. Furniture design is one of the focal points of this studio's work. From 1998 to 2005, Aisslinger was professor of design at the Karlsruhe State Academy of Design. He worked with Vitra to develop the Level 34 range of office furniture which was premiered in 2004.

JOSEF ALBERS
(1888–1976)

was both a student and a teacher at the Bauhaus until 1933, when he emigrated to the United States to continue his career as an artist and university teacher. He rose to international fame mainly thanks to his series of pictures entitled "Homage to the Square". However, Albers also worked as a designer of furniture and graphic designer during his Bauhaus period. 1926/1927 saw the creation of his nesting tables with glass panels tinted in various colours, which have been produced by the Vitra Design Museum as a → re-edition since 2004.

EMILIO AMBASZ
(*1943)

studied architecture at Princeton University. From 1970 to 1976, he was curator of design at the Museum of Modern Art in New York, where his achievements included staging the legendary exhibition "Italy. The New Domestic Landscape" in 1972. As well as his wide variety of teaching activities, Ambasz has made a name for himself as a designer, architect and urban planner. In 1982, Vitra launched the Dorsal chair, jointly designed by Ambasz and Gian Carlo Piretti. This was followed in 1998 by VoX, a multifunctional seating unit.

TADAO ANDO
(*1941)

started out as a professional boxer before teaching himself architecture. He travelled extensively in Europe, America and Africa to deepen the knowledge of architecture he had gained from textbooks. He set up his own office in Osaka in 1969. He focused on residential buildings and churches at the start of his career, but from the late 1980s onwards began designing other buildings including a series of museums. Ando was awarded the Pritzker Prize in 1995. The hallmarks of his work are simple, basic geometric forms and formal reduction which sometimes conveys a hint of asceticism, counterbalanced by great attention to detail and sensitive handling of construction materials. He is famous for his work with exposed concrete where he manages to impart a textile-like structure to this material, largely through masterful light distribution. Ando's introverted, tranquil buildings cannot be attributed to any particular school or style; they represent a synthesis of specifically Japanese traditions and modern Western elements. Tadao Ando designed the Conference Pavilion on the → Vitra Campus in → Weil am Rhein for Vitra. This building, completed in 1993, was Ando's first work outside Japan.

RON ARAD
(*1951)

attended the Jerusalem Academy of Art from 1971 to 1973, going on to study at London's renowned Architectural Association until 1979. In 1981, he opened his first design studio in London – One Off Ltd. This is where he began producing his unconventional, sculptural, handcrafted furniture, which he liked to weld together from steel plate. Arad's architectural and interior design work has also attracted much attention: examples include the room sculpture which he completed in the Foyer of the Tel Aviv Opera House in 1990. Since the end of the 1980s, Arad has also been designing furniture and other articles for mass production. Arad's cooperation with Vitra started with a → Vitra Edition collaboration, for which he designed the Well-Tempered Chair, the School Chair (both dating from 1987/1988) and the Schizzo pair of chairs (1989). He led one of the first → workshops at the Vitra Design Museum in 1990. Other projects he has completed with Vitra include the Tom Vac chair (1999) and the Bad-Tempered Chair (2002). Ron Arad was also involved in → Vitra Edition 2007.

RICHARD ARTSCHWAGER
(*1923)

started out studying biology, but then decided to become an artist. The works of this American painter and sculptor resist traditional classification. They occupy the middle ground between art and furniture, pictures and sculptures, with elements of both abstract and objective representation; they question established modes of perception. In the same way, his Chair/Chair, part of → Vitra Edition 1987, can be read both as an item of furniture and as a sculpture.

DOROTHEE BECKER
(*1938)

is a self-taught designer. She was married to the lighting designer Ingo Maurer from 1962 until 1976, and in the late 1960s and early 1970s she designed a series of lamps and other objects for his Design M label. Her most famous work is the Uten.Silo wall container dating from 1969, which the Vitra Design Museum re-launched as a → re-edition in 2001.

MARIO BELLINI
(*1935)

studied architecture at Milan Polytechnic. From 1961 to 1963, he was design director of La Rinascente, the Italian chain of department stores. In 1963 he moved to → Olivetti, where he designed calculators and typewriters (including the Divisumma in 1972) into the 1980s. At his own studio in Milan, he created furniture, lighting, electrical appliances and other devices which were produced by renowned Italian design firms. Alongside his practical design work, which included designs for exhibitions and fairs, he was editor-in-chief of "Domus" magazine from 1986 to 1991. From the 1960s onwards, he also accepted numerous professorships at design colleges. The 1980s saw the focus of Bellini's work shifting increasingly towards architecture. He undertook projects in Europe, the United States, Japan, the United Arab Emirates and Australia. Bellini has been working with Vitra since the late 1970s. His first office chairs – Figura, Persona and Imago – were launched in 1984, followed by the Metropol office furniture range (from 1988), the Onda visitor's chair (1990), the Memo storage system (1992), the Forma (1994) and Summa visitor's chairs (2000) and the office chairs designed in cooperation with his son Claudio, Ypsilon (2001) and Headline (2006).

HANS BELLMANN
(1911–1990)

studied at the Bauhaus in Dessau and Berlin after serving his apprenticeship as an architectural draughtsman in Baden, Switzerland, from 1931 to 1933. After his return to Switzerland, he worked at Wohnbedarf in Zurich and in various architectural practices. Bellmann became a freelance architect and designer in 1946. He created Typenmöbel (type furniture) which was sold by Wohnbedarf, as well as designs for exhibitions and houses. Alongside these practical activities, Bellmann also held academic posts (Zurich University of the Arts, the Ulm School of Design and elsewhere). The Vitra Design Museum relaunched the Colonial Table which he designed in 1945/1948 as a → re-edition in 2004.

SEBASTIAN BERGNE
(*1966)

studied industrial design at London's Central School of Art and Design and at the Royal College of Art. He started work as a freelance designer in London in 1990, since when he has designed various objects, lamps and furniture which are manufactured by international design companies. Though simple in form, his work is often typified by a surprising and sometimes humorous reinterpretation of functional conventions. In 1999, Bergne developed the IXIX Universal Table in cooperation with Vitra.

JURGEN BEY
(*1965)

studied at the Design Academy in Eindhoven. He has been running the Jurgenbey design studio in Rotterdam since 1998, achieving prominence with furniture and lighting designs (for Droog Design, among others) as well as interior design work. Bey was invited to submit a design for → Vitra Edition 2007 and participated in the Vitra Design Museum's "MyHome" exhibition project.

MAX BILL
(1908–1994)

was one of the twentieth-century's most versatile artists and designers. In the course of his lengthy career, he worked not only as an architect, designer and exhibition designer, but also as a painter, sculptor, graphic artist and typographer. In addition, he was a prominent journalist, university teacher and theorist. After completing his apprenticeship as a silversmith, Bill studied at the Bauhaus in Dessau from 1927 to 1928. On his return to Zurich, he started working mainly as a commercial artist and exhibition designer. His first sculptures and buildings, including his own studio and home in Zurich-Höngg, were created at this time. In 1951, he was one of the co-founders of the Ulm School of Design, becoming its first principal as well as designing its buildings. During the 1950s, Bill developed into one of the most prominent exponents of 'concrete art'. His furniture includes the Ulmer Hocker, designed together with Hans Gugelot in 1954, which the Vitra Design Museum has been marketing since 2002.

IRMA BOOM
(*1960)

studied at the Academy of Art (AKI) in Enschede and went on to work as a designer at the Dutch state printing works for several years. In 1991, she opened the Irma Boom Office in Amsterdam, which has attracted much attention ever since, especially for its book designs. Irma Boom designed → "Workspirit" for Vitra in 1998.

RONAN & ERWAN BOUROULLEC
(*1971, 1976 respectively)

launched their joint career in 1997 at the Salon du Meuble in Paris, when Ronan (who had just completed his studies at the École Nationale des Arts Décoratifs) presented his Disintegrated Kitchen project. He was assisted by his brother Erwan who was still a student at the École des Beaux-Arts in Cergy-Pontoise. Since 1999, they have been running a design studio in Paris as equal partners. The Bouroullec brothers work in areas ranging from small household objects to architectural projects. As well as designing furniture for the home and office, vases, porcelain-ware, jewellery and various home accessories, their creative work focuses on space and spatial design. Projects which have won them much attention in this field include shopfitting designs (such as their Paris boutique for Issey Miyake's A-Poc collection in 2000) as well as fair designs (such as the "Ideal House" installation at the Cologne Furniture Fair in 2004) or the → Vitra Home Collection exhibit at the Milan Furniture Fair in La Pelota (2005). Their spatial work also led to the creation of Algues, one of their most unconventional productions. The brothers' cooperation with Vitra started with the Joyn office furniture range which they designed and continued to develop between 2000 and 2002, at the invitation of → Rolf Fehlbaum. Alongside → Jasper Morrison and → Hella Jongerius, they have since made a major contribution to the → Vitra Home Collection. The Bouroullec brothers were participants in → Vitra Edition 2007 and in the "MyHome" exhibition at the Vitra Design Museum.

CONSTANTIN BOYM
(*1955)

studied at the Moscow Institute of Architecture and at the Domus Academy in Milan. In 1986, he established his own practice in New York, working chiefly in the field of product and exhibition design. Boym has also worked as a university lecturer, is the author of several books, and designed the Neocon → Showroom in Chicago for Vitra in 1999.

ANDREA BRANZI
(*1938)

studied architecture at the University of Florence and was one of the founders of the Archizoom group in 1966 (→ Paolo Deganello). Since the early 1970s, Branzi has worked on numerous projects in the fields of urban planning, architecture and design, sometimes independently and sometimes in cooperation with others. He has also worked frequently as a journalist and university lecturer. Branzi worked with Vitra in the early 1990s on the → "Citizen Office" project.

EGON BRÄUNING
(*1943)

is head of Vitra's → product development. He works closely with designers to devise appropriate solutions for each design in terms of structure, choice of materials and manufacturing processes. Bräuning's work is the fruit of decades of experience, meticulous care and an inventive mind, and although little of it is evident to the outside world, his contribution

towards the → quality of Vitra's products is decisive. Before joining the firm in 1963 as a designer of plastic tools, Bräuning had completed an apprenticeship as a toolmaker and had also trained as a mechanical engineer. When → Willi Fehlbaum set up a development department focusing on furniture in 1971, he appointed Bräuning as its manager. Since then, Bräuning has provided support and assistance to almost all the Vitra designers from his department in the Vitra Center in → Birsfelden.

SCOTT BURTON
(1939–1989)

was a sculptor who mainly made his name with art projects in public spaces. In formal terms, his works were committed to the tradition of classical modernism; most of them trod the borderlines between art and design, and they often revolved around the subject of 'sitting'. This American artist designed the Soft Geometric Chair for → Vitra Edition in 1987.

FERNANDO & HUMBERTO CAMPANA
(*1961, 1953 respectively)

Two Brazilian brothers who achieved renown through their furniture designs. Before setting up their joint studio in São Paulo in 1983, Fernando studied architecture while his older brother Humberto graduated in law. They make repeated use of unusual materials or combinations of materials in their furniture designs. The Campana brothers participated in the "MyHome" exhibition on show at the Vitra Design Museum in 2007 as well as → Vitra Edition 2007.

DAVID CHIPPERFIELD
(*1953)

studied architecture at Kingston School of Art and the Architectural Association in London. After graduating, Chipperfield worked at the practices of Douglas Stephen, Richard Rogers and Norman Foster, and in 1984 established his own studio, which currently maintains locations in London, Berlin and Milan as well as a representative office in Shanghai. Chipperfield's wide-ranging projects are

defined not by a uniform formal vocabulary, but by a design approach ensuing from the particular context and function. His most renowned structures include the River and Rowing Museum in Henley-on-Thames, the Museum of Modern Literature in Marbach and the City of Justice in Barcelona. He also attracted considerable attention with his plan for the restoration of the Neues Museum on Museum Island, Berlin. In 1999, Chipperfield designed the Vitra Showroom in London.

ANTONIO CITTERIO
(*1950)

studied architecture at the Milan Polytechnic. In 1972, he established his studio in the same city, where he has since worked on numerous projects as architect, interior planner and designer. Administrative and industrial buildings as well as hotels figure prominently among his architectural projects. His design work includes furniture for the home and office, lighting, bathroom fittings and other furnishings. Restrained in form, Citterio's designs convincingly combine functional qualities with elegance and precision. Citterio has taken on numerous teaching posts in the last few decades and in 2006 he became a professor at the Academy of Architecture of the Università della Svizzera Italiana in Mendrisio. Antonio Citterio has maintained exceptionally close ties with Vitra since 1985. This period has seen the creation of numerous office chairs (including models AC 1, AC 2 and AC 3 (1988), Visavis and Axion (1992), T-Chair (1994), Axess (1996), Oson C and Oson S (2002), furniture for waiting areas, storage furniture and, in particular, the Ad Hoc range of office furniture. Citterio has also worked as an architect for Vitra: a production building which he designed was completed at Neuenburg (Germany) in 1992, and another production building to his design will be built at the same location in 2008.

CHRISTIAN COIGNY
(*1946)

attended the photography class at the École des Arts Appliqués in Vevey and then spent several years in San

Francisco. On his return to Switzerland, he was the house photographer for "Annabelle" magazine in the mid 1970s before setting up as a freelance fashion and advertising photographer, initially in Lausanne and then in Lutry. As well as his commercial work, he has also produced still lifes, portraits and nude photographs. Coigny photographed the 'Personalities' campaign for Vitra between 1987 and 1997.

COMA

is the name of the practice set up in 1996 by Cornelia Blatter and Marcel Hermans, which is active in the field of graphic design with studios in Amsterdam and New York. Cornelia Blatter (*1960) studied at the Zurich School of Art and Design and at Yale University School of Art in the United States. Marcel Hermans (*1961) studied graphic design at the Rietveld Akademie in Amsterdam. Book designs (including a monograph on → Hella Jongerius) account for many of the numerous projects which have brought COMA to prominence since then. COMA attracted international attention with the editorial design for "FRAME" (2003–2005), a design magazine published in the Netherlands. COMA designed → "Workspirit" 2006 for Vitra, as well as publications on Vitra products ("Worknest" and "BaObab").

COOP HIMMELB(L)AU

is an architectural practice established in Vienna in 1968 by Wolf D. Prix (*1942) and Helmut Swiczinsky (*1944); it is one of the foremost advocates of deconstructivism. This office has attracted international attention ever since it converted the attic storey of an old Viennese building into an attorneys' office in 1988, and it has undertaken numerous projects of ever-increasing scope in recent years. Wolf D. Prix, who studied at Vienna Technical University, is a prominent theorist and university teacher alongside his hands-on work. Coop Himmelb(l)au designed the Vodöl armchair in 1989 for → Vitra Edition.

PAOLO DEGANELLO
(*1940)

studied architecture in Florence and was one of the founders of the Archizoom group in 1966 together with → Andrea Branzi. Considered as part of the Italian Radical Design movement, the group questioned the social role of design and of the designer, as well as considering issues related to architecture and urban planning. Its best-known works include the Safari sofa object, inspired by Pop art. After Archizoom was disbanded in 1972, Deganello worked as a university lecturer and journalist, as well as in other fields. He established his own design studio in Florence in 1981. He designed the Documenta Chair for → Vitra Edition in 1987 when it was also presented at the art exhibition of the same name in Kassel.

WOLFGANG DEISIG
(*1946)

studied design at the University of Fine Arts in Kassel. He began working as a freelancer in 1971, and in 1989 he set up the Deisig Design practice in Berlin, primarily to design office furniture but also sanitary equipment. In 1976, he collaborated with Vitra to produce the Vitramat, the first office chair developed by Vitra.

E-TEAM

A Zurich-based design studio, established in 1995 by Jochem Willemse (*1968), Kyeni Mbiti (*1967) and Peter Kancsár (*1968), who met while studying industrial design together at the Zurich School of Art and Design. In 2001, they designed the X-Tend storage system for Vitra.

CHARLES & RAY EAMES

Charles Eames (1907–1978) was an architect. Ray Eames (1912–1988), whose name at birth was Bernice Alexandra Kaiser, studied art with the German painter Hans Hofmann in New York and Provincetown during the 1930s. Charles and Ray Eames began their collaboration in 1940 when they met at the Cranbrook Academy of Art, which was then a major centre of American design. The couple married in 1941 and moved to Los Angeles where they set up a joint practice. Their collaboration was to last almost four decades, during which it produced many pioneering furniture designs, as well as important buildings, exhibitions, films, toys, graphic works, textile designs and countless photographs. The Eameses' creative work was exceptionally varied, and it was a key factor in shaping the concept of → design which gained general currency at Vitra as well as the company's understanding of the designer's mission. After Charles Eames's death in 1978, Ray finished several projects begun while he was still alive; Ray Eames died in 1988. Vitra's involvement with Charles & Ray Eames was of fundamental importance. The production of their designs in 1957 marked the start of the company's history as a furniture manufacturer. But it was not just the Eames products which helped to shape Vitra's development. It was their understanding of design which played a decisive part in determining the company's values and orientation. Vitra produced furniture by Charles & Ray Eames from 1957 to 1983 as a licensee of → Herman Miller. In 1984, the rights to the Eames furniture for Europe and the Middle East were transferred to Vitra. The Vitra Design Museum, which also owns the three-dimensional estate of Charles & Ray Eames, produced a touring exhibition on Charles & Ray Eames in 1997.

FEHLBAUM FAMILY

Vitra is a family enterprise established by Willi Fehlbaum (1914–2003) that was mainly involved in shopfitting during the first phase of its existence. Together with his wife Erika (*1918), Willi Fehlbaum started developing the furniture division in 1957 when he took over the license rights to the designs of → Charles & Ray Eames and → George Nelson. Their sons Rolf, Peter and Raymond Fehlbaum took over the business in 1977. When Peter Fehlbaum left the company in 1992, Rolf and Raymond Fehlbaum divided the responsibilities between them: Rolf Fehlbaum took on the furniture division while Raymond assumed responsibility for the shopfitting division. Both divisions later became independent companies (Vitra and → Vitrashop), with close cooperation between the brothers in the two firms. A management team has been employed to manage the companies' operations for some years now. Since then, Rolf and Raymond Fehlbaum have focused their activities on the boards of directors of these companies. Rolf Fehlbaum is intimately involved with → product development and corporate strategy at Vitra. Vitra intends to continue as a family business.

ROY FLEETWOOD
(*1946)

completed his architecture studies in Liverpool and Rome. From 1973 until 1976, he worked as a partner in → Norman Foster's practice, where he was responsible for the Hong Kong and Shanghai Bank project in Hong Kong, among other assignments. He founded the Office for Design Strategy in Cambridge in 1986, followed two years later by the Sugimura Fleetwood architects' practice in Tokyo. He works as an architect, product designer and university teacher. He developed the Wing sofa with Vitra in 1990.

NORMAN FOSTER
(*1935)

studied at the Manchester University School of Architecture and at Yale University in New Haven. Starting in 1963, he worked with his wife Wendy and with Su and Richard Rogers in the Team 4 practice before founding Foster Associates in 1967 and launching the career which has brought him worldwide success. Together with → Nicholas Grimshaw and Richard Rogers, Foster is one of the foremost exponents of British high-tech architecture, and he was awarded the Pritzker Prize in 1999. Of the countless buildings he has produced, particular attention has been focused on the Hong Kong and Shanghai Bank in Hong Kong (1985), the Chek Lap Kok airport, also in Hong Kong (1998), the rebuilding of the Reichstag in Berlin (1999) and the Swiss Re Tower in London (2003). Foster developed the AIR LINE seating system for waiting areas with Vitra in 1998.

NAOTO FUKASAWA
(*1956)

studied product design at Tama Art University. After working for many years as a staff designer at Seiko-Epson and at the IDEO design agency in San Francisco and Japan, he established the Naoto Fukasawa Design practice in Tokyo in 2003. He is primarily concerned with designing clear and minimalist household articles. Fukasawa was invited to contribute to the 2007 → Vitra Edition.

RICHARD BUCKMINSTER FULLER
(1895–1983)

is one of the most individualistic figures in the history of design and ideas in the twentieth century. Although he never underwent any academic training, the varied work of this inventor and visionary lateral thinker met with respect and recognition in many academic and scientific fields. His most important inventions include the geodesic dome which he created in the 1940s. This is a lightweight cupola structure based on simple geometric bodies which achieves maximum stability and span with minimum use of materials. The design principle for the domes (patented in 1954) is an excellent example of Richard Buckminster Fuller's call for materials and energy to be used efficiently, not least for reasons of environmental protection. In 2000, a Buckminster Fuller "Dome" used for exhibitions and events was set up on the → Vitra Campus in → Weil am Rhein.

JAKOB GEBERT
(*1965)

studied interior planning and product design at the School of Design in Basel. He has been running his own industrial and exhibition design studio in → Weil am Rhein since 1994. After holding teaching posts at various design colleges, Gebert was appointed professor at the Kassel University of Fine Arts in 2005. He produced the Taino chair with Vitra in 2001.

FRANK GEHRY
(*1929)

studied architecture at the University of Southern California in Los Angeles and Harvard University in Cambridge (Mass.). In 1962, he set up as a freelancer in Los Angeles and started a career which climaxed in spectacular large-scale projects such as the Guggenheim Museum in Bilbao (1999). Alongside his numerous architectural projects, Gehry (who was awarded the Pritzker Prize in 1989) has often produced furniture and lighting designs. Gehry has had links with Vitra since the early 1980s. Their first joint project was the Little Beaver chair made of cardboard, designed in 1987 for → Vitra Edition. Vitra also took over production of the Easy Edges series at a later stage. Gehry's first building with Vitra was the Vitra Design Museum in → Weil am Rhein – his first project in Europe, which was completed in 1989. At the same time as the Museum, a factory building including a canteen, → showroom and offices was built to Gehry's plans on the → Vitra Campus. The Vitra Center in → Birsfelden, completed in 1994, was the company's third building to be designed by Gehry. Gehry also participated in → Vitra Edition 2007.

GINBANDE DESIGN

Uwe Fischer (*1958) and Klaus-Achim Heine (*1955) studied industrial design and design at the College of Design in Offenbach. From 1985 until 1995, they worked together under the brand Ginbande Design. The pair chiefly designed furniture, lighting and exhibition installations. Ginbande cooperated with Vitra to develop the Nexus table range and for → Vitra Edition and also produced the Tabula Rasa and Tabula Varia tablebench combinations in 1987/1988 and the Stool in 1988. Since 2001, Fischer has been a professor at the State Academy of Fine Arts and Design in Stuttgart, as well as heading a design studio in Frankfurt am Main which he set up in 1993. Heine was appointed professor at Berlin's University of the Arts in 1993, and he heads a design studio based in Frankfurt and Berlin.

ALEXANDER GIRARD
(1907–1993)

Together with his close friends → George Nelson and → Charles and Ray Eames, Alexander Girard is numbered among the defining figures in post-war American design. His creative work focused on designing textiles: he expressed his love of colours, patterns and textures in hundreds of designs for furniture fabrics and decorative materials. Girard, a qualified architect, also rose to prominence as a designer of furniture, graphics, exhibitions and interiors. His legendary achievements in these fields include the decor to the La Fonda del Sol restaurant in New York City and his work for Braniff Airlines, where he played a key part in developing the firm's corporate design. Girard's work enriched twentieth-century design by adding a sensual and playful element which had hitherto been absent from the classical development of the modernist movement. One of Girard's essential sources of inspiration was his involvement with popular art in South America, Eastern Europe and Asia. His extensive collection is on show in a wing of the Museum of International Folk Art, which he designed in Santa Fe, New Mexico – his chosen home. In Vitra's early days, Girard (who headed → Herman Miller's textile department at that time) exerted a major influence on the company's → colour worlds. Several of Girard's textile designs have now been reintroduced into the Vitra programme and the Vitra Design Museum relaunched Girard's Wooden Dolls as a → re-edition in 2006.

KONSTANTIN GRCIC
(*1965)

was apprenticed as a cabinet-maker before studying design at the Royal College of Art in London. In 1991, he established the Konstantin Grcic Industrial Design (KGID) practice in Munich. His concept-based designs for furniture, lighting and interior furnishings are manufactured by renowned design firms. Grcic contributed a design to → Vitra Edition 2007.

APRIL GREIMAN
(*1948)

studied graphic design at the Kansas City Art Institute, going on to attend the 'further education class' at the School of Design in Basel. Her teachers there included Wolfgang Weingart, who exerted a lasting influence on her. During the 1980s, Greiman was one of the pioneers of digital communication design in the United States, being one of the first to use the Apple computer as a design tool. She was also a leading figure in the New Wave style which broke with the dogmas of modernism. She designed the first edition of → "Workspirit" for Vitra in 1988.

NICHOLAS GRIMSHAW
(*1939)

studied at Edinburgh College of Art and the Architectural Association in London. In 1965, he was the co-founder with Terry Farrell of the Farrell Grimshaw partnership, which lasted until 1980, and has since worked under the name of Grimshaw & Partners. At the outset, his interest was mainly focused on construction with prefabricated and standardized elements: industrial buildings gave him ideal scope for this work. But even after the horizons of his architectural projects had become much broader, unusual and sophisticated designs, exuding a comparatively cool, technical aura, continued to be hallmarks of his buildings. As well as factory buildings (for which his clients included → Herman Miller UK), Grimshaw won international acclaim for numerous projects such as the British Pavilion at the World Exposition in Seville (1992), the Waterloo International Terminal in London (1993) and the Ludwig-Erhard-Haus in Berlin (1997). In 1981, Nicholas Grimshaw designed the first building for the → Vitra Campus in → Weil am Rhein after the major fire, followed by his master plan for the site and another factory building.

WILLI GUHL
(1915–2004)

was one of Switzerland's most important twentieth-century furniture designers. After training as a cabinet-maker, he attended the interior design course at the Zurich University of the Arts before opening his own studio in that city in 1939. The Eternit beach chair which he designed in 1954 has a firm place in the history of design. Guhl exerted a major influence on the development of design in Switzerland through his teaching work at the Zurich University of the Arts, where he lectured from 1941 until 1980. The Vitra Design Museum is marketing a → re-edition of the "Furniture Game" which he designed in 1948/1949.

ZAHA HADID
(*1950)

initially read mathematics at the American University in Beirut and went on to study architecture at the Architectural Association in London. After many years of cooperation with OMA/Rem Koolhaas, Hadid started out on her freelance career in London in 1980. She soon became known thanks to successes in competitions in the field, but her dynamic and expressively serrated architecture – made even more dramatic by her unique style of presenting plans – were often regarded as impossible to realize. This changed after the completion of her first building, the Fire Station on the → Vitra Campus in → Weil am Rhein, between 1989 and 1993. This keynote deconstructivist building received an enthusiastic welcome from the critics and brought Hadid international fame. Since then, she has undertaken major projects throughout the world, including the much-acclaimed Contemporary Arts Center in Cincinnati (2003) and the Phaeno Science Center in Wolfsburg (2005); she was awarded the Pritzker Prize in 2004. As well as her architectural practice, Hadid has also risen to prominence as a designer of furniture, interior furnishings and exhibitions. Zaha Hadid also took part in → Vitra Edition 2007.

HANS HANSEN
(*1940)

was apprenticed as a lithographer and went on to study graphic art at the Düsseldorf Art Academy; then, with no formal training in the field, he started work as a freelance product and stills photographer in 1962. Having set up his studio in Hamburg in 1967, he developed a style which he himself described as "photography using graphic methods". Hansen works for many international corporations, renowned periodicals and book publishers. The product photographs he has produced for Vitra since 1990 have played a key part in the development of this furniture.

HERZOG & DE MEURON

Jacques Herzog and Pierre de Meuron, both born in 1950, studied architecture together at the ETH in Zurich and established their joint practice (Herzog & de Meuron) in Basel in 1978. Awarded the Pritzker Prize in 2001, the Basel architects' many projects that have won international acclaim include the Tate Modern in London (2000), the Schaulager near Basel (2003), the Olympic Stadium in Beijing which is currently under construction, and the planned Elbphilharmonie in Hamburg, to name but a few. In 2005, Herzog & de Meuron designed the Hocker for the → Vitra Home Collection. They have also planned the VitraHaus on the → Vitra Campus in → Weil am Rhein which is due for completion in 2009.

CHRISTOPH INGENHOVEN
(*1960)

studied architecture at RWTH Aachen and the Düsseldorf Academy of Arts. In 1985, he set up his own independent practice, Ingenhoven Architekten, based in Düsseldorf. His work chiefly focuses on the design of office buildings, though he has drawn the most international acclaim for his ecological approach and dedication to the concept of sustainability. His most prominent works include the RWE high-rise in Essen, the Burda Media Park in Offenburg, the Lufthansa Aviation Center in Frankfurt as well as the prizewinning design for the Main Station in Stuttgart, which will begin construction in 2010. In 2007, Ingenhoven worked with Vitra on the development of the Terminal table system, which was first used in the project for the Lufthansa Aviation Center.

EVA JIRICNA
(*1939)

studied architecture at Prague Technical University, after which she attended the Academy of Art in the Czech capital. In 1968 she emigrated to Britain where she worked for the Greater London Council and in the offices of Louis de Soissons and Richard Rogers. In 1982, Jiricna established her own London practice which has since undertaken numerous projects, mainly in the field of interior design. In particular, her shopfitting designs – often featuring dramatic staircases built of glass and steel – have achieved international renown. In 1988, Jiricna designed the entire entrance area for the → Vitra-shop administrative building in → Weil am Rhein. Among the special features of this project was a roofed, bridge-like staircase.

HELLA JONGERIUS
(*1963)

studied industrial design at the Design Academy in Eindhoven. She attracted international attention during the 1990s thanks to her cooperation with the Dutch Droog Design label. In 2000, she set up the JongeriusLab design studio in Rotterdam, where she produces and markets many of her own designs. Jongerius' works often tread the borderlines of design and handicraft, art and technology. Traditional and contemporary influences are fused in her designs, which she produces with a combination of high-tech processes and traditional craftsmanship. Jongerius primarily designs crockery, vases, textiles and furniture. She began working with Vitra in 2004. Their very first joint project – the Polder Sofa for → Vitra Home – met with an excellent response. Alongside other furniture projects, she is working on a new → colour world for Vitra. Jongerius participated in → Vitra Edition 2007 and in the "MyHome" exhibition at the Vitra Design Museum.

TIBOR KALMAN
(1949–1999)

was born in Budapest, but following the Hungarian uprising of 1956, he and his parents emigrated to the United States. After abandoning journalism studies at New York University, he started his career as a designer in the graphic department of Barnes & Noble, which was still a small bookstore at that time. In 1979 he was one of the founders of the M&Co practice which caused a sensation with its work for the Talking Heads band, among others. In the late 1980s, Kalman was creative director of "Interview" magazine founded by Andy Warhol; from 1990–1995 he edited "Colors" magazine sponsored by the Benetton clothing company, which rose to fame because of his provocative yet easily understandable visual language and his frequently explosive choice of subjects. After illness forced him to withdraw from "Colors", Kalman revived the M&Co studio where he was active until his death in 1999. Tibor Kalman maintained a close relationship with Vitra – leading most notably to the → "Chairman Rolf Fehlbaum" book published in 1998. Kalman also designed → "Workspirits" in 1994 and 1996, as well as other printed materials for Vitra.

SHIRO KURAMATA
(1934–1991)

studied architecture at Tokyo Technical College and trained as a cabinet-maker at the Kuwasawa Institute of Design. After working at Tokyo's Maysuya department store for several years, he set himself up as a freelance interior designer in 1965, since when he has designed countless restaurants and bars. Kuramata devoted increasing attention to furniture design in the 1970s. His designs (for Memphis among others) attracted much attention, due especially to his unusual choice of materials. In the 1980s, Kuramata worked closely with Issey Miyake for whom he fitted out several boutiques. In 1987, he created the How High The Moon armchair made of expanded metal for → Vitra Edition.

ARIK LEVY
(*1963)

studied industrial design at the Art Center College of Design, La Tour de Peilz (Switzerland) and in 1997 he founded the Parisian L design studio with Pippo Lionni; this practice focuses mainly on product, communication, shop and exhibition design. Arik Levy created the abc office furniture range with Vitra in 2004.

GREG LYNN
(*1964)

studied architecture and philosophy at Princeton University and elsewhere. He worked in Peter Eisenman's practice from 1990 to 1994. In 1994, he set up in business on his own with the Greg Lynn FORM practice, where his complex computer-generated designs very soon drew international attention. Lynn, who is nowadays regarded as one of the foremost representatives of 'blobitecture' (buildings with an organic, amoeba-shaped, bulging form), holds numerous teaching posts at architecture colleges in the United States and Europe. He designed the Ravioli Chair for → Vitra Home in 2005. He also participated in → Vitra Edition 2007 and the "MyHome" exhibition on show at the Vitra Design Museum.

M/M (PARIS)

Michael Amzalag (*1968) and Mathias Augustyniak (*1967) founded M/M (Paris) in 1992 as a communication and design studio at the crossroads of the stakes of contemporary creation. Regularly working as visual designers in the art, fashion and music worlds, they have designed productions for theatres, ad campaigns (for Balenciaga, Yohji Yamamoto and Calvin Klein Jeans), and served for two years as the art directors for French Vogue. Amzalag and Augustyniak have been teaching visual communication and graphic design at Ecal, Ecole Cantonale d'Art in Lausanne since 1997. In 2002, Vitra commissioned them to create the launch campaign for its Jean Prouvé re-editions.

BRUCE MAU
(*1959)

studied at the Ontario College of Art & Design in Toronto, although he left the college in 1980 before his examinations to work with the Fifty Fingers group of designers. After various assignments with other practices, he established the Bruce Mau Design Studio in Toronto in 1985; the studio has since made a name for itself with book designs and exhibition projects in particular. Mau's most important works include the "S, M, L, XL" book created with Rem Koolhaas/OMA and published in 1995, and the "Life Style" book in 2000, which documents the work of his own studio. Bruce Mau designed →"Workspirit" 2000 for Vitra, and in 2000 he cooperated with the → Barragan Foundation to develop the concept for the exhibition entitled "Luis Barragán. The Quiet Revolution".

JÜRGEN MAYER H.
(*1965)

studied architecture at Stuttgart University, the Cooper Union School of Art in New York and Princeton University. In 1996, he established his own practice in Berlin which, as he says, works on the interfaces between architecture, communication and new technologies. To date, Jürgen Mayer H. has completed several major projects, including the City Hall in Ostfildern and a university refectory in Karlsruhe. In 2006, he was invited to submit a design for → Vitra Edition. He also participated in the "MyHome" exhibition on show at the Vitra Design Museum.

ALBERTO MEDA
(*1945)

studied mechanical engineering at Milan Polytechnic. After starting work as a freelancer in 1979, he worked not only as a technical design consultant but also as an industrial designer. His ideal: simple well-thought-out products that make our complex daily lives both easier and richer. Like his great predecessors → Jean Prouvé and → Charles and Ray Eames, he consistently succeeds in achieving a synthesis of modern, timeless formal language, sophisticated structural design and advanced technology. These are also the hallmarks of his cooperation with Vitra which began in 1994 and has since led to a complete family of products, starting in 1996 with Meda Chair, an office chair. This was followed by Meda Conference, the MedaPro, MedaPal and Spiro office chairs, and the MedaSlim and MedaShell office/conference chairs. Vitra's Meda range is completed by the Meda Executive Group range of office furniture and the MedaMorph conference table. Meda also participaed in → Vitra Edition 2007.

PIERRE MENDELL
(*1929)

studied graphic design at the Basel School of Design and founded the Mendell & Oberer studio with Klaus Oberer in Munich in 1961. The internationally renowned studio is active in all areas of graphic design and visual communications and, in addition to numerous other commissions throughout the decades, created the visual identities of the Neue Sammlung (New Collection: National Museum for Design and Applied Arts) in Munich and the Bavarian State Opera. In 1976, Pierre Mendell designed the first catalogue for the Vitramat office chair range and devised the Vitra logotype with its distinctive full stop in 1990. He has designed many publications for Vitra over the years, including → "Workspirit" series (1990 and 1992).

ALESSANDRO MENDINI
(*1931)

is a designer, architect and publicist; he is both a pioneer and one of the chief protagonists of postmodernism. After completing his architecture studies at the Milan Polytechnic, he worked for several years in an architect's studio. From 1970 to 1976, he was editor-in-chief of "Casabella" magazine. In 1977, Mendini became one of the founders of the Alchimia group, the cradle of many defining postmodern impulses. Mendini's preferred medium in graphic design is collage. He caused a particular stir with his irreverent, ironic reinterpretations of famous designs. In the 1980s, he returned to journalism and worked as editor-in-chief of "Domus" from 1980 to 1985. During this time, he also excelled as an architect, designing the Casa della Felicità for Alessi (1983–1988) and the Groningen Museum (1988–1994). He designed two armchairs and a sofa for →Vitra Edition in 1988, calling them Maracatu.

J. ABBOTT MILLER
(*1963)

studied design at the Cooper Union School of Art in New York. He founded the firm Design/Writing/Research with Ellen Lupton in 1989. Following the designer as author principle, the pair develop form and content in the same step of the design process rather than separating the two. Since 1999, Miller has been one of the managing partners of the New York office of Pentagram, working mainly in print. In addition to his work as a designer, Miller is also a design critic and university professor. In 1997 and 2007, he designed publications about → Charles & Ray Eames for Vitra.

JASPER MORRISON
(*1959)

studied at Kingston Polytechnic and the Royal College of Art in England, completing a master's degree in 1985. He moved to the College of Arts in Berlin on a scholarship, then founded his own design studio back in London in 1986. He first rose to fame through two space installations, "Reuters News Centre" for Documenta 8 in Kassel in 1987 and "Some New Items for the Home" in the DAAD

Ron Arad, Richard Artschwager, Scott Burton, Coop Himmelb(l)au, Paolo Deganello, Frank Gehry, Ginbande, Shiro Kuramata, Alessandro Mendini, Jasper Morrison, Gaetano Pesce, Denis Santachiara, Borek Sipek, Ettore Sottsass, Philippe Starck

Participants of the Vitra Edition 1987

Gallery in Berlin in 1988. Both works were impressive in their crystal-clear concept and their minimalist tone. In his reaction against exuberant postmodern forms, Morrison was a pioneer of New Simplicity, a more modest, serious approach to design which prevailed during the 1990s. In addition to furniture, Morrison has designed lights, interior design accessories, textiles and a tram for the city of Hanover in Germany. He has been working with Vitra regularly since 1989. Some of the most important projects Morrison has completed for Vitra include the Ply-Chair, the SIM chair and the ATM office furniture series. Morrison also participated in → Vitra Home and → Vitra Edition 2007.

LARS MÜLLER
(*1955)

studied graphic design and philosophy in the USA and Holland. In 1983 he began publishing books on typography, design, art, photography and architecture. Following in the tradition of → Pierre Mendell, Lars Müller planned and designed numerous publications for Vitra between 1996 and 2000, some of them in collaboration with → Tibor Kalman. He also designed catalogues and posters for the Vitra Design Museum. The book → "Chairman Rolf Fehlbaum" was printed by Lars Müller Publishers in 1998. Lars Müller has also produced several publications on designers and architects that have worked with Vitra, including → Zaha Hadid and → Jasper Morrison.

GEORGE NELSON
(1908–1986)

completed an architecture degree at Yale University from 1925 to 1931, which at that time was still firmly rooted in fine arts. From 1932 to 1934, he was in Europe on a scholarship. During this period, Nelson met the major exponents of modernism and familiarized himself with their works, returning to the United States as a wholehearted supporter of the movement. In 1935, he began working for "Architectural Forum" as an editor, staying with the publication until 1944. That year he published an article outlining his thoughts on domestic housing and furniture design, which caught the attention of D. J. DePree, chief executive officer of the furniture manufacturer → Herman Miller. Shortly after publication of this article, George Nelson was appointed creative design director at Herman Miller. He stayed in that role until 1972, becoming a key figure in American design history. He brought in designers → Charles & Ray Eames, → Isamu Noguchi and → Alexander Girard who collectively created one of history's greatest furniture collections. Nelson's own design studio was active in various fields throughout the decades. The core of his work was furniture, some of which, like Marshmallow Sofa and the Coconut Chair, have become icons of the mid-century modern style. His graphic design work, including the Miller logo, the Bubble Lamps series and the Clocks, which the Vitra Design Museum distributes as part of its → re-edition series, has also become very well known. Nelson's work also focused on architecture, especially single-family homes and exhibition design. He was an important mentor to → Rolf Fehlbaum and played an essential role in shaping the latter's design philosophy. Vitra has been manufacturing George Nelson's designs since 1957 and has had exclusive rights to his furniture in Europe and the Middle East since 1984. Nelson's archives were entrusted to the Vitra Design Museum after his death.

ISAMU NOGUCHI
(1904–1988)

was at one time or another a sculptor, stage designer, interior decorator, a designer of furniture, lighting and industrial design and a landscape architect, all without having had a formal education. The sculptural approach running through his pieces is the only thing that unifies his heterogeneous oeuvre. Noguchi frequently fused artistic disciplines, built bridges between East and West, tradition and modernity, craft and industrialism. As a designer, he focused especially on lighting and furniture. His Akari lamps – light sculptures with traditional, hand-made paper shades and bamboo rods – brought him international fame. Noguchi began developing these lamps in 1951. Over the years, he designed over a hundred models, of which about sixty are still being produced today. Just as important as the Akari lamps are Noguchi's furniture designs for → Herman Miller, such as the Coffee Table (1944), an icon of the Organic Design movement. Vitra manufactured Noguchi furniture in the late 1950s and 1960s. In 2001, the Vitra Design Museum hosted a retrospective of his work, and has since been producing some of his more important designs as → re-editions in cooperation with the Noguchi Foundation in New York.

ADRIANO OLIVETTI
(1901–1960)

is one of the most important entrepreneurs of the twentieth century. Revolutionizing the Ivrea office machinery factory he inherited from his father in the northern Italian provincial town of the same name, he turned the company into a global player within a few short decades. His success was rooted in technological innovation, social engagement, progressive management techniques and a strong cultural vision. Working together with the leading designers and architects of his time, Olivetti established a corporate culture that permeated not only the company's products but its buildings and visual identity. Olivetti's business model, which integrated culture, design and architecture, served as a role model for Vitra.

VERNER PANTON
(1926–1998)

studied at the Technical University of Odense and completed a degree in architecture at the Royal Danish Academy of Art in Copenhagen. He worked in Arne Jacobsen's atelier from 1950 to 1952, when he set up his own architecture and design studio. He first came to the attention of the international design world with his strictly geometric Cone Chair series of furniture manufactured by Plus-Linje. He went on to design innumerable chairs and lamps. Panton's predilection for vibrant colours and geometric forms was especially evident in his substantial oeuvre of textile designs. His interior design for the Komigen Inn (Langsö, 1958) and the Astoria restaurant (Trondheim, 1960) showcased his holistic approach to design, which sought to weld ceiling, walls and floor, as well as furniture, lighting, textiles and wall panels of enamel or plastic, into a single, self-contained unit of space. The Visiona ships designed for the Cologne Furniture Fair and the Spiegel publishing house in Hamburg in 1969, as well as the Varna restaurant (Aarhus 1970) are the most famous manifestations of this philosophy. Panton began working with Vitra in the 1960s, and the collaboration turned out to be of seminal importance for both parties. The Panton Chair, first presented to the public in 1967 and developed in collaboration with Vitra, is his most famous design and the first product Vitra commissioned directly. Today, Vitra produces → re-editions of the designer's pieces and the Vitra Design Museum hosted a retrospective of his work in 2000.

SEVIL PEACH
(*1949)

completed her studies in interior design at Brighton University in 1972, and joined Sir Frederick Gibberd & Partners, London. She set up her own independent practice in 1985 and was later invited to become a design director to lead the Interior Design Division of the YRM Partnership in 1988. In 1994, she and Gary Turnbull founded "SPGA", a studio for architecture and design, and in 1997 her collaboration with Vitra began. Her first project was → Vitra's Network Office in → Weil am Rhein, completed in 2000. Sevil Peach has designed numerous showrooms for Vitra and their presence at various fairs, and is an important partner, advising Vitra on the creation of new office concepts and products.

GAETANO PESCE
(*1939)

studied industrial design and architecture in Venice. He became famous in the 1960s for his Pop art-inspired foam furniture. Plastic is Pesce's raw material of choice. In addition to furniture, he has designed fixtures and jewellery, and has been involved in several architecture projects. He created the Greene Street Chair for → Vitra Edition in 1987 and the Vitra Design Museum showcased his work in 2005 with "Gaetano Pesce – il rumore del tempo".

JEAN PROUVÉ
(1901–1984)

completed an apprenticeship as an ornamental blacksmith and opened his own atelier in Nancy in 1924. He stayed true to his roots, working with metal throughout his career, and his foundation as a craftsman is evident even in his later designs. His workshop produced numerous items of furniture in the 1930s, as well as the prefabricated architectural elements for the Maison du Peuple in Clichy – a collaboration with the architects Beaudoin and Lods which caused a sensation due to their highly futuristic glass-steel construction. Prouvé opened the Maxéville factory in 1947 where he produced not only furniture but prefabricated houses and schools. In 1953, however, after a dispute with the majority shareholder, Prouvé left the company. He moved to Paris and worked as an engineering consultant on numerous prestigious projects, including the Aluminium Centenary Pavilion in Paris (1954) and exhibition halls in Grenoble (1968). He continued to specialize in system building and prefabricated facade elements. Prouvé was professor at the Conservatoire National des Arts et Métiers (CNAM) from 1954 to 1970. In 1971, he once again made architectural history: as chairman of the jury for the Pompidou Centre, he lobbied hard for Renzo Piano and Richard Rogers's design to be chosen. Prouvé's oeuvre includes almost everything that requires an industrial production method, from letter openers, door and window mountings, lamps or furniture, facade elements, prefabricated houses and modular construction systems, to large installations for exhibitions and fairs. In most of his designs, Prouvé managed to marry the complex requirements of mass production with his own self-imposed requirements for design to be functional, true to its material, and economical (using as little material and being as simple as possible). It is this aesthetic of necessity that makes his work so timeless. Working closely with the Prouvé family, Vitra has been producing some of the great designer's work as → re-editions since 2002.

MICHAEL ROCK
(*1959)

trained at the Rhode Island School of Design. In 1994 he founded 2x4 in New York along with Susan Sellers and Georgianne Stout and worked for numerous cultural organizations and design firms. In addition to his design work, Rock has made a name for himself as a univer-sity lecturer and design critic. He designed the 2002 and 2004 editions of → "Workspirit" for Vitra, helped create the company's → showroom in New York and has contributed to a range of other Vitra publications.

THORSTEN ROMANUS
(*1963)

is a graphic designer and economist living and working in Binzen, Germany. Romanus has collaborated with Vitra since 1990 on various projects, designing catalogues and print products for the company and the Vitra Design Museum, including "Verner Panton – Complete Works", "Isamu Noguchi – Sculptural Design", and "Marcel Breuer – Design and Architecture".

LINDY ROY
(*1963)

Upon completing studies in architecture in her native Cape Town and at Columbia University in New York, Lindy Roy worked in the office of Peter Eisenman. She subsequently taught at a number of American universities before founding her own studio ROY Co. in 2000, which handles both interior design and building projects. For Vitra, she designed the company's new showroom in New York's Meatpacking District in 2001–02.

SANAA

is an architecture practice founded by Kazuyo Sejima and Ryue Nishizawa in Tokyo in 1995 which, within a few short years, has become internationally renowned for its minimalist yet poetic structures. SANAA's most important projects include the Dior Building in Tokyo, the 21st Century Museum of Contemporary Art in Kanazawa and the Zeche Zollverein School of Management and Design in Essen. Kazuyo Sejima (*1956) studied

Ron Arad, Jurgen Bey, Ronan & Erwan Bouroullec, Fernando & Humberto Campana, Naoto Fukasawa, Frank Gehry, Konstantin Grcic, Zaha Hadid, Hella Jongerius, Greg Lynn, Jürgen Mayer H., Alberto Meda, Jasper Morrison, Jerszy Seymour, Tokujin Yoshioka

Participants of the Vitra Edition 2007

architecture at the Japan Women's University and started working in Toyo Ito's atelier before opening her own studio in 1987. Her partner Ryue Nishizawa (*1966) completed his architecture studies at Yokohama National University and, in addition to collaborating with Sejima, has run his own practice since 1997. A factory building for → Vitrashop, designed by SANAA and due for completion in 2009, is currently under construction on the → Vitra Campus in → Weil am Rhein.

DENIS SANTACHIARA
(*1950)

is in many ways an anomaly whose works fall into the in-between zone between design and art. In 1986/1987 he produced his experimental chairs The Sisters, which remained one-offs, as part of → Vitra Edition. In 1990–1991 the Vitra Design Museum presented the exhibition "Denis Santachiara. Goods and Animations". His Santachair was integrated into the Vitra collections in 1999.

WOLFGANG SCHEPPE
(*1955)

studied philosophy and linguistics at Ludwig-Maximilians University in Munich. He works as an author and graphic designer. In addition to writing adverts for Joyn by the Bouroullec brothers and Aluminium Chair by Charles & Ray Eames, Scheppe has written an extensive publication for Vitra on the history of the office chair. The book, "Growing a Chair. The Past and Future of Office Seating", which was also designed by Scheppe, was published in 2004.

JERSZY SEYMOUR
(*1968)

grew up in a multi-ethnic part of London which developed into a kind of laboratory for youth culture during the 1980s. It was here that Seymour began his career as a DJ and designer of club flyers. He received a scholarship to the Royal College of Art where he discovered his love for design and sculpture. His work, which inhabits a cross-over zone between disciplines, is inspired by Pop culture. Seymour, who now lives in Berlin, was asked in 2006 to produce a design for → Vitra Edition. He was also involved in the Vitra Design Museum's "MyHome" exhibition.

BOREK SIPEK
(*1949)

studied furniture design at the Prague School of Art, and architecture and philosophy in Hamburg and Stuttgart. He has worked as a freelance designer and university professor since 1979. He was appointed professor of architecture at the University of Applied Art, Prague, in 1990. Sipek designed his Ota Otanek chair (1988), his Wardrobe (1989/1991) and his Paper Basket (1989) for → Vitra Edition. His Sipek office desk and Sedlak chair were created in 1992. The Vitra Design Museum presented an exhibition entitled "Borek Sipek – Die Nähe der Ferne" (literally, "The Nearness of the Far") in 1992.

ÁLVARO SIZA
(*1933)

studied architecture at the Escola Superior de Belas Artes in Porto and then began working in the studio of his teacher, Fernando Távora. After winning a competition he set up his own practice in 1958 and has since become one of Portugal's pre-eminent contemporary architects. He is known for the simplicity of his buildings, for their classical modern forms and for the care he takes to integrate them into urban and natural settings. Siza's work focuses on residential dwellings, university buildings, such as the architecture faculty in Porto (1986–1995), and cultural pieces such as the Museum of Art in Santiago de Compostela (1988–1994) and the Portuguese pavilion at the Expo 1998 in Lisbon. Siza is also active in designing furniture, lamps and interiors. In 1994, this distinguished architect, who won the 1992 Pritzker Prize, designed a factory building at the → Vitra Campus in → Weil am Rhein.

ETTORE SOTTSASS
(1917–2007)

studied architecture at the Turin Polytechnic but initially devoted his energies to artistic projects. It was not until the 1950s that he began turning his attention to design and architecture. Sottsass has created numerous works for companies like → Olivetti and Alessi. As a founder of Studio Alchimia and the Memphis group, he became one of the leading proponents of postmodernism. Since the 1980s, Sottsass has also built up a successful architecture practice. He created the Theodora chair for → Vitra Edition in 1987. Sottsass contributed to the Vitra Design Museum's → "Citizen Office" exhibition in 1993.

PHILIPPE STARCK
(*1949)

was educated in Paris at the École Nissim de Camondo. He worked for a brief period as art director at Pierre Cardin before setting up his own interior and product design studio and embarking on a stellar career in both market segments. Since striking out on his own, Starck has gone from strength to strength. Helped by his shrewd sense for self-promotion, he has become an internationally renowned design star with a bewilderingly large portfolio of projects to his name. He has collaborated with Vitra since the early 1990s. He created the W. W. Stool for → Vitra Edition in 1992 and the Louis 20 chair came to market the same year. A series of products followed, including the Dr Oola foot rest and the Louise table (1994), the Hula Hoop swivel office chair (2001), the Loulou chair (2003) and the BaObab desk (2006).

DIETER THIEL
(*1947)

studied design at the University of Visual Arts in Hamburg. Between 1976 and 1993 he worked freelance with designers Andreas Christen in Zurich and → Mario Bellini in Milan. Thiel has designed showrooms and fair installations for Vitra and → Vitrashop since 1985 and has regularly helped design exhibitions for the Vitra Design Museum since 1989. Thiel now lives and works as a freelance exhibition designer in Basel. While working in → Mario Bellini's atelier, Thiel was heavily involved in creating the Figura, Imago and Persona office chairs (all 1984), the Onda (1990) and Forma (1994) visitor's chair, the Metropol office furniture system (1988) and the Memo cupboard series (1994).

MAARTEN VAN SEVEREN
(1956–2005)

studied architecture at the Ghent Art Academy in the 1970s before opening his own studio there in 1987. Van Severen made a name for himself designing and manufacturing small batches of furniture. For many years, unity of design and production was central to Van Severen's work which was dominated by a preoccupation with a few archetypal furniture types: chairs, tables, sofas, shelves and cupboards. His designs were always the result of extensive research into form, materials and construction. In addition to his furniture, Van Severen worked on many interior design projects. His collaborations with Rem Koolhaas/OMA, including a house in Floriac, Bordeaux (1999), were particularly notable. Van Severen's partnership with Vitra, which began in 1996, was an important break in his career, enabling him to branch out into new materials and production techniques and reach a much wider audience. His .03 chair was the first fruit of this collaboration with Vitra. Although Van Severen did work with other industrial partners in the years before his premature death, the relationship with Vitra remained very intense. He worked on a series of new designs for the company, which have since entered mass production, right to the end.

ALEXANDER VON VEGESACK
(*1945)

began designing and organizing a range of cultural projects on a freelance basis early in his career. Since the mid 1970s he has increasingly concentrated on furniture design, and established a reputation as a collector (particularly of plywood and steel-pipe models), exhibition curator and publicist. He has organized several large touring exhibitions in the United States and advised major museums in France, Germany and Austria on how best to expand their collections. Von Vegesack has worked with Vitra since 1988. Initially hired to advise the company on extending its furniture collections, he was appointed founding director of the Vitra Design Museum in 1989. Under his leadership, the Museum has evolved into an internationally renowned cultural institution in a remarkably short time. In addition to its attractive programme of exhibitions and substantial output of publications, the Museum's design → workshops, initiated by von Vegesack and conducted at the idyllic Domaine de Boisbuchet country estate in France since 1996, have made a major contribution to the organization's success.

CORNEL WINDLIN
(*1964)

studied visual communication and graphic design at Lucerne School of Art and Design and started his career with Neville Brody in London. In 1990 he became art editor for the magazine "The Face" and consequently set up his studio in London and from 1993 in Zurich, specializing in editorial design, book and poster design and typography. In 1999 he launched Lineto.com, an internationally acclaimed platform for contemporary type design. He is known in particular for his work for the Zurich Museum of Design under Martin Heller, the Schauspielhaus Zurich under Christoph Marthaler as well as the Tate Museums in London. Windlin has been responsible for the launch campaign of Vitra's Home Collection in 2004, for which he since art directed and designed three extensive volumes ("Select, Arrange").

SORI YANAGI
(*1915)

After completing an art degree at the Tokyo Academy of Arts, Yanagi soon turned his attention to design and architecture. He has worked freelance since 1950 and created an exceptionally diverse oeuvre during his long career. His work ranges from cutlery to furniture and technical devices to car bodywork and civil engineering projects. Yanagi, who was honoured by the emperor of Japan as a "living cultural treasure" in 2002, is famous above all for his efforts to fuse centuries-old Far Eastern notions of form with traditional Western aesthetics. The Butterfly Stool and Elephant Stool, both designed in 1954, illustrate this unique combination of elegance and purism perfectly. The Vitra Design Museum has continued to sell the Butterfly Stool unmodified since 2001. In 2004, Yanagi launched a → re-edition of the Elephant Stool, this time made of polypropylene, in conjunction with the Vitra Design Museum.

TOKUJIN YOSHIOKA
(*1967)

studied at the Kuwasawa Design School in Tokyo and completed his training in the studios of →Shiro Kuramata and Issey Miyake. He has worked freelance since 1992 and founded the Tokujin Yoshioka Design Office in 2000. He has made a name for himself with his shop and exhibition designs (for Issey Miyake, among others) and his sculptural furniture (Tokyo-pop). Yoshioka was invited to contribute to the 2007 → Vitra Edition.

Mathias Remmele wrote the captions, chronology and glossary for this book. After studying history, literature and philosophy in Berlin and Vienna, he worked as a freelance journalist. Following this, he was a guest curator at the Vitra Design Museum where he oversaw exhibits on Verner Panton and Marcel Breuer. Remmele has been a professor at the University of Art and Design in Basel since 2000.

PHOTOGRAPHERS

BARBIERI, BASILICO, CHIARAMONTE, DE PIETRI

In 1996, Vitra invited the Italian photographers Olivo Barbieri, Gabriele Basilico, Giovanni Chiaramonte and Paola de Pietri, all of whom are well known for their interest in portraying architecture and urban landscapes, to explore and interpret the Vitra Campus. Each one was asked to depict the site overall but also to investigate it in order to find their favourite object or theme. A small selection of the previously unpublished photographs in the "Sites" chapter shows the exceptional complexity and complementarity of their perspectives.
→ p. 12–54

MAURICE SCHELTENS AND LIESBETH ABBENES

The photographer Maurice Scheltens is based in Amsterdam and his work oscillates between the worlds of art, fashion and commerce. In their 'trompe-l'œil' tableaux, Scheltens and long-time collaborator Liesbeth Abbenes often leave evidence of their construction, thus referring to the artificiality of the process while at the same time capturing the viewer's eye through the contemplative quality of their images. For this book, Scheltens and Abbenes staged various elaborate settings to capture the essence of each designer's work. Assisted by Eke Kriek, with thanks to Connie Hüsser.
→ p. 66–99

BRUNS/UEBERSCHÄR/WOOTTON

Malte Bruns, Jyrgen Ueberschär and Tobias Wootton are art students majoring in photography at the Hochschule für Gestaltung and Zentrum für Kunst und Medientechnologie in Karlsruhe. Led by professor Armin Linke, the trio formed a team and embarked on a study project to photograph parts of the Vitra Design Museum's extensive furniture collection for the first time. The raw photographic material was amalgamated into a single image by Philipp Engelhardt, Kilian Ochs and Joscha Steffens and was then lithographically optimized by Günter Hansmann.
→ p. 272–298

PICTURE CREDITS

We would like to thank all individuals and institutions that kindly made picture material available for reproduction in this book. We have done our utmost to locate all copyright holders. Should we not have been successful in individual cases, copyright claims should be addressed to the publishers.

Courtesy ALCOA Aluminium Company of America: 156
Nacho Alegre: 131 (top r.), 135 (top. l.)
Lena Amuat: 131 (top. l. and bott. r.), 133 (bott. l) 136 (top. l. and bott. r.), 340 (1st row r.)
Tadao Ando: 173
asbl Atomium vzw/Jan Bitter: 108 (1st row)
Nicole Bachmann: 135 (top r.), 182, 185, 210
Theodora-Cristina Balauru: 26–27

Alberto Balsalm: 58 (r.), 157 (top r., m. and bott.), 167
Olivo Barbieri: 14–17, 30–33, 44–51, 54
Barragan Foundation, Birsfelden/ProLitteris, Zürich: 308–309
Gabriele Basilico: 38–43
BBC: 116 (bott.)
Mario Belllini Associati: 203 (top), 205
Bibliothèque Publique d'Informations – Centre Pompidou: 108 (4th row l. and m.)
Jan Bitter: 105 (4th row m. and r.), 106 (3rd row), 110 (4th row r.), 317 (4th row l. and 5th row r.), 318 (1st row l. and and row l.)
Anna Blau: 109 (1st row l.)
Luc Boegli: 110 (2nd row l.)
Ronan Bouroullec: 195 (m.), dust jacket
Ronan & Erwan Bouroullec: 193–195
Serge Brison: 113 (2nd row l. and m.)

Ivan Brodey: 105 (4th row l.)
Melissa Brown courtesy Herman Miller Inc.: 153 (bott. l.)
Malte Bruns, Jyrgen Ueberschär, Tobias Wootton: 272–298, dust jacket
David Burdeny: 105 (3th row l. and m.)
Santi Caleca: 249 (m.)
Benny Chan: 112 (2nd row)
Giovanni Chiaramonte: 18–19, 28–29, 52–53, 242–245
Courtesy Antonio Citterio and Partners: 206–209
Niall Clutton: 109 (4th row r.), 112 (4th row r.), 113 (1st row r.)
Christian Coigny: 335–338
Margit Cosper: 349 (2nd row 3rd from l., 3rd row 2nd from l.)
Geoffroy Cottenceau: 192
West Dempster courtesy Herman Miller Inc.: 154

APPENDIX

Marc Detiffe: 109 (4th row m.), 110 (3rd row r.)
Deutscher Bundestag/Lichtblick/ Achim Melde: 110 (1st row l.)
Donato Di Bello: 112 (3rd row)
Willem Diepraam/Architectuurstudio Herman Hertzberger: 126
Thomas Dix Foto-Design: 59 (l.), 249 (bott., m. and l.), 250–254, dust jacket
Duffy: 217
Eames Office LLC: 141–150, 155, 330 (1st row 3rd from l., 4th row l.), 331 (2nd row l.), 340 (3rd row l.)
Charles Eames courtesy Herman Miller Inc.: 162
Ray Eames courtesy Herman Miller Inc.: 150 (m.)
Marc Eggimann: 59 (r.), 110 (2nd row r.), 113 (3rd row r.)
Lizzie Finn: 349 (2nd row m.)
Alan Fletcher: 340 (4th row l.)
Liz Fletcher: 332
Fotostudio DSP Belgique: 112 (1st row l.)
Gaia Gambiaggi: 109 (1st row 3rd from l.)
Herbert Gehr: 157 (top. l.)
Herbert Gehr/Getty Images: 158
Gehry Partners LLP: 169–171
GRRRR: 349 (3rd row l., 5th row 2nd from l.)
GRUNDFLUM: 266
Andreas Gursky © 2007 ProLitteris, Zurich/Courtesy Galerie Sprüth/Magers: 319
Zaha Hadid Architects: 181
Richard Hamilton © 2007 ProLitteris, Zurich: 347
Hans Hansen: 211, dust jacket, 352
Michael Heilgemeir: 202
Courtesy Herman Miller Inc.: 153 (bott. r.), 159–161, 163 (top.), 164, 165 (top and m.), 340 (2nd row r.)
Herzog & de Meuron: 61 (l.), 220–221
Melanie Hofmann: 129 (bott. l.)
Karl Holmqvist/Courtesy Galerie Giti Nourbakhsch, Berlin: 348
Peter Inselmann: 247 (top)
Johan Jacobs: 186
Mikael Jansson/Tod's: 334 (top)
JongeriusLab, Hella Jongerius: 183–184
Andreas Jung: 249 (top r.)
Oliver Jung: 105 (1. row), 108 (2nd and 4th row), 109 (4th row l.)
Maira Kalman: 166
Nick Kane: 113 (1st row l. and m.)
Keystone/AP/J. W. Green: 321
Nick Knight/Vogue © The Condé Nast Publications Inc.: 333, dust jacket
Niki Lackner: 108 (3rd row)

Dieter Leistner: 110 (1st row m.), 112 (1st row m. and r.)
J. Lepard: 163 (bott.)
Armin Linke: 106 (1st and 2nd row)
M/M (Paris), photo Jodokus Driessen: 197
Tobias Madörin : dust jacket
Walter Maier: 110 (4th row l. and m.), 316 (3rd row m.)
Studio Makkink & Bey: 117
Ari Marcopoulos: 129 (top r.), 328 (4th row l.), 330 (1st row 2nd from l.), dust jacket
Peter Marlow/Magnum Photos: 117
Dylan Martorell: 349 (1st row l., 4th row 3rd from l.)
Peter Mauss/Esto: 170
Ian McKinnell: 246
Alberto Meda: 212–213
Guy Meldem/Körner Union: 349 (2nd row r., 3rd row 3rd from l.)
Ralph Morse/Stringer/Life Magazine © Time Inc.: 168, dust jacket
Samuel Nyholm/Reala: 349 (1st row 2nd from l., 4th row l. and r., 5th row r.)
100% Orange: 349 (4th row m.), dust jacket
Panton Design Basel: 214–215, 219
Eduardo Perez: 109 (2nd row m. and r.), 112 (4th row l. and m.), 113 (4th row)
Josh Petherick: 349 (3rd row r., 5th row l.)
Photofest: 114
Photo service "L'Osservatore Romano": 325
Paola de Pietri: 12–13, 20–25, 34–37, dust jacket
Robert Polidori: 109 (2nd row l.)
ProLitteris, Zurich/Centre G. Pompidou, Bibliothèque Kandinsky, Fonds J. Prouvé/ADAGP: 198–201, dust jacket
Engelbert Reineke/Presse und Informationsamt der Bundesregierung: 314
Dale Rooks, courtesy Herman Miller Inc.: 118
Lukas Roth: 110 (1st row r.)
Alexis Saile: 349 (1st row r., 2nd row l.), dust jacket
SANAA/Kazuyo Sejima & Ryue Nishizawa: 61 (r.), 175
Maurice Scheltens: 66–99, dust jacket
Marco Schillaci: 203 (top l. and bott. l.) 204 (m.)
Louis Schnakenburg, Copenhagen: 218, 328 (3rd row r.), 330 (2nd row 1st and 2nd from l.)
Oliver Schuh: 109 (3rd row r.)
Nigel Shafran: 176
J. Paul Getty Trust, Julius Shulman Photography Archive, Research Library at the Getty Research Institute: 146 (bott.)

Filip Slapal: 106 (4th row m. and r.)
Margherita Spiluttini: 110 (2nd row m.)
Erik Steinbrecher: 340 (4th row 2nd from l.), 344
Studio Frei: 247 (bott. l. and bott. r.), 248 (top r.)
Gordon Summers: 169 (bott.)
Andreas Sütterlin: 58 (l.), 267, 352 (2nd row l.)
Paul Tahon and Ronan & Erwan Bouroullec: 194 (m. and bott.), 195 (top),
Yoshio Takase/GA Photographers: 174
Tino Tedaldi: 109 (1st row 2nd from l.)
Juergen Teller and Contemporary Fine Arts, Berlin: 339, dust jacket
Nicolas Tikhomiroff/Magnum Photos: 116 (bott.)
Courtesy Wolfgang Tillmans/Galerie Daniel Buchholz, Cologne: 341
Isabel Truniger: 129 (top l.), 133 (top, bott. r.), 135 (bott.), 136 (top r. and bott. l.) 328 (1st row r.)
Gary Turnbull: 109 (3rd row m.), 113 (2nd row r., 3rd row l. and m.)
Alexander Van Berge: 109 (3rd row l.)
Inez Van Lamsweerde & Vinoodh Matadin: 334 (bott.)
Bart Van Leuven: 189
Maarten Van Severen: 188, 190–191, dust jacket
Barbara Visser courtesy Annet Gelink Gallery: 343
Vitra Archives: 120, 122, 152, 159, 171, 315–318, 320, 323–324, 326–331, 342, 345, 350, 353
Vitra Design Museum: 165 (bott.), 216, 307, 340 (3rd row r.), dust jacket
Vogue: 340 (1st row l.)
Christopher Wahl: 105 (2nd row)
Hans-Jörg Walter: 354–356, dust jacket
Ian Wright: 349 (5th row 3rd from l.)
Atelier Erwin Wurm: 351
Miro Zagnoli: dust jacket
ZDF: 322

The Vitra world map was designed by Rafael Koch.

APPENDIX

Editors	Cornel Windlin and Rolf Fehlbaum
Concept	Cornel Windlin
Coordination	Maja Baumgartner
Text editing	Basil Rogger
Copy-editing	Harriet Graham
Translation	German/English: Richard Hall, Barbara Hauss, Julia Taylor Thorson
	Spanish/German, English: Caleidos
	Dutch/German, English: Taalwerk
Design, layout, production	Cornel Windlin, Rebecca Stephany, Marco Müller
Archival research, picture editing	Rebecca Stephany
Scanning, retouching, proofing	GZD, Ditzingen; Licht+Tiefe, Berlin
Printing, binding	Kösel GmbH & Co. KG, Altusried-Krugzell
Publisher	Birkhäuser Verlag AG
	Basel · Boston · Berlin
	P.O. Box 133, CH-4010 Basel/Switzerland
	Part of Springer Science+Business Media
	www.birkhauser.ch
	First, corrected reprint 2008
	© 2008 Birkhäuser Verlag AG

We would like to thank for their help and assistance:

Mario Bellini, Erwan Bouroullec, Ronan Bouroullec, Antonio Citterio, Hella Jongerius, Alberto Meda, Jasper Morrison.
Olivo Barbieri, Gabriele Basilico, Giovanni Chiaramonte, Paola de Pietri, Federica Zanco.
Liesbeth Abbenes, Eke Kriek, Maurice Scheltens.
Malte Bruns, Jyrgen Ueberschär, Tobias Wootton.
Nicole Bachmann, Theodora Balauru, Laurenz Brunner, Thomas Freitag/Buchbinderei Burkhardt, Günter Hansmann/Licht+Tiefe, Connie Hüsser, Rafael Koch, Tobias Madörin, Stephan Müller/Lineto.
Wolfgang Beyer, Eames Office (David Hertsgaard), Herman Miller Archives (Linda Baron, Mike Stuk), Maira Kalman, Marianne Panton, Catherine Prouvé, Vitra Design Museum (Serge Mauduit, Andreas Nutz).
Lena Amuat, Sophie Ballmer, Alberto Balsalm, Mirjam Daubé, Simone Gerber, Charmian Griffin, Ruth Kunz, Aude Lehmann, Tan Wälchli.
Stefano Boeri, Paul Elliman, Max Küng, Armin Linke.

Special thanks to Maja Baumgartner and to Martin Heller.

Printed on acid-free paper produced from chlorine-free pulp TCF ∞
Printed in Germany

ISBN 978-3-7643-8593-4

This book is also available in a German language edition: ISBN 978-3-7643-8592-7

9 8 7 6 5 4 3 2

Library of Congress Control Number: 2007936763

Bibliographic information published by the German National Library:
The German National Library lists this publication in the Deutsche Nationalbibliografie; detailed bibliographic data are available on the Internet: http://dnb.d-nb.de.

This work is subject to copyright. All rights are reserved, whether the whole or part of the material is concerned, specifically the rights of translation, reprinting, reuse of illustrations, recitation, broadcasting, reproduction on microfilms or in other ways, and storage in data bases. For any kind of use, permission of the copyright owner and Vitra must be obtained.

www.vitra.com

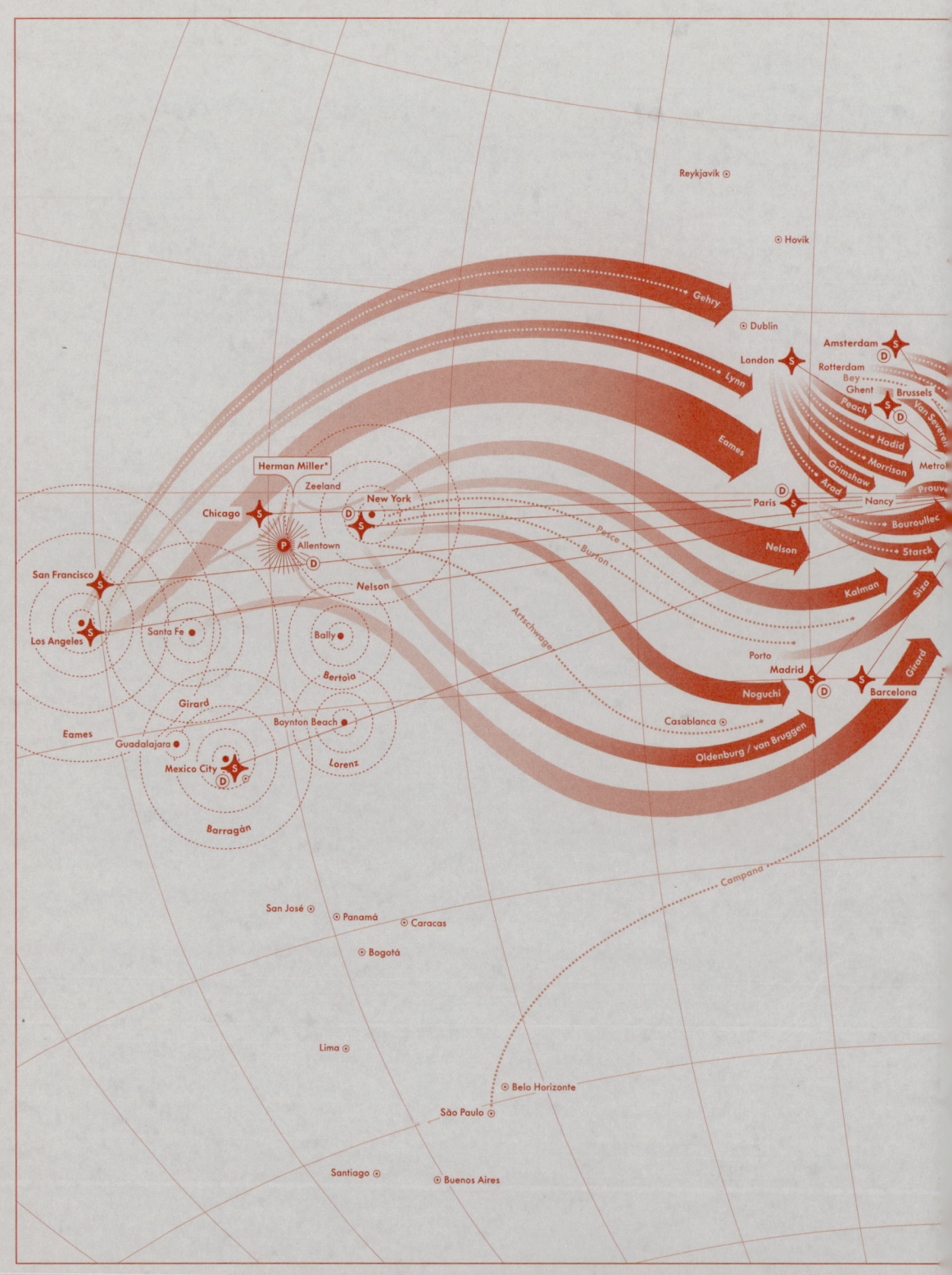

PROJECT VITRA   The world according to Vitra: network and relations   III

Vitra headquarters, MetroBasel
Management; Research & Development (Birsfelden/Switzerland)
Production; Vitra Design Museum, Vitra Campus (Weil am Rhein/Germany)
Production (Neuenburg/Germany)

PROJECT VITRA — Index

Legler, Gian Franco 305
Lelli, Angelo 303, 305
Levy, Arik 225, 385
Lichtenstein, Roy 338
Linke, Armin 394
London 61, 109, 112-113, 176, 265, 374
Loos, Adolf 299, 305
Lorenz, Anton 301, 305-306
Los Angeles 56, 59, 112, 141, 144, 147, 168
Love Investigation 226, 372
Luckhardt, Hans & Wassili 305
Lynn, Greg 87, 226, 355, 385

M

M/M (Paris) 197, 386
Mackintosh, Charles Rennie 302, 305
Magistretti, Vico 305
Mallet-Stevens, Robert 305
Mangiarotti, Angelo 305
Mari, Enzo 305
Matadin, Vinoodh 334
Matheson, Bruno 278-283
Mau, Bruce 386
Mauduit, Serge 301
Maurer, Ingo 253, 303, 305
Mayer H., Jürgen 226, 355, 386
Mazza, Sergio 305
McArthur, Warren 305
Meda, Alberto 88-89, 120, 140, 210-213, 235, 386
Memphis 260, 296-298, 302, 305
Mendell, Pierre 370, 386
Mendelson, Erich 305
Mendini, Alessandro 225, 305, 352, 386
MetroBasel 4, 7, 11, 373
Meuron, Pierre de 55, 220, 384
Mexico 237, 260, 308-309
Mies van der Rohe, Ludwig 56, 51, 272-277, 299, 302, 305-306
Miller, Abbott J. 386
Miniatures 5, 264, 266-267, 373
Miyake, Issey 335
Moholy-Nagy, László 306
Mollino, Carlo 302, 305
Morrison, Jasper 24, 27, 57, 59, 76-77, 140, 176-179, 233-234, 305, 352, 357, 359, 386, 388
Moscow 141, 155, 306
Moss, Kate 333
Mouille, Serge 303, 305
Mourgue, Olivier 305
Müller, Lars 388
Mumbai 112

N

Nakashima, George 305
Nancy 196, 201
Napoleon 59
Nauman, Bruce 339
Nelson, George 4, 7, 65, 70-71, 84-85, 118, 119, 125, 128, 139-140, 153-161, 228-229, 232-233, 237, 300-301, 305-306, 357-359, 386, 388
Netherlands 305

Net 'n' Nest 124, 237, 373
Network Office 373
Neuenburg 58
Neutra, Richard 305
Newson, Marc 296-298, 305
New York 165, 226, 228, 258
Nishizawa, Ryue 55, 57, 174, 389
Noguchi, Isamu 84-85, 86-87, 156, 252, 305, 357, 388

O

Obuchi, Keizo 314
Oldenburg, Claes 24, 26, 28, 36, 59, 60, 262, 359
Olivetti 121, 388
Orgatec 373

P

Pacific Palisades 132
Panton, Marianne 218
Panton, Verner 74-75, 84, 120, 140, 214-219, 229-230, 251, 260, 290-295, 301-303, 305, 306, 332-333, 348, 350, 351, 359, 388-389
Pardo, Jorge 361
Paris 108, 109, 110, 176, 259
Paulin, Pierre 305
Peach, Sevil 126, 389
Perriand, Charlotte 302, 305, 306
Pesce, Gaetano 225, 253, 260, 305, 352, 361, 389
Pietri, Paola de 12-13, 20-23, 25, 34-37, 394
Piretti, Giancarlo 305
Pollack, Sidney 55
Ponti, Gio 302, 305
Pope John Paul II 325
Product development 120, 210, 222, 373
Propst, Robert 119, 126, 127, 153
Prouvé, Jean 24, 27, 57, 59, 72-73, 140, 196-201, 210, 230-231, 254, 260, 265, 300, 302, 305, 389
Pucci, Emilio 165

Q

Quality 373
Quasar 305

R

Rahm, Berta 305
Rams, Dieter 305
Rasch, Heinz & Bodo 305
Re-edition 5, 373
Rehberger, Tobias 361
Remmele, Mathias 392
Restoration laboratory 373-374
Rey, Bruno 305
Rhode, Gilbert 305
Riemerschmid, Richard 305
Rietveld, Gerrit 272-277, 300, 302, 305
Rietveld, Wim 305
Rock, Michael 389
Romanus, Thorsten 389
Roth, Alfred 305
Rotterdam 182
Roy, Lindy 389

S

Saarinen, Eero 301, 302, 305
Sagnot, Louis 305
Saint-Simon, Henri de 58
Salas Portugal, Armando 308, 310
SANAA 24, 25, 26, 57, 61, 62, 140, 174-175, 389, 391
Santachiara, Denis 225, 248, 305, 391
Santa Fe 162, 163, 306
Santer, Jacques 314
Sarfatti, Gino 303, 305
Sartoris, Alberto 253
Scandinavia 302, 303, 305
Scheltens, Maurice 66-99, 394
Scheppe, Wolfgang 391
Schindler, Rudolph 305
Schinkel, Karl Friedrich 305
Schröder, Gerhard 314
Sejima, Kazuyo 55, 57, 174, 389
Seville 60
Seymour, Jerszy 226, 391
Shaker 305
Showroom 307, 374
Sipek, Borek 225, 249, 352, 391
Siza, Álvaro 24, 25, 27, 44-47, 50-51, 57, 60, 391
Sottsass, Ettore 125, 225, 260, 297, 305, 391
Spasski, Boris 321
Stam, Mart 299, 305
Starck, Philippe 86-87, 225, 305, 337, 391
Steiger, Flora 305
Steinbrecher, Erik 344
Steiner, Rudolf 58
Sudjic, Deyan 257-268
Summers, Gerald 305
Switzerland 11, 153, 305

T

Tati, Jacques 114
Teller, Juergen 339
Thiel, Dieter 391
Thonet, Michael 249, 260, 299, 305
Thorsen, Kjetil 360
Thut, Kurt 305
Tillmans, Wolfgang 341
Tokyo 57, 174
Transversality 374
Trial & error 145, 227, 235, 374
Tüllinger 52-53, 374

U

United Kingdom 258, 259, 305
United States 119, 127, 302, 305

V

Valérien, Harry 322
Van Bruggen, Coosje 24, 26, 28, 36, 59
Van de Velde, Henry 305
Van Lamsweerde, Inez 334
Van Severen, Maarten 78-79, 140, 186-191, 222, 231, 305, 357, 392
Vegesack, Alexander von 257, 260, 261, 264, 268, 299-304, 392

Venice 62, 265
Venice (California) 147, 301, 307
Venturi, Robert 305
Vienna 109, 233, 258, 304
Vigano, Vittorio 305
Vintage 374
Visser, Barbara 343
Vitra (name) 374
Vitra Campus 5, 11, 23, 24, 25, 54, 55, 173, 175, 181, 220-221, 241, 262, 268, 374, 376
Vitra Center 9, 11, 12-20, 58, 171, 185, 222
Vitra Design Museum 4, 5, 6, 8, 11, 23, 25, 26, 28-33, 36-37, 40, 55, 57, 60, 84-85, 125, 170, 221, 226, 238, 239, 241, 242-254, 257-268, 269, 299, 300, 303, 304, 306
Vitra Edition 7, 194, 224, 225, 226, 228, 313, 352-356, 360, 361, 362, 363, 376
VitraHaus 57, 61, 220-221
Vitra Home 58, 128, 129, 130, 131, 132, 133, 134, 135-136, 238, 376
Vitra Office 112-113, 114-127, 376
Vitrashop 61, 175, 376

W

Wagenfeld, Wilhelm 303, 305
Wagner, Otto 305
Warhol, Andy 361
Weber, Kem 305
Wegner, Hans J. 302, 305
Weil am Rhein 4, 11, 21, 22-23, 24, 25-54, 55, 56, 58, 60, 106, 175, 180, 181, 241, 262, 301, 307, 376
Welles, Orson 116
Wettstein, Hannes 225, 305
Wilder, Billy 114, 261
Wilson, Robert 261, 305
Windlin, Cornel 392
Windsor 305
Wirth, Armin 305
Workshops 6, 123, 261, 268, 374, 376
Workspirit 377
Wright, Frank Lloyd 251, 302, 305
Wurm, Erwin 351

Y

Yanagi, Sori 84-85, 305, 392
Yeltsin, Boris 314
Yoshioka, Tokujin 305, 392

Z

Zanco, Federica 166, 310, 371
Zanuso, Marco 305
Zeeland 152
Zittel, Andrea 361
Zoelly, Pierre 305
Zürich 219

Reference to image
Reference to text